BUNYAN IN OUR TIME

Bunyan in Our Time

Edited by Robert G. Collmer

THE KENT STATE UNIVERSITY PRESS
Kent, Ohio, and London, England

© 1989 by The Kent State University Press, Kent, Ohio 44242
All rights reserved
Library of Congress Catalog Card Number 89-33452
ISBN 0-87338-391-5
Manufactured in the United States of America

Library of Congress Cataloging-in-Publication Data

Bunyan in our time / edited by Robert G. Collmer.
    p. cm.
  Bibliography: p.
  Includes index.
  ISBN 0-87338-391-5 ∞
  1. Bunyan, John, 1628–1688—Criticism and interpretation.
I. Collmer, R. G., 1926–
PR3332.B8   1989
828′.407—dc20

                                                      89-33452
                                                           CIP

British Library Cataloging-in-Publication data are available.

For Roger Sharrock
". . . let me be
Thankful, O good Interpreter, to thee."

Contents

ROBERT G. COLLMER

Introduction

At the tercentenary of John Bunyan's death, occasions present themselves to acclaim the author of the one book that has passed through more editions and into more foreign languages than any other book written in English. Not only do studies and celebrations stress *The Pilgrim's Progress,* but they must also recognize the voluminous writings of the autodidact of Bedford, who in his sixty years of life produced some sixty treatises. Beyond the writings, the activities of Bunyan that proclaimed the struggle between religious convictions and governmental oppression in the seventeenth century sound familiar to persons in the late twentieth century who witness the clash between church and state in many forms.

Acceptance of Bunyan as a respected writer has been long delayed. He is the only major English author who, first adopted by ordinary readers, had to wait at least a century and a quarter until the literati acknowledged his writing skills. That is, not until the Romantics rescued him from isolation and ridicule did he rise in reputation. And even throughout much of the Victorian period and the early twentieth century, to some ears he sounded too much like an unenlightened Evangelical. In our own century, as the religious heritage from which he sprang gains respect or toleration on its intellectual and social grounds and is distanced through a diminished emotional opposition, Bunyan can be seriously studied by literary critics and historians.

The eight essays of *Bunyan in Our Time* provide views from the New World, for all the authors are from either the United States or Canada. Thus, this collection of original essays parallels a similar collection cele-

brating the 300th anniversary of the publication of *The Pilgrim's Progress,*
which contained essays from English and Scottish critics exclusively.
The earlier collection was published by Liverpool University Press in
1980 and well edited by Vincent Newey. The only links between these
two collections lie in the participation of Roger Sharrock (who continues to make Bunyan's works available to the scholarly community
and whose writings on Bunyan make good sense) in the previous collection and in the dedication that the present collection offers to him. The
starting-point for these essays was a special session on Bunyan sponsored
by the Conference on Christianity and Literature at the 1982 meeting of
the Modern Language Association of America in Los Angeles. There
three papers that culminated in their present state for this collection
were read by Dayton Haskin, U. Milo Kaufmann, and Brainerd P.
Stranahan.

The essays in this book reflect various ways of interpreting Bunyan
and his writings. They reach back into Bunyan's floating word hoard of
the proverb through George W. Walton's opening study and into the
present for a measuring of structure by setting Bunyan next to the
twentieth-century C. S. Lewis in Kaufmann's analysis. A glance at each
essay will show the cohesion of the collection yet the preservation of the
individuality of the authors.

As hinted above, Walton analyzes the proverb for stylistic elements
in various works by Bunyan. The seventeenth century showed the first
serious attempts in English to make lists of proverbs; witness the works
by George Herbert and John Ray. Compiling such catalogs usually suggests that an oral tradition is becoming obsolescent; fearing its loss, persons try to preserve it in writing. For Bunyan, however, the proverb was
alive and available as a tool to capture the minds of his readers. Walton
goes behind the seventeenth century to set forth the classical and biblical
origins of the proverb. His study shows that Bunyan used the proverb
for embellishment rather than as an authoritative source for wisdom.
Even in the melding of biblical and folk proverbs, Bunyan never substi-
tuted the wisdom of people for what he believed was the truth revealed
by the Bible. The twentieth century, more open than some earlier periods to the genius of the language of the folk, has admitted the proverb as
a legitimate form of literature, as the late Charles G. Smith's identification of proverbs in such respected authors as Shakespeare and Spenser
has shown.

Stranahan's and Haskin's essays test Bunyan's handling of his key source of knowledge, the Bible, to define the nature and function of satire in *The Pilgrim's Progress* (Stranahan's study) and the use Bunyan made of the Book of Acts (in Haskin's essay). Stranahan finds satire in the First Part and Second Part but with different objects, the first the conduct of worldly figures who attempt to evade God's judgment and the second the "unwillingness of Christians to accept God's mercy and love." The two different objects reflect the shift in tone between the First Part and the Second Part. Regardless of the butt of the satire, however, the technique is an outgrowth of the art of the sermon, and its medieval ancestry can be traced. Stranahan's study has two consequences, the first of which is the defacing of the image of Bunyan as a "stern and sober Puritan." Of course the sternness and soberness may have been a misperception anyway, a distortion foisted upon Puritanism by post-Victorians. The other consequence is an altering of Bunyan's place in the development of English literature by finding satirical elements reminiscent of the satire that characterized English folk attitudes as far back as medieval protests.

The analysis of the structure of *The Pilgrim's Progress* reopens, in Haskin's essay, the question of whether the Book of Hebrews or the Book of Acts determined the form. To answer this question, Bunyan's method of interpretation must be defined. An issue in recent literary criticism concerns the tension between source and discourse, that is, between the original material and the narrator's recasting. According to Haskin, Bunyan's "work as an interpreter has not commanded much in the way of systematic attention." The controversies between Bunyan and radicals like the Quakers appear here, for Bunyan had to decide whether further light comes forth from the Bible or in addition— even in opposition—to the Bible. He committed himself to the nonradical position, yet he utilized his memory—for example, his recollection of "grace abounding"—to reinterpret the past. The method of interpretation which appears in Walton's study of Bunyan's proverbs rises again in Haskin's work with Bunyan and parts of the Bible. The complexity in Bunyan is exacerbated in that he was both a believer (hence committed to a system of truth) and a creator of literature (hence aware of his potential readership). Further studies may measure whether Bunyan stands closer to the secular narrator of Wayne C. Booth or the biblical narrator of Meir Sternberg.

Continuing the topic of Bunyan's method, James F. Forrest and
Barbara A. Johnson take up the matter of allegory. Each essayist pays
attention to the "Apology" that Bunyan placed before the First Part of
The Pilgrim's Progress; each employs, though Forrest with obviously more
detail, Spenser's *The Faerie Queene.* Forrest shows how Spenser and Bunyan attempted to influence the minds of their readers; Johnson explains
that in the "Apology" Bunyan sets forth a staircase of increasing sophistication toward his book in relation to its readers. Though Forrest cites
the ancestry of "dark conceits," he does not claim that Bunyan knew
late-medieval and Renaissance books similar to *The Pilgrim's Progress.*
Johnson claims that Bunyan was aware of traditional Renaissance literary traditions though she does not claim any direct connections. She
offers examples from contemporaneous religious writings to show Bunyan's uniqueness. Forrest applies the modern fascination with literature
as game to Bunyan's works and concludes that allegory for him became
"sacred sport." Johnson treats some of the issues encountered by Stranahan and Haskin, namely, the extent to which Bunyan imitated the Bible or practiced the spirit that produced Holy Writ.

The next two essays deal with Bunyan as activist rather than as literary dreamer. Of course, the term "activist" applied to Bunyan creates a
distortion, for Bunyan's long imprisonments (twelve years in one period
plus a later six months) were products of what since Thoreau's time we
call "civil disobedience." Richard L. Greaves as a historian defines Bunyan's attitude toward the Stuart state. Rejecting views of William York
Tindall and Christopher Hill, who find antimonarchical and proletarian
elements in Bunyan, Greaves is nevertheless far from allowing Bunyan
to be what George Offor claimed, a proponent of "high monarchial
principles." Greaves chooses the term "passive disobedience" to describe Bunyan's conduct. Citing *The Holy War,* which, incidentally,
Greaves and Forrest jointly edited, Greaves notes that Bunyan was opposed neither to kingship nor to aristocracy. The question of the extent
to which groups such as the Levellers and Diggers influenced Bunyan
pervades Greaves's study. Bunyan, for Greaves, did not want to pull up
the monarchy root and branch. His opposition to violent action sprang
from his belief that temporal authorities acted as the agents of God and
that suffering was "virtually an act of worship." Thus, Bunyan's militancy was of the spirit, not of the sword—the tension suggested by the
title for the essay.

David Herreshoff's essay surveys modern radical views toward the politics of Bunyan. Using as a starting-point Jack Lindsay's 1937 book, which is both Marxist and Freudian in view, Herreshoff traces the interpretations down to the conference on Bunyan at Humboldt University in East Germany in 1978 celebrating the 350th anniversary of Bunyan's birth. It is significant to note than in 1988 the tercentenary of Bunyan's death was celebrated with a conference on "Bunyan and Puritanism" at Durham University, England, at which one of the principal speakers was the distinguished Marxist historian Christopher Hill. Matters such as Bunyan's professed concern to find the way from this world to the next world and the tension between individual salvation and group action exercise Marxist interpreters. The key writer in the seventeenth century for Marxist critics is the Leveller Gerrard Winstanley, against whom Bunyan must be measured. Hill, for example, finds Winstanley superior, citing his "better way of thinking than Bunyan's." Most Marxist critics of Bunyan emphasize content in the works and his own actions, but at least one stresses form and reader response—again the issue raised by Forrest and Johnson in their essays. The world has indeed turned upside down when a writer long identified as merely religious can offer substance for study by dialectical materialists.

The final essay, U. Milo Kaufmann's conclusions about C. S. Lewis's *The Pilgrim's Regress* and the influences of its antecedent, is the most traditionally religious in this collection. Curiously, however, the tensions Marxists find between the individual and the group appear here also. Contemporary favorite catchwords like "ambiguity" and "journey" also exist for study. In a one-way quest the individual moves to the infinite, not the communal; yet even this path has communal elements with companionship en route and an anticipated gathering in the Celestial City. A two-way journey, Kaufmann claims, has a hero leaving one group to recover traditional and shared forms of thought and worship within another group. An ultimate irony is that even in a one-way quest, Kaufmann concedes, the world beyond is a transfigured vision of this world.

Bunyan in our time still speaks. His testimony through his willingness to endure imprisonment rather than to compromise beliefs may inspire a generation looking for examples. His writings, now arrayed with critical apparatus, reappear on some university reading lists and attract the learned student. The methods of creating literature from surrounding pieces, the means for appealing to the reader, the self-conscious literary artist standing before his task, the place of the writer in a society that is needful of change, and the ambiguous journey in which everyman or everywoman is engaged—these issues still remain compelling three centuries later. This collection of essays can offer directions and stimuli for Bunyan's claim to increasing scholarly attention.

The editor owes debts to many persons. Roy W. Battenhouse of Indiana University and Roland Mushat Frye of the University of Pennsylvania provided suggestions and judgments on the essays. Marie Wolfe checked documentation and sources. Michael Ragland aided in compiling the index. Deborah J. Rhoads typed with precision and patience. The University Research Committee of Baylor University provided financial assistance. My wife, Alys, has sympathized with my delays and yet has encouraged me on to completion. But the ultimate and greatest debt is to the eight authors whose willingness to cooperate and generosity to forgive procrastination have made our walk together with Bunyan a happy experience.

GEORGE W. WALTON

Bunyan's Proverbial Language

Readers have long recognized Bunyan's use of proverbial language in his successful writing, some critics going so far as listing, cataloguing, or even discussing several of the phrases that apparently flowed naturally from his brimming reservoir of folk-speech.[1] George Offor, Bunyan's enthusiastic nineteenth-century editor, claimed expansively that in *The Pilgrim's Progress* the "mechanick" preacher borrowed no phrases from any book "except the quotations from the Bible, and the use of common proverbs."[2] Surprisingly, however, while recent readers have noted the varying degrees of influence exerted upon Bunyan's content, method, and style by the traditions of allegory, popular romance, folk-tale, emblem, riddle, homiletics, hermeneutics, meditation, spiritual autobiography, theological treatise (the list goes on), few have remarked at any length on his skillful handling of the proverb, which has its own legitimate tradition. Our late twentieth-century predilection for complexities has perhaps led us to overlook one part of a style which Bunyan himself thought to be the distingushing feature of his writing, a style he refers to in "The Author's Way of Sending Forth His Second Part of the Pilgrim" as he tells his book how it may prove that it is not yet another unauthorized, counterfeit sequel to the First Part:

> *If such thou meetst with, then thine only way*
> *Before them all, is,* to say out thy say,
> *In thine own native Language, which no man*
> *Now useth, nor with ease dissemble can.* (PP, 168, lines 24–27)

The proverb was an ingredient in this "native Language" which Bunyan consciously drew upon, and there is evidence that he used it with genuine craftsmanship. My purpose in this essay, then, is not merely to enumerate Bunyan's proverbial allusions and phrases, since, as Maurice Hussey has properly cautioned, to do so is to court the "danger that we may relegate the language and imagery of a popular writer to the folkmuseum along with the metal fiddle and the tinker's irons still preserved in the Bunyan Museum in Bedford."³ Instead, I shall try to point out an additional argument for viewing Bunyan as a conscious artist, first by chalking out those inherent qualities traditionally ascribed to the proverb which made it a serviceable rhetorical figure for Bunyan's purposes, and then by tracing his developing attitude toward and use of the figure up through the First Part of *The Pilgrim's Progress.* By isolating this one pattern in Bunyan's style, we should be able to perceive yet another reason why a seventeenth-century sectarian can still attract the human interest of more secular twentieth-century readers.

The Definition and Tradition of the Proverb

An authoritative definition of the proverb—one with firmly drawn demarcations to suit the collector's needs—is impossible to come by. It is "too difficult to repay the undertaking," Archer Taylor has said, encouraging the reader to "be content with recognizing that a proverb is a saying current among the folk."⁴ Bartlett J. Whiting has attempted a more specific description by dividing proverbial material into three groups (proverbs, proverbial phrases, and sententious remarks) and tackling each one separately. Even so, the description of only the first group confirms Taylor's contention that a single definition is not entirely adequate; however, Whiting's attempt is valuable for its suggestions:

> A proverb is an expression which, owing its birth to the people, testifies to its origin in form and phrase. It expresses what is apparently a fundamental truth,—that is, a truism,—in homely language, often adorned, however, with alliteration and rhyme. It is usually short, but need not be; it is usually true, but need not be. Some proverbs have both a literal and a figurative meaning, either of which makes perfect sense; but more often they have but one of the two. A proverb must be venerable; it must bear the sign of antiquity, and, since such signs may be counterfeited by a clever literary man, it

should be attested in different places at different times. This last requirement we must often waive in dealing with very early literature, where the material at our disposal is incomplete.[5]

Obviously, from the number of qualifications which Whiting has attached to his definition, the province of the collector's proverb has some fuzzy borders.

The *Oxford English Dictionary*, perhaps more useful to noncollectors, offers three definitions of the substantive form of "proverb" which complement and expand Whiting's. The first is the most familiar meaning of the term: "A short pithy saying in common and recognized use; a concise sentence, often metaphorical or alliterative in form, which is held to express some truth ascertained by experience or observation and familiar to all; an adage, a wise saw." The second, as we shall see later, derives from a special Hebraic term: "A common word or phrase of contempt, a byword; . . . hence *transf.* a person or thing to which such a phrase is applied. . . ." The third, developing from Greek almost as much as from Hebrew, is particularly suggestive in relation to Bunyan: "An oracular or enigmatical saying that requires interpretation; an allegory, a parable."

These definitions, of course, are the summation of a long history of usage, including theoretical discussions of rhetoric in which the proverb received considerable attention. The inherent potentials of the figure for logical and rhetorical purposes first attracted Aristotle's interest; for even though it was often banal, *paroimia* (which etymologically suggests a wayside saying, a common expression that is heard on the road) could be used effectively in argument before vulgar hearers who delighted in generalizations suited to their prejudices. Proverbs were thus "in the nature of evidence"; but Aristotle also observed that when a speaker applied a proverb to a specific situation, it could assume a figurative attribute and thus become appropriate as illustration or embellishment. With this aspect of their nature in mind, he said that proverbs are "metaphors from species to species. Suppose, for instance, that one introduces something in the expectation of profiting by it himself, and then is injured, he says, 'This is like the Carpathian and the hare';—since both he and the Carpathian have had the fate in question."[6] Demetrius Phalereus (c. 350 B.C.), who also noticed this mode of operation within certain sayings, quoted some of them in his discussion of allegory, a significant fact since the allegorical nature of many proverbs became the chief feature of most Greek and Latin definitions. Diogenianus (A.D. 125), for example, drew an interesting, though doubtful, comparison between *paroimia* ("wayside saying") and *paromoios* ("nearly like"). Not so questionably, Varro (c. 125 B.C.) compared certain proverbs and fables, and Eustathius (c. A.D. 1175) defined the fable as an "unfolded proverb."[7] Hence the classicists tended to emphasize not only the argumentative but also the figurative functions of the proverb.

Later rhetoricians encouraged other uses. According to medieval textbooks, proverbs were appropriate as introductions and conclusions, and as amplifications of subject matter. They also served admirably as introductions and conclusions to other types of amplification, notably the *exemplum,* whose moral could be heightened by an apt adage.[8] This advice, together with the grammarians' quoting of proverbs to facilitate the teaching of Latin, made these sayings the stock in trade of educated men; and, as G. R. Owst has indicated, proverbs were formally popularized by their inclusion in medieval sermons in the vernacular.[9] During the Renaissance the collection and use of such material reached its zenith (F. P. Wilson found twenty-one collections published in England between 1640 and 1670, a list which he thought to be incomplete[10]); however, the rhetoricians' statements on the proverb's nature and function offered no startlingly novel insights, but generally recapitulated and amplified earlier notions. George Puttenham, whose book *The Arte of English Poesie* (1589) was primarily an analysis of figurative language, included the proverb in a list of figures which draw the mind "from plainnesse and simplicitie to a certaine doublenesse."[11] In *The Garden of Eloquence* (1593) Henry Peacham described it as embellishment and also as a type of *apodixis* (a figure which grounds argument on general or common experience), as opposed to *martyria* (the martyr's proof, which confirms a statement by reference to one's own experience).[12] He extolled its persuasive, logical, and didactic qualities:

> Among all the excellent forms of speech there are none other more brief, more significant, more evident or more excellent than apt Proverbs: for what figure of speech is more fit to teach, more forcible to perswade, more wise to forewarne, more piercing to imprint? Briefly, they are most profitable, and most pleasant, & may well be called, The Summaries of maners, or, The Images of humane life: for in them there is contained a generall doctrine of direction and particular rules of all duties in all persons. (29)

But James Howell's sonnet introducing one of his collections claimed the highest authority for the proverb:

> The Peeples voice the *Voice of God* we call,
> And what are *Proverbs* but the Peeples voice?
> *Coin'd* first, and current made by *common* choice;
> Then sure, they must have *weight* and *Truth* withall;
> They are *a publike Heritage* entayled
> On every Nation, or like *Hirelomes* nayld,
> Which passe from Sire to Son, and so from Son
> Down to the Grandchild till the world be don.
> They are *Free-denisons* by long descent,
> Without the Grace of Prince or Parlement;
> The truest *Commoners and Inmate* Guests,
> We fetch them from the Nurse, and Mothers brests,
> They can prescription plead 'gainst King or Crown,
> And need no *Affidavit* but their own.[13]

To be sure, not all sixteenth- and seventeenth-century critics looked so favorably upon the proverb. George Gascoigne, for one, objected to the idea that *vox populi vox Dei est* on the grounds that God would never stoop to crass vulgarities.[14] But generally the proverb had both appeal and worth for the common and the educated man alike, being functional as argument and as embellishment. It became incorporated into biographies written to illustrate virtue rewarded and vice punished;[15] it contributed to the witty stereotypes developed in the "character" (at least seven proverbs and proverbial phrases appear in the very brief Overburian "A Tinker," for instance); it often served as the kernel of an emblem;[16] and, as studies almost too numerous to acknowledge have confirmed, it became a legitimate, highly effective rhetorical device in the writing of some of the best essayists, dramatists, and fiction writers of the English Renaissance.[17]

Precedents for Bunyan's Use of the Proverb

Though the proverb has had a long history in rhetorical theory and practice, and though a running look at that history may illuminate the potential literary uses of the figure, Bunyan himself was probably unaware of any sophisticated definitions and distinctions made by the theorists, since throughout his writing career he made repeated disclaimers concerning his education or his dependence upon secular learning. Typical is this remark from his fourth publication, *The Doctrine of the Law and Grace Unfolded* (1659):

> Reader, if thou do finde this book empty of Fantastical expressions, and without light, vain, whimsical Scholar-like terms, thou must understand, it is because I never went to School to *Aristotle,* or *Plato,* but was brought up at my fathers house, in a very mean condition, among a company of poor Countrey-men. But if thou do finde a parcel of plain, yet sound, true, and home sayings, attribute that to the Lord Jesus, his gifts and abilities, which he hath bestowed upon such a poor Creature, as I am, and have been. (Oxford Bunyan, 2: 16)

But certainly Bunyan absorbed particular rhetorical methods available in the plain style of the Puritan sermon, which relied heavily on the proverb;[18] and he could hardly overlook Arthur Dent's method in *The Plaine Mans Path-way to Heauen* (1601), one of two books his first wife brought to the marriage. Dent generally used the proverb in what Janet Heseltine has described as the typical mode of most Elizabethan writers: either by direct quotation or by ornate elaboration to effect emphasis or comparison (xv). This practice sometimes overwhelms the reader as when Dent unleashes Theologus in his attack on liars:

> Men now adayes studie the Arte of lying, flattering, fawning, glosing and dissembling: they haue a heart and a heart. *They haue hony in their mouth; and gall in their heart.* Their tongues are *as soft as butter and oile:* but their hearts are full of bitternesse, poison, and wormwood. They are full of outward courtesie and ciuility, full of *court holy water,* when there is no truth nor plaineness in their inward affection. *They will speake you faire, when they would cut your throats.* They will shew you a good countenance; when *they would eate your heart with garlicke.* . . . This viperous brood do but watch their times & opportunities, till they can *get a man upon the hip:* and then they will sting him & worke their malice upon him. These fauning *curs will not barke till they bite.* They will lurke, and lie close, til they spie their vantage, and then they will shew themselues in their kinde: then they will hoist a man, and turne him ouer the perke, if they can. These men are like *the waters, which are most deepe, where they are most calme:* like a dangerous rocke, hid under a calme sea; or, as the Heathen say, like the Syrens song, which is the Sailers wrecke; like the Fowlers

whistle, which is the birds death; like the *hid bait,* which is the fishes bane; like
the Harpyes, which have virgins faces, and Vultures tallons; or like Hyena,
which speaketh like a friend, and deuoureth like a foe. . . .[19]

And on it goes, and this is only half the passage. Here proverbs, classical
allusions, natural history, and Scripture combine to illustrate and emphasize with a kind of verbal overkill.

One could, with equal ease, find passages exemplifying Dent's reliance on proverbs as introductions or conclusions to other forms of
amplification. For instance, "Sweet meat will haue sower sawce, and a
dramme of pleasure, a pound of sorrow" (Dent, 58; M839 and D582) is
Theologus' confirmation of Philagathus' remarks upon lust. Occasionally Dent even placed proverbs in the arguments of antagonists for the
apparent dramatic purpose of letting them expose their own personalities. For instance, Asunetus verifies his choice of ignorance when he
offers up facile proverbs justifying his evasion of the Word: "We cannot
liue by the Scriptures," he argues, *"they are too high for vs, we will not meddle
with them"* (Dent, 27; T206; emphasis mine). Similarly, Antilegon's
choice of proverbs indicates his dedication to self-gratification and self-
justification, as when he says, "Oh sir you must beare with youth, youth
you know is fraile; and *youth will be youthfull,* when you haue said all that
yon [sic] can" (Dent, 57; Y48 and C337; emphasis mine); and again when
he responds, "I shall answer for mine owne faults, and *euery fat shall stand
on his own bottome"* (Dent, 274; T596; emphasis mine), a proverb which
Bunyan's Presumption carelessly mutters in his sleep.

Dent thus provided Bunyan an example of using the proverb for embellishment, emphasis, and dialogue; but more important as immediate
influences on Bunyan are the biblical formulae derived from the Old
Testament Hebrew *mashal* and the New Testament Greek *paroimia* (usually translated as "proverb" in the Authorized Version). He could find
"proverb" used as a common, pithy adage based on general experience,
illustrated by 1 Samuel 24.13 in the Old Testament ("As saith the
proverb of the ancients, Wickedness proceedeth from the wicked") and
by 2 Peter 2.22 in the New ("But it is happened unto them according to
the true proverb, The dog *is* turned to his own vomit again; and the sow
that was washed to her wallowing in the mire"). He could also find it
used to indicate a person who has become a widely recognized word of
reproach, as seen in Deuteronomy 28.37 ("And thou shalt become an

astonishment, a proverb, and a byword, among all nations whither the Lord shall lead thee"). And finally he could find the term used in the sense of a mysterious or prophetic saying, an enigma, a riddle, an allegory; something which needs interpreting, as seen in Proverbs 1.6 ("To understand a proverb, and the interpretations; the words of the wise, and their dark sayings") and in John 16.25 ("These things have I spoken unto you in proverbs: but the time cometh, when I shall no more speak unto you in proverbs, but I shall shew you plainly of the Father").

Bunyan used all meanings of the term in one case or another in *The Pilgrim's Progress*. In the First Part, for instance, Faithful clearly intends a short, pithy adage when he says to Talkative, *"The Proverb is true of you, which is said of a Whore; to wit, That she is a shame to all Women; so are you a shame to all Professors"* (*PP*, 84). Earlier, however, he uses it to indicate a person who has become a notoriously bad example, whose very name has become a term of reproach, when he says of Pliable, "I think God has stired up even his enemies to hiss at him, and make him a Proverb, because he hath forsaken the way" (*PP*, 68). And in the Second Part Christiana draws upon the word in its oracular or allegorical sense:

> God speaks once, yea twice, yet man perceiveth it not. In a Dream, in a Vision of the Night, when deep sleep falleth upon men, in slumbering upon the Bed. *We need not, when a-Bed, lie awake to talk with God; he can visit us while we sleep, and cause us then to hear his Voice. Our Heart oft times wakes when we sleep, and God can speak to that, either by Words, by Proverbs, by Signs, and Similitudes, as well as if one was awake.* (*PP*, 233)

Without having read Aristotle or any of the subsequent rhetoricians, then, Bunyan had at hand examples of the multiple uses of the proverb in most of its various meanings.

Bunyan's Attitude toward the Proverb as Evidence

It is important, as we turn to investigate Bunyan's employment of the proverb, first to clarify his attitude toward the authority of the figure. Speaking of Bunyan's command of popular proverbs in *The Life and Death of Mr. Badman* (1680), Roger Sharrock makes these provocative remarks:

The standard of reasonable conduct laid down in the book is supported as much by these dogmatic propositions of popular culture as by Biblical references, and as a result one has the impression that Wiseman is pronouncing the common judgement of the folk rather than the voice of theological authority. The principle that masters and parents should tread carefully in front of their children and servants is enforced by the merely prudential maxim: "Hedges have eyes and little Pitchers have ears."[20]

Although, as Sharrock has said, one hears Wiseman's folk authority more than Scripture in certain passages of *Mr. Badman,* we should be wary of concluding that Bunyan himself was taking folk wisdom as his own authority. Christiana did tell Mercy that God could speak to his people through proverbs, but there is no reason to infer that Bunyan thought that proverbs (in all meanings of the word) necessarily expressed the mind of God in a given situation. Even to be persuasive, not to say authoritative, proverbs must be applied most judiciously to specific situations since, unapplied, they often stab each other in the back: "Out of sight, out of mind" annihilates the truth of "Absence makes the heart grow fonder," for instance. But proverbs have a way of being true in the proper place at the proper time. "A proverb always tells a truth but not necessarily the truth," writes Christopher Ricks in his review of *The Concise Oxford Dictionary of Proverbs.*[21] Bunyan's pilgrims, however, tell the merchants in Vanity Fair, *"We buy the Truth"* (*PP,* 90). Bunyan and his kind seek an unadulterated truth applicable to all situations and all times and all conditions of people. The Way never changes, though it is open to all who come. It has a way of being absolute and relative at once, as the Second Part of *The Pilgrim's Progress* especially illustrates.

All of this is to place in relief what one would expect: Bunyan did not take the folk origin of proverbs as being sufficient reason to trust such sayings implicitly. He was not so class-oriented as that. Proverbs were a part of earthly witness,[22] and Bunyan's final authority—at least his professed one—was heavenly witness, the doctrine of the twelve apostles who were not only filled with the Spirit but also did "feel, see, handle, and receive conviction, even by their very carnal senses, which others did not . . ." (*The Holy City,* Offor, 3: 419). Though experience was an important source of evidence for Bunyan, traditional experience like that contained in proverbs was not inherently convincing, not like *martyria.* In Bunyan's thinking, when heavenly witness (the truth contained

in the book which Graceless reads in the City of Destruction) operates
to produce personal witness (the encounter with the Cross, or the overwhelming conviction by the Spirit that one is saved by the righteousness
of Christ), then the heavenly and personal experiences combine to become a source of ultimate knowledge and a place of argument as well.
Then the Christian, like Gaius in the Second Part of *The Pilgrim's Progress,*
can say, "Nothing teaches like Experience . . ." (*PP,* 263). Possession
of only one of the experiences leaves a character powerless to persuade
Christian, as we see both in the case of Talkative with his knowledge of
Scripture unattended by conviction, and in the case of Ignorance with his
heart-felt conviction unaccompanied by knowledge. Bunyan's epistemology is strict; common experience is not so trustworthy as is personal
experience, but even the latter is suspect if it does not conform to the
truth of Scripture interpreted by the Holy Spirit within the sanctified
believer. He had learned from John Gifford that he should not take up
"any truth upon trust, as from this or that or another man or men, but to
cry mightily to God, that he would convince us of the reality thereof,
and set us down therein, by his own Spirit in the holy Word . . ." (*GA,*
37). And he was even reluctant to allow his own private experiences to
be more authoritative than Scripture, for not until the third edition of
Grace Abounding did he include his account of the "strange dispensation"
in which he heard a note "as if" of a rushing wind, "as if" of a speaking
voice silencing the accusing hellhounds in his heart, "as if" of an angel
that had come upon him. Even in an account given almost twenty years
after the event, Bunyan writes, "But, I say, concerning this dispensation, I know not what yet to say unto it; which was also in truth the cause
that at first I did not speak of it in the Book. I do now, also, leave it to be
thought on by men of sound Judgment. I lay not the stress of my Salvation thereupon, but upon the Lord Jesus, in the Promise . . ." (*GA,* 53).
The nature of his final authority, as he understood it, may thus be illustrated by his words to the learned reader in the "Epistle to Four Sorts of
Readers" preceding *The Holy City* (1665):

> Sir, What you find suiting with the Scriptures take, though it should not suit
> with authors; but that which you find against the Scriptures, slight, though it
> should be confirmed by multitudes of them. Yea, further, where you find the
> Scriptures and your authors jump, yet believe it for the sake of the Scrip-
> ture's authority. I honour the godly as Christians, but I prefer the Bible

before them; and having that still with me, I count myself far better furnished than if I had without it all the libraries of the two universities. Besides, I am for drinking water out of my own cistern; what God makes mine by the evidence of his Word and Spirit, that I dare make bold with. (Offor, 3: 398–99)

Therefore in *A Few Sighs from Hell* (1658) Bunyan rejects the conventional wisdom of "A fair death honors the whole life" (D151) when others misapplied it to unrepentant sinners: "Now, by this one thing doth the devil take great advantage on the hearts of the ignorant, suggesting unto them that because the party deceased departed so quietly, without all doubt they are gone to rest and joy . . ." (Offor, 3: 682). Similarly, in *The Doctrine of the Law and Grace Unfolded,* his belief in the perseverance of the saints leads him to oppose the idea expressed in "Young saint old devil" (S33): "[S]ome through ignorance of the vertue of the offering of the body of Jesus Christ do say a man may be a child of God to day, and a childe of the Devil to morrow, which is gross ignorance . . ." (Oxford Bunyan, 2: 199). Clearly, personal experience of the Word and the Spirit operating together was the only evidence on which Bunyan could confidently establish the truth of any proposition; and yet, having established that truth, he could confirm or support it through a properly applied proverb—whether a wise saying of folk origin, a term of reproach, or an oracular communication. As a rhetorical device which could sum up a situation, a person, or an argument in witty and rhythmical speech, the proverb became as useful to Bunyan as did the language of similitude in general.

The chronological sweep of Bunyan's writing career repeats in broader strokes this progressive relationship between Bunyan's first determining the truth by Scripture and then confirming the truth by rhetoric, for the lively colloquial language which marks the best works of his later career is conspicuously more subdued in most of his early treatises, polemic as well as homiletic. Any number of explanations might answer why, ranging from Caroline Richardson's suggestion that one of Bunyan's disciples might have edited his early material to prevent the scorn of the educated clergy, to W. Fraser Mitchell's observation that the Puritan style formulated by William Perkins discouraged human comment and advocated letting the Bible speak for itself.[23] But Richard Weaver offers another explanation of stylistic development which is consonant with the mentality undergirding Bunyan's epistemology. With only a slight transposition of meaning, one can apply to Bunyan's career the terminology by which Weaver describes the honest rhetorician's progress. He says that "there is no honest rhetoric without a preceding dialectic," a stage often characterized by "semantically purified speech." And yet,

> when the disputed terms have been established, we are at the limit of dialectic. How does the noble rhetorician proceed from this point on? That the clearest demonstration in terms of logical inclusion and exclusion often fails to win assent we hardly need state; therefore, to what does the rhetorician resort at this critical passage? It is the stage at which he passes from the logical to the analogical, or it is where figuration comes into rhetoric.[24]

Bunyan's dialectic occurred in such early works as *Some Gospel-Truths Opened* (1656) and *The Doctrine of the Law and Grace Unfolded* (1659), with the "semantically purified speech" being the language of Scripture, which he often quoted and strung together with the barest of personal comment as he established his truth. To be sure, even in *Some Gospel-Truths Opened* he was cognizant of the utility of analogy: "Now let me give you a Similitude," he said, "for it is warrantable; for both Christ and his Apostles did sometimes use them, to the end that soules might be the better informed . . ." (Oxford Bunyan, 1: 75–76). However, by the time he published *The Resurrection of the Dead* (1665), he was so confident of his doctrinal position that he now felt free to praise another, though secondary, book, that is, the world of nature, upon which he might base his arguments for the truth:

> This book of the creatures, it is so excellent, and so full, so easy, and so suiting the capacity of all, that there is not one man in the world but is catched, convicted, and cast by it. This is the book, that he who knows no letters may read in; yea, and that he who neither saw New Testament, nor Old, may know both much of God, and himself by. 'Tis this book, out of which generally, both Job and his friends did so profoundly discourse of the judgements of God; and that out of which God himself did so convincingly answer Job. Job was as perfect in this book, as we are, many of us in the scriptures; yea, and could see further by it, than many now adays do see by the New Testament and Old. This is the book out of which, both Christ, the prophets, and apostles, do so frequently discourse by their *similitudes, proverbs,* and *parables,* as

being the most easy way to convince the world, though by reason of their ignorance, nothing will work with them, but what is set on their heart by the Holy Ghost. (Offor, 2: 111–12; emphasis mine)

And after publishing *The Strait Gate* (1675), in which the analogies begin to sparkle out with such frequency as to outshine the "semantically purified speech," Bunyan found himself at the critical stage described by Weaver, faced with the decision of retaining the "logical" Scripture-quoting style or of crossing over into a mode in which analogy becomes the prime carrier of meaning while Scripture (though still the authority) is consigned to the margin. In the language of U. Milo Kaufmann's discussion elsewhere in this book (pp. 186–99), Bunyan was prepared to select *mythos* rather than *logos* as the fit vessel of truth.

The Proverb as Embellishment in Bunyan's Early Works

A brief look at Bunyan's use of the proverb in his early works will reveal that, within the overall pattern of his rhetorical development, factors more ordinary than epistemology operated upon his selection of language, the most obvious being audience, subject, and purpose. For instance, in *Some Gospel-Truths Opened,* he addressed the Quaker doctrine concerning the nature of Jesus Christ in order to argue that the Quakers emphasized a belief in an inner Christ at the expense of Scripture. His text, though polemic, is thus expository in nature, comprising little more than the quotation of passage after passage of Scripture; and consequently, remarkably few proverbial formulae of any sort operate in this work. But after the Quaker Edward Burrough had replied to the first discourse, Bunyan responded in *A Vindication of Some Gospel-Truths Opened* (1657) with a more polemic tone, more personal and more colloquial in nature since he now had before him a single opponent whom he knew, one who had attacked Bunyan and his minister, John Burton. Although he did attempt to answer Burrough's objections with Scripture, he was prepared to resort to the common enough seventeenth-century practice of attacking the man as well as the idea. Apparently not expecting to convert Burrough, Bunyan was nevertheless worried that others might believe the Quaker doctrine, for "those that are carried away, are such as are not able to discerne between fair speeches declared by hereticks, and sound Doctrine declared by the simple-hearted servants of Jesus" (Oxford Bunyan, 1: 124). For such people, Bunyan felt obliged to expose Burrough's method in order to expose his character and thus refute his doctrine. The proverb could become an effective instrument under such circumstances. As Archer Taylor has observed, "A proverb is often a ready-made epigram, sums up the situation effectively, drives home the point, and appeals to the reader's or hearer's sense of humor. Consequently proverbs are much used in ages of controversy and satirical criticism" (172). Accordingly, Bunyan directed his proverbs against Burrough, often with unabated sarcasm: "Now I say therefore, do not thou thus accuse the Brethren, for speaking good of the Name of *Jesus,* least thou be *troubled at thy end for thus spending thy beginning* . . ." (136; B261; added emphasis in this quotation and in those immediately following is mine); "Friend, what harme is it to joyne a *Dog* and a *Woolfe* together? *a fawning Dog,* and *a Woolfe in sheepes clothing,* they differ a little in outward appearance, but they can *both agree to worrie Christs Lambes* . . ." (138; S704, W614, and W619); "Friend, here like a man in the dark, *in seeking to keep thy self out of one ditch thou art fallen into another*" (184; M988); "Again, to defend thy self *thou throwest the dirt in my face* . . ." (184; D650); "It is well thou doest recant so much, as *to eat thy first words* at the last . . ." (186; W825); "*Friend,* how doest thou *run about the bush,* seeking to scrable up an answer . . ." (190; B742).

A similar use of the proverb emerges in *A Defence of the Doctrine of Justification by Faith* (1672), published in the final year of Bunyan's off-and-on imprisonment as a reaction to Edward Fowler's *Design of Christianity* (1671). Fowler was an educated man (B.A. Oxford, 1653; M.A. Cambridge, 1655) who had been a Presbyterian during the Commonwealth, had obtained the parish of Norhill in Bedfordshire in 1656, but (unlike his father and brother, who were also Nonconformist churchmen) had become an Anglican in response to the Act of Uniformity in 1662, thus retaining his church position. His argument in the *Design,* summed up by William York Tindall, was that

> the aim of Christianity was the establishment of a holy, moral life of which the first principles were written in the hearts of all men, heathen and Christian, and corroborated by Scripture. To establish these first principles, made known by "Revelation, nature, or the use of Reason," had been the chief end

of the Saviour, who had promoted holiness by example rather than by expiation.[25]

For a man like Bunyan—who had little education, who placed his confidence in the Word only, who gave up almost everything he had rather than to give up his sectarian preaching, and who painfully experienced his need for the imputed righteousness that Christ made possible through his sacrifice (not example)—Fowler was everything that a Christian should not be. In *A Defence* Bunyan thus turns the proverb against the character of this man, first by accusing him of planning "*to spit* [*his*] *. . . venom* at Christ . . ." (Offor, 2: 294; 129; added emphasis in this quotation and those immediately following is mine), and then by charging him with learning "to dissemble with words, that thereby [his] own heart-errors, and *the snake that lieth in* [*his*] *bosom*, may yet there abide the more undiscovered" (294; V68). Fowler was "*making a very stalking-horse* of the Lord Jesus Christ" (312; S816), being one of "*such bats as cannot see*" the power of the gospel (313; 092). Seizing upon Fowler's opportunism in conforming to Anglicanism, Bunyan leaves his opponent pinned and wriggling on the wall, labeled by the appropriate formulated proverbial phrases. Fowler, he writes, would fall into the customary religion of any country in order "*to sleep in a whole skin* . . ." (322; S530). He is "a glorious Latitudinarian, that can, as to religion, *turn and twist like an eel* on the angle, or rather *like the weather-cock* that stands on the steeple" (322; E60 and W223).

Bunyan thus used the proverb in controversy not to support doctrine so much as to distill the character of his opponent to its perceived essence. But he also drew heavily upon the figure in hortatory sermons, especially those like *A Few Sighs from Hell* (1658) and *The Barren Fig-tree* (1673), which were based upon parables (the Lazarus-Dives story from Luke 16 and the fruitless-tree story from Luke 13). Like his expository and catechistic treatises, Bunyan's hortatory sermons still convince from Scripture, laying down doctrine and buttressing it with book, chapter, and verse; and yet in their attempts to arouse in the reader an awareness of his sinfulness sufficient to persuade him to action, these sermons frequently draw upon the proverb for embellishment. For example, in *The Barren Fig-tree* one becomes increasingly aware that, as a representation of the proverb "A tree is known by the fruits and not by the leaves" (T498), the fig tree is one of those monuments or emblems that appear in the book of the creatures to persuade those who know how to interpret the oracular nature of a universe which, though silent, speaks to those with ears to hear. Bunyan exposes the hidden meanings and warnings—the proverb—of the tree to persuade fruitless professors (those who profess to be Christians) to mend their ways. Again, several proverbs, when gathered together, help formulate the essential character of such Christians in a way similar to that used on Burrough and Fowler: in a vain attempt to hide their sin, these professors *"make religion their cloak,* and *Christ their stalking-horse"* (Offor, 3: 566; C419 and S816; added emphasis in this quotation and those immediately following is mine); they *"are only saints* before men when they are *abroad,* but are *devils* and vipers *at home;* saints by profession, but devils by practice; saints in word, but sinners in heart and life"(568; S31). They are nothing but "cumber grounds": "The cumber ground is a very drone in the hive, that eats up the honey that should feed the labouring bee; he is *a thief in the candle,* that wasteth the tallow, but giveth no light; he is the unsavoury salt, that is fit for nought but the dunghill" (574; T114).

Besides contributing to something like the emblem and the "character," the proverb in *The Barren Fig-tree* also functions within a miniature drama that anticipates one situation—and the overall method—of *The Life and Death of Mr. Badman.* The dramatic narrative begins with the gardener (God) coming to examine the productivity of the fig tree (man), only to find it barren:

> What have I here? saith God; what a fig-tree is this, that hath stood this year in my vineyard, and brought me forth no fruit? I will cry unto him, Professor, barren fig-tree, be fruitful! I look for fruit, I expect fruit, I must have fruit: therefore bethink thyself! At these the professor pauses; but these are *words, not blows,* therefore off goes this consideration from the heart. (Offor, 3: 579; W763; emphasis mine)

Here the professor has evaluated God's remarks by the proverb "He is a word and a blow," and, finding that God does not strike immediately, has dismissed God's words with the wisdom of the folk. The scene repeats itself a second year; but at the end of the third year, when the tree is still unproductive and the gardener calls for Death, then the sinner repents with innumerable vows, and God graciously relents. Again the professor shifts into his proverbial wisdom:

At this the poor creature is very thankful, praises God, and fawns upon him, shows as if he did it heartily, and calls to others to thank him too. He therefore riseth, as one would think, *to be a new creature* indeed. But by that he hath put on his clothes, is come down from his bed, and ventured into the yard or shop, and there sees how all things are *gone to sixes and sevens,* he begins *to have second thoughts,* and says to his folks, What have you all been doing? How are all things out of order? I am I cannot tell what behind hand. One may see, if a man be but a little to a side, that you have neither wisdom nor prudence to order things. And now, instead of seeking to spend the rest of his time to God, he doubleth his diligence after this world. Alas! all must not be lost; we must have provident care. And thus, quite *forgetting* the sorrows of death, the pains of hell, the promises and vows which he made to *God* to be better; *because judgment was not now speedily executed,* therefore the heart of this poor creature is fully set in him to do evil. (580; M170; A208; T247, and D31; emphasis mine)

The inclusion of the proverbial and colloquial material produces an undeniably vivid little drama, but it is more important to note that the entire passage expands the wisdom of a proverb which the narrator all but quotes: "The danger past and God forgotten" (D31). First by his speech ("These are words, not blows") and now by his action, the professor obviously evaluates his situation by the conventional wisdom expressed in proverbs, and not by the word of God. Both his speech and action, in fact, as consistently formulated by the proverbs, betray a personality which places no value in words—neither God's warnings nor the sinner's own vows.

But the drama has not ended. Again God afflicts the professor, who again attempts to dismiss God with a bit of proverbial logic: "Lord, try me this one time more; take off thy hand and see; *they go far that never turn*" (580; R210; emphasis mine). And so once again God spares him and once again the professor forgets his promise, but this time the gardener cuts down the barren tree—not quickly and not mercifully, but slowly and painfully since, as Bunyan appropriately observes in an ironic application of another proverb, "the tree is not felled at one blow" (584; T496). God apparently knows how to counter proverb with proverb. In *The Barren Fig-tree,* then, one perceives a variety of ways Bunyan has learned to use the proverb: (1) he has used the parable-proverb to develop an emblem; (2) he has drawn upon traditional proverbs and phrases to produce something approaching the "character," though not so compact;

(3) he has created a miniature drama in which the professor himself speaks a proverbial wisdom which further delineates his personality; and (4) he has used the proverb as a pointed summary of his *exemplum*. The figure has become much in little in this sermon; and, though no doubt the work is characterized by "pulpit rhetoric of the cruder sort,"[26] much of the folk material coheres so remarkably well that one must acknowledge a degree of conscious artistry at play.

In *The Strait Gate* (1675), the minor work preceding the First Part of *The Pilgrim's Progress,* proverbs play an almost indispensable part in Bunyan's developing artistry. This work is another exhortation based upon the explication of the figurative text found in Luke 13.24: "Strive to enter in at the strait gate: for many, I say unto you, will seek to enter in, and shall not be able." Consisting of two major sections (a phrase-by-phrase commentary upon the text, followed by observations), the sermon follows traditional Puritan rhetorical practice by becoming intensely hortatory in the "use and application of the whole" which comes at the end of the second section. It is here that Bunyan's embellishment, including his use of proverbs, becomes most pronounced as part of his characterizing technique. In early controversial works such as *A Vindication* and *A Defence,* Bunyan had made scattered proverbial remarks concerning the character and method of his opponents, and in *The Barren Fig-tree* he had plotted a more unified proverbial drama characterizing a single imaginary scriptural character, the fruitless professor. But now in the final pages of *The Strait Gate* he writes his own abbreviated "character" book which compactly delineates an entire cast of professors unable to enter the strait gate: the talkative professor, the covetous professor, the wanton professor, the opinionist, the formalist, the legalist, the libertine, the temporizing latitudinarian, the willfully ignorant professor, the professor who compares himself to others, the anything-professor who serves both God and the devil, and such professors as the free-willer, the Socinian, and the Quaker (Offor, 1: 388–89). Here are the characters whose ancestors are Burrough, Fowler, and other opponents, and whose progeny will later populate the worlds of *The Pilgrim's Progress* and *The Holy War.*

Some of the more vividly drawn professors are those whose essential characteristics are defined by one or more proverbs. For example, the covetous professor uses even his religion "to bring grist to [his] mill"

(388; A122). The formalist "is a man that *hath lost all but the shell* of religion. He is hot, indeed, for his form; and no marvel, for that is *his all to contend* for" (388; K18; added emphasis here and following is mine). The temporizing latitudinarian receives the identical proverb given to Edward Fowler, his prototype: "He is a man that hath no God but his belly, nor any religion but that by which his belly is worshipped. His religion is always, *like the times, turning* this way and that way, *like the cock on the steeple;* neither hath he any conscience but a benumbed and seared one, and is next door to a downright atheist . . ." (389; T343 and W223). And when Bunyan begins depicting the anything-professor, he pulls out a plentiful stock of proverbial metaphors, though without overwhelming the reader as did Arthur Dent's Theologus:

> There is yet another professor; and *he is for God and for Baal too; he can be anything for any company; he can throw stones with both hands;* his religion alters as fast as his company; he is a frog of Egypt, and can live in the water and out of the water; he can live in religious company, and again as well out. Nothing that is disorderly comes amiss to him; *he will hold with the hare, and run with the hound; he carries fire in the one hand, and water in the other;* he is a very anything but what he should be. (389; M322, M233, H115, H158, and F267; also cp. F319)

Without claiming too much for the proverb, we can nevertheless discern in Bunyan's early works certain effects to which it contributed. Expressed by Bunyan/the narrator, it identifies through its parabolic nature the spiritual core of objects, characters, and events, whether a barren fig tree ("A tree is known by the fruits and not by the leaves"), an anything-professor ("He bears fire in one hand and water in the other"), or slow-but-certain processes and consequences ("The tree falls not at the first stroke"). But when Bunyan places the proverb in the mouth of one of his characters, then something else begins to happen. Rather than simply being a spiritual kernel, the proverb then becomes a part of realistic folk speech by which characters reveal their own natures, as the fruitless professor does when he implies his short-term pragmatism with such sentiments as "these are words, not blows." In this respect the very ordinary proverb contributes to Bunyan's rendering the world allegorically and realistically at once, and it becomes a gold mine for a writer on the verge of composing a parabolic drama such as *The Pilgrim's Progress.*

The Proverb as Embellishment in
The Pilgrim's Progress

By and large, the patterns by which proverbs occasionally operate in Bunyan's early writings recur with much greater frequency in the fictional works, a detail which indicates even more convincingly that for Bunyan the proverb was a rhetorical figure more suitable to fictional than to doctrinal truth, that is, more fitting for persuasive embellishment than for authoritative demonstration of his faith. This is not to denigrate fiction, embellishment, or the proverb, however; for as his apology in the First Part of *The Pilgrim's Progress* suggests, Bunyan had proceeded far down the road that Richard Weaver's honest rhetorician travels, and so Bunyan defends his analogical method at great length. Expositions of Scripture had settled him confidently upon his doctrine, and he now fell easily into a more gratifying vocabulary and method which, as it occurred to him later, could appeal more effectively to readers of all kinds. Thus even in the apology, while still appealing to Scripture to defend his method, he also draws from the book of the creatures for arguments, many of which are little more than expanded proverbial wisdom. For example, though some godly person might complain of the book's being "dark" (the same adjective used to describe the sayings of the wise in Proverbs 1.6), Bunyan suggests that *"Dark Clouds bring Waters, when the bright bring none"* (*PP*, 2, line 34), a modification of "All clouds bring not rain" (C443). Similarly he argues that his method might attract some who otherwise would not read: *"Some love the meat, some love to pick the bone . . ."* (2, line 29; M810). These are the fish which *"must be grop'd for, and be tickled too, / Or they will not be catcht, what e're you do"* (3.13–14), an allusion to the proverbial phrase "to catch one like a trout with tickling" (T537). In groping for this new audience, then, Bunyan perceived the utility of the proverb. It must have been appealing because it was figurative, but more importantly because it was set in language "really used by men." Bunyan knew what he was up to:

> *This Book is writ in such a Dialect,*
> *As may the minds of listless men affect:*
> *It seems a Novelty, and yet contains*
> *Nothing but sound and honest Gospel-strains.* (7.8–11)

Thus, as in *The Barren Fig-tree,* Bunyan builds upon proverbs in *The Pilgrim's Progress* to create significant events, objects, and characters.

Some proverbs in the book go directly into the composition of the narrative line in such a way that Bunyan appears to be creating the context out of which the original proverbs might reasonably have been expected to have developed. At such moments his story almost literally conforms to Eustathius' definition of the fable as an "unfolded proverb," adding new meaning to Bunyan's question in the apology, "*Wouldest thou see a Truth within a Fable?*" (7.3). And at such moments he rarely gives marginal evidence of his procedure, although the overall purpose of an episode, combined with its language, provides clues of the proverbial truth to be ascertained. In his own world of words, the reader of *The Pilgrim's Progress* must learn to extract the hidden order of its riddling episodes much as Christian, in his world informed by words and the Word, learns from the Interpreter to comprehend unaided such dramatic presentations as that in the fifth room, where the valiant man hacks his way to the palace.[27] How Christian acquires this important verbal experience is well illustrated in the events of the third dramatic presentation involving the boys Passion and Patience. Here the Interpreter guides Christian from the proverbial wisdom of "men of this world" like Passion, who believe that *"A Bird in the hand is worth two in the Bush"* (31; B363), to the proverbial truth of "the world to come"—more subtly visible both in the world and in the text.

In this third scene, the governor of the two boys asks them to wait a year before receiving their "best things." While Patience meets the request with equanimity, Passion angrily demands and receives his portion immediately, scorning the composure of Patience and quickly running through his wealth until he has "nothing left him but Rags." Then the Interpreter begins teaching Christian how to read:

> *Int.* So he said, These two Lads are Figures; *Passion,* of the Men of *this* World; and *Patience,* of the Men of *that* which is to come: For as here thou seest, *Passion will have all now,* this year; that is to say, in *this* World; So are the Men of this World: they must have all their good things now, they cannot stay till next *Year;* that is, untill the *next* World, for their Portion of good. That Proverb, *A Bird in the Hand is worth two in the Bush,* is of more Authority with them, then are all the Divine Testimonies of the good of the world to come. But as thou sawest, that he had quickly

> lavished all away, and had presently left him, nothing but Raggs; So will
> it be with all such Men at the end of this world.
> Chr. *Then said* Christian; *Now I see that* Patience *has the best Wisdom, and
> that upon many accounts.* 1. *Because he stays for the best things.* 2. *And also
> because he will have the glory of* His, *when the other hath nothing but Raggs.*
> Int. Nay, you may add another; to wit, The glory of the *next* world
> will never wear out; but *these* are suddenly gone. Therefore *Passion* had
> not so much reason to laugh at *Patience,* because he had his good things
> first, as *Patience* will have to laugh at *Passion,* because he had his best
> things *last;* for *first* must give place to *last,* because *last* must have his time
> to come, but *last* gives place to *nothing;* for there is not another to suc-
> ceed: he therefore that hath his Portion *first,* must needs have a time to
> spend it; but he that hath his Portion *last,* must have it lastingly. There-
> fore it is said of *Dives, In thy life thou receivedst thy good things, and likewise
> Lazarus evil things; but now he is comforted, and thou art tormented.* (31–32)

The two arguments Christian offers for preferring the wisdom of
Patience have the aura of proverbs breathing through them. The first
reason, *"Because he stays for the best things,"* carries the spirit and language
of "He that can stay obtains" (S835) as well as that of "All things may
come soon enough if we can have the patience to stay for them" (T172).
Christian's second reason, *"And also because he will have the glory of His,
when the other hath nothing but Raggs,"* has its parallel in "He that has no
patience has nothing" (P103). The Interpreter then adds a third argument in support of the wisdom of Patience—namely, the permanence of
the inheritance he chose; and as the Interpreter speaks, proverbial allusions appropriate to the hidden order of things begin to proliferate:
"Better is the last smile than the first laughter" (S560); "Win at first and
lose at last" (F297); "He that comes last makes all fast" (A186). The
proverbial wisdom thus illustrates and explains the scriptural principle
that confirms it.

    Like the Interpreter, the narrator presents significant episodes in
which Christian and his companions unknowingly enact parabolic dra-
mas which the reader must learn to interpret correctly. Since the material generated in these episodes is often proverbial, the answer to the
riddle of each episode is likewise often couched in a proverb, sometimes
even whispered to the reader out of the margin. For instance, Christian's
falling asleep and losing his roll in the arbor on Hill Difficulty elicits the
gloss *"He that sleeps is a loser,"* a close variant of "He that sleeps much gets

nothing" (42; N273). Christian's stumbling and falling after "vain-gloriously" smiling at having "gotten the start of his brother" (66; S828) rather obviously dramatizes "Pride will have a fall" (P581); Christian and Hopeful's digression from "the Kings High-way" (59) into "By-Path-Meadow" evokes associations with the proverb "A man must not leave the king's highway for a pathway" (M281); Hopeful's drawing Christian's mind from thoughts of suicide in Doubting Castle (115–18) expands the proverb "Hope keeps him alive" (H604) in the same way that his efforts "to keep his Brothers head above water" in the river (157) acts out the idea in "It is hope holds up his chin" (H606). Situations like these in *The Pilgrim's Progress* are almost too numerous to mention and hardly need pointing out.

But in several extended episodes proverbs associated with character, event, and object impressively spark associations by which Bunyan's reader contributes to the creation and the interpretation of the text. For example, a number of proverbial details related to Pliable's story combine to form a study in fickleness. Most explicit is Pliable's name, which suggests the phrase "as pliable as wax" (W135). Then there is his forsaking Christian at the Slough of Despond, which recalls another phrase, "to leave in the mire" (M989), with all its attendant connotations of callous betrayal: "And with that [Pliable] gave a desperate struggle or two, and got out of the Mire, on that side of the Slow which was next to his own House. . . . Wherefore *Christian* was left to tumble in the Slow of Despond alone . . ." (14–15). Again, after returning to his home and receiving the various judgments of his neighbors, Pliable eventually moves among them with such assurance that he inspires a certain fickleness in them as well. Bunyan expresses this subtle transference with a witty play on a proverbial phrase which associates Pliable's cowardly inconstancy at the Slough—his turning tail—with their fickle evaluations of Pliable and Christian: "But at last [Pliable] got more confidence, and then they all turned their tales, and began to deride poor *Christian* behind his back" (16; T16). Yet the final reading of Pliable and his neighbors comes much later after Christian hears from Faithful the news of Pliable's return to the city and of the neighbors' having apparently changed their tales again: "Oh, they say, Hang him; he is a Turn-Coat, he was not true to his profession: I think God has stirred up even [God's] enemies to hiss at [Pliable], and make him a Proverb, because he hath forsaken the way" (68). In thus transforming Pliable into a verbal monument, Faithful appropriately labels him with another proverbial phrase, "A very turncoat" (T621); but Christian inscribes the permanent epigraph, a scriptural proverb from 2 Peter 2.22 (first appearing in Proverbs 26.11): *"Well, at my first setting out, I had hopes of that Man; but now I fear he will perish in the overthrow of the City, for it is happened to him according to the true Proverb, The Dog is turned to his Vomit again, and the Sow that was Washed to her wallowing in the mire"* (68; D458). Christian has finally read Pliable correctly, although the proverbial hints were there all the time. Correspondingly, by being alert to the progression of proverbs associated with Pliable, the reader can perceive that the fickle abandonment of Christian in the Slough has, ironically enough, ultimately served to fix Pliable eternally in the sow's mire.

Christian's ability to read character appears to be most successful toward the middle part of his journey, especially when he and Faithful encounter Talkative. But even before Christian begins to play the role of the Interpreter for Faithful in this episode, the reader can hear his own guide addressing him in the narrator's voice, preparing him at the outset for one set of proverbs (having to do with distance and proximity) by which Christian will eventually resolve the riddle of Talkative. The narrator's italicized language leading into the sequence involving Talkative is important as it anticipates this first cluster: "Moreover, I saw in my Dream, that as they went on, *Faithful,* as he chanced to look on one side, saw a Man whose name is *Talkative,* walking at a distance besides them, (for in this place there was enough room for them all to walk). *He was a tall Man, and something more comely at a distance then at hand* . . ." (75).

Faithful's first impression of Talkative is most favorable, and he is taken by surprise when Christian describes the new pilgrim as "a sorry fellow."

> Faith. *Well, he seems to be a very pretty man.*
> Chr. That is, to them that have not through acquaintance with him, for he is best abroad, near home he is ugly enough: your saying, That he is a *pretty man,* brings to mind what I have observed in the work of the Painter, whose Pictures shews best at a distance; but very near, more unpleasing. (77)

Here the narrator's original hints to the reader receive confirmation by Christian's allusion to the first proverb of the distance-proximity set: "On painting and fighting look aloof," or as the example from Benjamin Franklin has it, "Paintings and Fightings are best seen at a distance" (P29). But Christian has not yet unveiled the central proverb of this set. The metaphoric thread emphasizing Talkative's distant prettiness is woven neatly into the conclusion that Bunyan's marginal comment identifies as *"The Proverb that goes of him"*: "He is the very stain, reproach, and shame of Religion to all that know him; it can hardly have a good word in all that end of the Town where he dwells, through him. Thus say the common People that know him, *A* Saint *abroad, and a* Devil *at home* . . ." (78; S31). Changing the sense of the proverb only slightly, Bunyan has managed to leave the reader with a consistent picture of the hypocrite who from a distance ("abroad") looks fair, but up close ("at home") is monstrous.

Christian's initial response to Faithful's queries concerning Talkative also sets in motion a second series of proverbs extracting another attribute of the hypocrite, the contrast between saying and doing. Christian's identifiction of Talkative as "the Son of one *Saywell*" (77) reestablishes the new arrival's double nature by alluding clearly to the proverb "Say well is good but do well is better" (S123). This allusion leads naturally to Christian's "further discovery of him: This man is for any company, and for any talk . . ." (78; M233), causing him to remind Faithful of the "proverb" in Matthew 23.3: "Remember the Proverb, *They say and do not* . . ." (78; cp. T64). Having thus received the benefit of Christian's experience, Faithful draws the appropriate conclusion: "*Well, I see that Saying, and Doing are two things, and hereafter I shall better observe this distinction*" (79; S119), a proverb which not only further delineates Talkative, but indicates a new stage in Faithful's spiritual/verbal progress as well.

Faithful proceeds to engage Talkative in a discussion of the power of religion, for, as Christian notes, a subject of this sort is bound to reveal the hypocrite's true colors and send him packing. After asking Talkative to describe the effects of the grace of God in a man's life, Faithful corrects each of his faulty answers, gradually reducing Talkative's windy phrases to sporadic—and increasingly cooler—responses. As Talkative realizes that Faithful is not being fooled by his religious verbiage, he finally responds with his own stripped-down, unpretentious (and proverbial) analysis of Faithful's method: "You lie at the catch, I perceive" (81; C188), a phrase he falls back on as he retreats before Faithful's

plainer, but superior, verbal skills. Finally, when Faithful challenges
Talkative to judge whether religion is truly active in his life by warning
him to "*say no more then you know the God above will say* Amen *to . . .*" (84;
A137), this final proverb of the saying-doing cluster leaves Talkative
completely identified and momentarily speechless. If he were to say
what God would say about his religion, he could say only nothing, which
is precisely what he says. Consequently, after he evades a direct response, Faithful labels the hypocrite with a final over-arching summary
that moves to a conclusive proverb:

> *They say You are a spot among Christians, and that Religion fareth the worse for your*
> *ungodly conversation, that some already have stumbled at your wicked ways, and that*
> *more are in danger of being destroyed thereby; your Religion, and an Ale-house, and*
> *Covetousness, and uncleanness, and swearing, and lying, and vain Company-keepings,*
> *&c. will stand together. The Proverb is true of you, which is said of a Whore; to wit,*
> *That she is a shame to all Women; so you are a shame to all Professors.* (84)[28]

Like Pliable, Talkative has been read. He has become a sign and a
proverb.

Other episodes in *The Pilgrim's Progress* draw heavily upon the proverb,
though the method and the effect of its use differ a bit from those of the
Pliable and Talkative scenes. In the frequently discussed meeting with
By-ends, for instance, By-ends himself supplies Christian and Hopeful
with his set of identifying proverbs as he names his family and describes
its religious position. His concluding remark about his family is a saying
that actually identifies all its members: "And to tell you the Truth, I am
become a Gentle-man of good Quality; yet my Great Grand-father was
but *a Water-man, looking one way, and Rowing another;* and I got most of my
estate by the same occupation" (99; W143; emphasis mine). All of his
kindred are two-faced opportunists (my Lord Turn-about, my Lord
Time-server, my Lord Fair-speech, Mr. Smoothman, Mr. Facing-both-
ways, Mr. Any-thing, and Parson Two-tongues) whose compromised
religious stance finds expression in a set of proverbs: "First, we never
strive against Wind and Tide" (99; W429); and "Secondly, we are al-
wayes most zealous when Religion goes in his Silver Slippers; we love
much to walk with him in the Street, *if the Sun shines,* and the people
applaud it" (99; cp. S991; emphasis mine). These identifying proverbs
lead Christian to suspect By-ends' identity; and he, with Hopeful, refuses to associate with the fair-weather pilgrim.

In the subsequent episode By-ends falls in with company more suited to his outlook. These men (Mr. Hold-the-World, Mr. Money-love, and Mr. Save-all) are all descendants of Edward Fowler. Being former schoolmates of By-ends, they agree whole-heartedly with his religious views, which Mr. Hold-the-World states succinctly in a famous set of proverbs:

> Ai, and hold you there still, good Mr. *By-ends,* for, for my part, I can count him but a fool, that having the liberty to keep what he has, shall be so unwise as to lose it. Let us be wise *as Serpents,* 'tis best to make hay when the Sun shines; you see how the Bee lieth still all winter and bestirs her then only when she can have profit with pleasure. God sends sometimes Rain, and sometimes Sunshine; if they be such fools to go through the first, yet let us be content to take fair weather along with us. (102)

This response echoes a number of proverbs: "A fool is he that has his choice and chooses the worst" (F464); "To have more of the serpent than the dove" (M1162); "Make hay while the sun shines" (H235); "God sends good luck and God sends bad" (G221); "He should be called a fool to his face that being well does put himself into danger" (F487); and "Fair weather after you" (W217). But the number of proverbs does not make Mr. Hold-the-World's position right; it only indicates how firmly he has identified with the wrong. His fair-weather logic, combined with Mr. Money-love's remarkable resolution of By-ends' case of conscience, proves to be a puff of wind, however, when Christian responds to it: "Then said *Christian,* Even a babe in Religion may answer ten thousand such questions. For if it be unlawful to follow Christ for loaves, as it is, *Joh.* 6. How much more abominable is it to make of him and *religion a stalking-horse* to get and enjoy the world" (105; R63; emphasis mine). Having thus expanded his scriptural principle with a proverb, Christian gives four biblical examples of "Heathens, Hypocrites, Devils, and Witches that are of [Money-love's] opinion" (105), and concludes by appealing to another proverb: "Neither will it out of my mind, but that that man that takes up Religion for the world, will throw away Religion for the world . . ." (106; cp. G234: "He that serves God for money will serve the devil for better wages"). Christian selects the proper scriptures and proverbs to unravel the riddle posed by Mr. Hold-the-World, and leaves the group "stareing one upon another" without an answer.

The effect of the folk sayings in *The Pilgrim's Progress* is not inconsequential. By their means Bunyan often provides the reader with sufficient clues to accept the challenge posed in "The Conclusion" to the First Part:

> *Now Reader, I have told my Dream to thee;*
> *See if they canst Interpret it to me.* . . . (164. 1–2)

Six years later in "The Author's Way of Sending Forth His Second Part of the Pilgrim," he is almost astounded by the popularity of his Pilgrim in seven countries among people of widely varied backgrounds. The one cause to which Bunyan attributes his book's success is that his Pilgrim

> . . . imparts
> His pretty riddles in such wholsome straines
> As yields them profit double to their paines
> Of reading. (170. 1–4)

Bunyan's effective rhetorical use of the popular proverb certainly contributed to this success as he progressed from being polemicist to becoming fabulist.

BRAINERD P. STRANAHAN

Bunyan's Satire
and Its Biblical Sources

Recently Brean S. Hammond has argued, "In an elastic sense of the term, most of *The Pilgrim's Progress* is satirical; indeed satire of a kind is the staple diet of the prose."[1] His essay calls attention to a neglected aspect of John Bunyan's most celebrated work: few commentators portray its author as seeking to reform human conduct through the power of laughter and ridicule. Sometimes they appear uncertain about whether such effects are indeed present; A. Richard Dutton, for example, remarks on the early behavior of Christian's neighbors: "[O]ne might almost be tempted to believe that Bunyan had his tongue in his cheek." Elizabeth Adeney believes he often does, yet even she concludes that "Bunyan's prose is uneven, in short—not always fully under control and, in the long run, not quite certain of its own attitudes, even in some of the most delightfully comic writing in the book."[2]

If we wish to understand John Bunyan, it is always helpful to take suggestions from the Book that guided both him and the true pilgrims of whom he wrote. Our appreciation of satiric elements in *The Pilgrim's Progress* becomes much clearer if we consider how Bunyan's biblical sources influence the behavior of his characters. With the single exception of the scenes involving Mr. Ignorance, his satire is remarkably consistent in its techniques and faithful to the precedents that were available for him in Scripture. The First Part attacks the conduct of worldly folk who stand under the threat of God's angry judgment; the Second Part criticizes, much more gently, the unwillingness of Christians to accept God's mercy and love.

Bunyan's usual method is to adapt a traditional homilist's device—the *exemplum* that illustrates the text of a sermon. Again and again, he creates characters and scenes whose concerns are summed up in particular scriptural verses. The Bible at times furnishes only the general suggestion for a particular passage in *The Pilgrim's Progress;* in other places, its language is incorporated directly into the new story, so that text and illustration become one. Bunyan has no uniform practice for annotating his debts to Scripture; occasionally his marginal commentary (often omitted from modern editions) is overassiduous in sending the reader to his sources, but often he will incorporate a direct quotation without any citation at all.[3] However, whether acknowledged or not, his satiric aims and premises are firmly grounded in the Bible.

William Congreve's most famous play provides an apt title for Bunyan's satire in the First Part. The main target is indeed "the way of the world"—as opposed to the way of the faithful followers of Christ. To Bunyan, "the world" is an expression charged with a particular meaning by the early Christian writers. For the King James Version of the Old Testament, "the world" usually means "the whole earth" or "everywhere." The New Testament, though, employs the term more often in the sense of "this world," with the implication that another is possible. It is certainly natural that a book entitled *The Pilgrim's Progress from this World to That which Is to Come* should follow the New Testament's usage and also favor its preference for the second world, as opposed to the present one.

In the First Part, Bunyan's satire incorporates the Bible's evidence about how worldly figures are likely to behave when they encounter Christians—and how they like to behave when they are by themselves. For each of these two main areas of inquiry, he satirizes three kinds of conduct: the world's three reactions to Christians (the true pilgrims), and the three lusts that its adherents prefer to gratify instead of seeking the world to come.

The World's Three Reactions to Christians

The New Testament suggests three distinct ways in which worldly people usually respond in the presence of Christians, and all three appear frequently in the First Part of *The Pilgrim's Progress.* First, and at worst, the followers of Christ can expect physical abuse—imprisonment, torture, exile, or even death—as befell the men of faith in Hebrews 11.37–38 who, like Abraham, "looked for a city . . . whose builder and maker is God":

> They were stoned, they were sawn asunder, were tempted, were slain with the sword: they wandered about in sheepskins and goatskins; being destitute, afflicted, tormented;
> (Of whom the world was not worthy:) they wandered in deserts, and in mountains, and in dens and caves of the earth.

Second, dedicated followers of Christ can expect to receive genuine scorn or even revulsion as a response to their faith, as did the Psalmist in the Old Testament: "All they that see me laugh me to scorn" (22.7). Bunyan follows the argument of the opening chapter of 1 Corinthians, where Paul makes a contrast between Christian and worldly wisdom:

> For the preaching of the cross is to them that perish foolishness; but unto us which are saved it is the power of God. . . .
> For after that in the wisdom of God the world by wisdom knew not God, it pleased God by the foolishness of preaching to save them that believe. (18–21)

Finally, true believers might merely expect to be laughed at, to be ridiculed by the rest of the world. According to the Book of Acts, Paul personally experienced this third reaction while a prisoner of the Romans:

> And as he thus spake for himself, Festus said with a loud voice, Paul, thou art beside thyself; much learning doth make thee mad.
> But he said, I am not mad, most noble Festus; but speak forth the words of truth and soberness. (26.24–25)

These attitudes of worldly persons towards Christians are presented vividly at the start of Bunyan's story, when the man in rags flees to seek "Eternal Life" after learning that he lives in the City of Destruction.[4] In the figurative meaning of the allegory, that city represents "this world," while the nondeparture of its inhabitants demonstrates that they prefer it to the uncertain prospect of a world to come. At first, the desire of the man in rags for salvation is diagnosed by his family as an acute case of insanity; as "they thought, that some frenzy distemper had got into his head" (9). Seeing him run from the city, his neighbors react in three distinct ways: "some mocked, others threatned; and some cried after him to return" (10). These responses represent the world's typical and unchanging views about Christians, just as the New Testament describes them, and such views are repeated faithfully throughout the First Part of *The Pilgrim's Progress.* Christians are either ridiculous (and so should be mocked), dangerous (and thus should be threatened with persecution), or mad (and so should be restrained from their folly). Within the gallery of worldly characters who are encountered by the true pilgrims, let us briefly consider the leading proponents of these attitudes.

After Christian's own family judges him to be insane, his fellow townsmen Obstinate and Pliable reach the same verdict; they overtake Christian with the intention of bringing him back to safety. Obstinate is soon confirmed in his opinion that this fledgling pilgrim has lost his mind: "*Come then, Neighbour Pliable, let us turn again, and go home without him; there is a company of these Craz'd-headed Coxcombs, that when they take a fancy by the end, are wiser in their own eyes than seven men that can render a reason*" (11).[5] He is incensed when Pliable is at first inclined to follow Christian's example: "*What! more Fools still? be ruled by me and go back; who knows whither such a brain-sick fellow will lead you? go back, go back, and be wise*" (12). Pliable's dedication to the way of pilgrimage is extinguished by the Slough of Despond; as he turns away, his final words are a rejection of the world to come: "*May I get out again with my life, you shall possess the brave Country alone for me*" (14). Since Christian's convictions are based on a Book whose author "cannot lye" (13),[6] the truly irrational behavior in this scene is that of Obstinate and Pliable.

The people of the town of Vanity have no intention of abandoning their temporal affairs, so it is not surprising that they react to the sight of true pilgrims much as Christian's neighbors did, "some mocking, some taunting, some speaking reproachfully, and some calling upon others to smite them" (90). This episode dramatizes the most hostile of the world's opinions: Christians should be persecuted, even to the point of putting them to death. At first Vanity's citizens also incline to the insanity theory: "they that were appointed to examine them, did not believe them to be any other then [sic] Bedlams and Mad" (91). But when (as happened with Pliable) some are drawn to the pilgrims' cause, and a riot breaks out, the leaders recognize that Christians endanger their worldly business and "that they should die, for the abuse they had done, and for deluding the men of the *fair*" (92). Testifying at the trial of Faithful, Pickthank puts the issue well:

> For he hath railed on our noble Prince *Beelzebub,* and hath spoke contemptibly of his honourable Friends, whose names are the Lord *Old man,* the Lord *Carnal delight,* the Lord *Luxurious,* the Lord *Desire of Vain-glory,* my old Lord *Lechery,* Sir *Having Greedy,* with all the rest of our Nobility; and he hath said moreover, that if all men were of his mind, if possible, there is not one of these Noble-men should have any longer a being in this Town. (94)

These names suggest, of course, what the citizens prefer instead of going on pilgrimage.

When the members of the jury are identified during the trial scene, satire in *The Pilgrim's Progress* reaches a kind of climax in its density of biblical allusions. Nearly all the jurors who condemn Faithful can trace their lineage to a particular biblical passage, and the total weight of Bunyan's catalogue makes a grim commentary on how Christians fare at the hands of worldly tribunals. These townsmen of Vanity exit after hearing the charge of the judge, Lord Hate-good:

> Then went the Jury out, whose names were Mr. *Blind-man,* Mr. *No-good,* Mr. *Malice,* Mr. *Love-lust,* Mr. *Live-loose,* Mr. *Heady,* Mr. *High-mind,* Mr. *Enmity,* Mr. *Lyar,* Mr. *Cruelty,* Mr. *Hate-light,* and Mr. *Implacable,* who every one gave in his private Verdict against him among themselves, and afterwards unanimously concluded to bring him in guilty before the Judge. (96)

Over half of these names seem to have occurred to Bunyan because they appear in biblical texts that denounce unjust legal proceedings. The presiding magistrate's title is found in the King James Version only in Micah 3, which is part of a vigorous denunciation of the ruling authorities of Israel.[7] This passage also forecasts the cruel execution which is decreed for Faithful at the end of his trial:

> And I said, Hear, I pray you, O heads of Jacob, and ye princes of the house of Israel; Is it not for you to know judgment?

Who *hate the good,* and love the evil; who pluck off their skin from off them, and their flesh from off their bones;

Who also eat the flesh of my people, and flay their skin from off them; and they break their bones, and chop them in pieces, as for the pot, and as flesh within the caldron. (1–3; emphasis here and in following passages is mine)

Mr. No-good appears to have sprung from Job's complaint about the unjust way in which God allows the present world's magistrates to persecute the innocent:

If the scourge slay suddenly, he will laugh at the trial of the innocent.

The earth is given into the hand of the wicked: he covereth the faces of the judges thereof; if not, where, and who is he?

Now my days are swifter than a post: they flee away, they see *no good.* (Job 9.23–25)

On the other hand, the name of Mr. Malice suggests that the innocent ought to endure this ill treatment. The verse before the occurrence of the word in Titus 3.3 anticipates the "meekness and patience" (92) with which Christian and Faithful meet their ordeal:

Put them in mind to be subject to principalities and powers, to obey magistrates, to be ready to every good work,

To speak evil of no man, to be no brawlers, but gentle, shewing all meekness unto all men.

For we ourselves also were sometimes foolish, disobedient, deceived, serving divers lusts and pleasures, living in *malice* and envy, hateful, and hating one another. (1–3)

The presence of Mr. Hate-light among the jurymen implies not only that these followers of Christ are innocent, but that it is their accusers who stand condemned by the justice of God:

He that believeth on him is not condemned: but he that believeth not is condemned already, because he hath not believed in the name of the only begotten Son of God.

And this is the condemnation, that light is come into the world, and men loved darkness rather than light, because their deeds were evil.

For every one that doeth evil *hateth the light,* neither cometh to the light, lest his deeds should be reproved. (John 3.18–20)

Mr. Implacable's name also suggests that the judgment should really be against the jury. In the King James Version his name is mentioned only in a Pauline catalogue of men who are "Without understanding, covenant breakers, without natural affection, *implacable,* unmerciful: Who knowing the judgment of God, that they which commit such things are worthy of death, not only do the same, but have pleasure in them that do them" (Romans 1.31–32).

Mr. Enmity's origin shows that such a worldly jury could bring in only a verdict of death: "For to be carnally minded is death; but to be spiritually minded is life and peace. Because the carnal mind is *enmity* against God: for it is not subject to the law of God, neither indeed can be" (Romans 8.6–7). Mr. Liar is mentioned in 1 Timothy 1.10, which says that God's law nevertheless applies "For whoremongers, for them that defile themselves with mankind, for mensteakers, for *liars,* for perjured persons, and if there be any other thing that is contrary to sound doctrine." This also suggests the character of the testimony that has been heard at the trial, as does the text in which Mr. Cruelty's nature is described: "Deliver me not over unto the will of mine enemies: for false witnesses are risen up against me, and such as breathe out *cruelty*" (Psalm 27.12).

The foreman, Mr. Blind-man, probably takes his inspiration from Ephesians 4, which, besides alluding to spiritual blindness, also mentions the name of his home town:

> This I say therefore, and testify in the Lord, that ye henceforth walk not as other Gentiles walk, in the *vanity* of their mind,
> Having the understanding darkened, being alienated from the life of God through the ignorance that is in them, because of the *blindness* of their heart:
> Who being past feeling have given themselves over unto lasciviousness, to work all uncleanness with greediness. (17–19)

Mr. Love-lust and Mr. Live-loose may be described in verse 19. They are the only members of the jury who cannot be traced with probability to a particular Scripture. Another origin for them may be among the companions of Mr. Heady and Mr. High-mind, who are listed in 2 Timothy 3 among

> Traitors, *heady, highminded,* lovers of pleasures more than lovers of God;

Having a form of godliness, but denying the power thereof: from such turn
away.
For of this sort are they which creep into houses, and lead captive silly
women laden with sins, led away with divers *lusts,*
Ever learning, and never able to come to the knowledge of the truth. (4–7)

Surely, being judged by a jury whose members are so steeped in vice
and injustice, no honest pilgrim could have expected a favorable outcome for his trial. The savage punishment visited upon Faithful reads
like a summary of the principal torments chronicled in Foxe's *Acts and
Monuments:*

They therefore brought him out, to do with him according to their Law; and
first they Scourged him, then they Buffetted him, then they Lanced his flesh
with Knives; after that they Stoned him with Stones, then prickt him with
their Swords, and last of all they burned him to Ashes at the Stake. Thus came
Faithful to his end. (97)

Happily the pilgrims encounter much more frequently the most be-
nign of the world's three reactions—laughter, which proceeds from the
conclusion that Christians are the funniest people to be encountered
anywhere. Immediately after he had left his great burden at the Cross,
Bunyan's hero meets with merriment as he tries to enlighten Formalist
and Hypocrisy: "To these things they gave him no answer, only they
looked upon each other, and *laughed*" (41). Perhaps the most striking
instance of this attitude in *The Pilgrim's Progress,* and the most penetrating
and subtle refutation of it, comes in the pilgrims' interview with Atheist. By this time, his behavior has become familiar:

Chr. *We are going to the Mount* Sion.
Then *Atheist* fell into a very great Laughter.
Chr. *What is the meaning of your Laughter?*
Atheist. I laugh to see what ignorant persons you are, to take upon you so
    tedious a Journey; and yet are like to have nothing but your travel for
    your paines. (135; emphasis in original)

Atheist tells them that, having given up the search for the Celestial City,
"I am going back again, and will seek to refresh my self with the things

that I then cast away, for hopes of that, which I now see, is not." The marginal note for this statement is "*The* Atheist *takes up his content in this world*" (emphasis in original).

Bunyan is unusually reserved in his satire of Atheist. Christian and his new companion Hopeful seem to realize that the threat personified in this figure is a particularly serious one, and they do not confront him with the fervor that Christian employs against other worldly characters.[8] Indirectly, however, Bunyan sets out to subvert Atheist's position from the moment of his appearance: "Now after a while, they perceived afar off, one comeing softly and alone all along the High-way to meet them. Then said *Christian* to his fellow, Yonder is a man with his back toward *Sion,* and he is coming to meet us" (134). With these words, Atheist has already been branded as a rather peculiar fellow. It is emphasized that he is travelling alone—in contrast even to such false pilgrims as Talkative and By-ends, who seem to have no difficulty in finding companions. And the spiritual geography of Bunyan's book provides an even more telling condemnation. Atheist is walking in the *opposite* direction from the way to the Celestial City, whereas even Mr. Worldy-Wiseman and the citizens at Vanity Fair stayed in one place and did not *increase* their distance from the pilgrims' goal.

Atheist is allowed to make what seems a straightforward statement of his present opinion:

Chr. *Why man? Do you think we shall not be received?*
Atheist. Received! There is no such place as you dream of, in all this World.
  (135)

Yet if "this World" means "the present world"—as it always has in the First Part—then Atheist has simply made a statement with which every true pilgrim can agree. Christian takes his words in the latter sense, replying that there *is* such a place "*in the World to come.*" His remarks are confined to such simple affirmations, but an accumulation of quiet ironies continues to undermine Atheist's position. The dialogue of the episode rings with echoes of the eleventh and twelfth chapters of Hebrews:[9]

Chr. *We are going to the Mount*	But ye are come unto mount
Sion. . . .	Sion. . . . (12.22)

Atheist. When I was at home in mine own Countrey, I heard as you now affirm, and from that hearing went out to see, and have been seeking this City this twenty years: But find no more of it, than I did the first day I set out. . . . I am going back again. . . .

For they that say such things declare plainly that they seek a country.

And truly, if they had been mindful of that country from whence they came out, they might have had opportunity to have returned.

But now they desire a better country, that is, an heavenly . . . (11.14–16)

Hope. . . . Did we not see from the delectable Mountains the Gate of the City?

These all died in faith, not having received the promises, but having seen them afar off . . . (11.13)

At the end of the interview, "they turned away from the man, and he, Laughing at them, went his way" (136). Christian and Hopeful are reenacting the journey of the men of faith in Hebrews, whereas Atheist—unlike them—is availing himself of the opportunity to return. The sharp edge of Bunyan's satire can be felt even if the reader does not catch the references to Hebrews. His narrative has already established that the whole of reality is composed of two worlds (or "countries") rather than one, and that the second can be reached only by those who have rejected the first because of their belief in the one that is still to come.

The Three Lusts of the World

Since worldly characters reject the behavior of Christians in the First Part of *The Pilgrim's Progress,* what do they prefer instead? To answer this basic question, Bunyan's satire takes its direction from one of many New Testament passages that sharply contrast the world's ways with those of Christians:

Love not the world, neither the things that are in the world. If any man love the world, the love of the Father is not in him.

For all that is in the world, the lust of the flesh, and the lust of the eyes, and the pride of life, is not of the Father, but is of the world.

And the world passeth away, and the lust thereof: but he that doeth the will of God abideth for ever. (1 John 2.15–17)

Bunyan seems to have understood "the lust of the flesh" as lechery, "the lust of the eyes" as the desire for riches, and "the pride of life" as the desire for rank and ease.[10]

Christian runs into these worldly attractions from the very beginning of the story. The fact that the world and its lusts pass away is one reason that his birthplace is called "The City of Destruction." When he tells two of his townsmen why he has gone off on pilgrimage, one makes his preferences very clear: "*What! said Obstinate, and leave our Friends, and our Comforts behind us!*" (11). Pliable is briefly attracted by the prospect of the world to come, but he, too, soon opts for a life of comfort. Christian's next acquaintance, Mr. Worldly-Wiseman, hails from the town of Carnal-Policy, which is evidently dedicated to the lust of the flesh. He puts the prospects for pilgrimage in the bleakest terms: "*[H]ear me, I am older than thou! thou art like to meet with in the way which thou goest, Wearisomness, Painfulness, Hunger, Perils, Nakedness, Sword, Lions, Dragons, Darkness; and in a word, death, and what not? These things are certainly true, having been confirmed by many testimonies*" (18). And he is equally confident about the better alternative: "*I could direct thee to the obtaining of what thou desirest, without the dangers that thou in this way wilt run thy self into: yea, and the remedy is at hand. Besides, I will add, that instead of those dangers, thou shalt meet with much safety, friendship, and content*" (19). Worldly-Wiseman's views are refuted at length by Evangelist, and in his margin Bunyan cites 1 John: "They are of the world: therefore speak they of the world, and the world heareth them. We are of God" (4.5–6). A better text for the origin of his name is 1 Corinthians 1.19, which links it with Christian's first address: "For it is written, I will destroy the wisdom of the wise, and will bring to nothing the understanding of the prudent."

The contrast between this world and the next one is stressed in several of the emblems witnessed by Christian at the Interpreter's House—especially in the scene depicting Patience and Passion, where the treasure sought by the latter turns to rags: "So will it be with all such Men at the end of this world" (31). The next important episode in which Bunyan uses these ideas for satiric purposes is the dialogue that results from the meeting between Christian and Faithful.

In this scene we learn more about the interests and opinions of the world. The influences that have hindered Faithful's own pilgrimage are described as a series of personifications. Before the Wicket Gate, he escaped the clutches of Madam Wanton, who certainly represents one of the world's principal lusts, that of "all carnal and fleshly content" (68). This temptation soon returned in another form, for Faithful's next assailant was Adam the first, who offered in marriage all three of his daughters: "*The lust of the flesh, the lust of the eyes, and the pride of life*" (69). This Adam is among the first individuals in *The Pilgrim's Progress* to condemn himself by speaking Scripture; in the passage already quoted from 1 John 2, the names of his daughters describe "all that is in the world." By obeying another biblical injunction to "put off the old man with his deeds" (Colossians 3.9), Faithful freed himself from the world and its preoccupations (70).

The last and most insistent of his antagonists was Shame—who links the mockery begun by Christian's neighbors with the themes of the lust of the eyes and the pride of life, for he notes that most wealthy and important people avoid going on pilgrimage:

> why he objected against Religion it self; he said it was a pitiful, low, sneaking business for a man to mind Religion; he said that a tender conscience was an unmanly thing, and that for Man to watch over his words and ways, so as to tye up himself from that hectoring liberty, that the brave spirits of the times accustom themselves unto, would make him the Ridicule of the times. He objected also, that but few of the Mighty, Rich, or Wise, were ever of my opinion; nor any of them neither, before they were perswaded to be Fools, and to be of a voluntary fondness, to venture the loss of all, *for no body else knows what.* (72)

Like the names of the daughters of Adam the first, some of Shame's words come directly from biblical passages that condemn the world. A portion of his last sentence is taken from the end of the first chapter of 1 Corinthians:

> For ye see your calling, brethren, how that not many wise men after the flesh, not many mighty, not many noble, are called:
> But God hath chosen the foolish things of the world to confound the wise; and God hath chosen the weak things of the world to confound the things which are mighty. (26–27)

Shame is therefore really engaged in a kind of self-mockery: Faithful cannot ridicule the pilgrims for their "unworldliness" without reaffirming the truth of Scripture, which denounces his own worldly point of view. Faithful says that he also remembered another text (Luke 16.15): "But at last I began to consider, *That that which is highly esteemed among Men, is had in abomination with God*" (73). He is thus able to reject the world's opinions as well.

After their interview with Talkative—who fails in his duty "*to promote holiness in the World; not by talk only*" (83) so that he is exposed as a worldling of false piety—the pilgrims arrive at Vanity. We have already considered the biblical basis for that town's eagerness to persecute Christians; but the episode also contains an acid account of the activities that the world prefers. Here, God's judgment is less imminent than it seemed in the City of Destruction, though no less certain. Instead of stressing the ultimate wrath to come, the narrative now grimly satirizes the temporal follies of worldly folk, as well as their wicked conduct toward Christians.

Bunyan builds up his portrait by fitting together a tight mosaic of scriptural references; his portrait of "the world" is going to be almost literally what the Bible says it is, for it will be based on the Bible's very words. In the opening sentences his tone is wryly humorous:

> Then I saw in my Dream, that when they were got out of the Wilderness, they presently saw a Town before them, and the name of that Town is *Vanity;* and at the Town there is a *Fair* kept called *Vanity-Fair:* It is kept all the year long, it beareth the name of *Vanity-Fair,* because the Town where tis kept, *is lighter then* Vanity; and also, because all that is there sold, or that cometh thither, is *Vanity.* As is the saying of the wise, *All that cometh is vanity.* (88)

The marginal citations account for the name of the town and suggest many details for the rest of the portrait. Isaiah 40.17 mentions "vanity" as a term for all the countries of the world: "All nations before him are as nothing; and they are counted to him less than nothing, and vanity." In the first chapter of Ecclesiastes, the speaker, surveying the whole world, finds it all "vanity" without any "profit":

> Vanity of vanities, saith the Preacher, vanity of vanities; all is vanity.
> What profit hath a man of all his labour which he taketh under the sun?
> (2–3)

The word "profit" seems to have given Bunyan the idea of making a commercial fair the main feature of the town of Vanity.

One of the "nations" mentioned later by Isaiah is Babylon. This fact has influenced the description of the merchandise for sale at the Fair, which contains representative samples of the lust of the flesh, the lust of the eyes, and the pride of life.

> Therefore at *this Fair* are all such Merchandise sold, as Houses, Lands, Trades, Places, Honours, Preferments, Titles, Countreys, Kingdoms, Lusts, Pleasures, and Delights of all sorts, as Whores, Bauds, Wives, Husbands, Children, Masters, Servants, Lives, Blood, Bodies, Souls, Silver, Gold, Pearls, Precious Stones, and what not.
>
> And moreover, at this Fair there is at all times to be seen Juglings, Cheats, Games, Plays, Fools, Apes, Knaves, and Rogues, and that of all sorts.
>
> Here are to be seen too, and that for nothing, Thefts, Murders, Adultries, False-swearers, and that of a blood-red colour. (88)

The device of mixing people and things indiscriminately shows that the merchants of the Fair, though preoccupied with wealth, are unable to distinguish true value. Bunyan's theme and technique, along with many of the particular items on sale, are derived from an uncited passage describing God's judgment on the worldly merchants of Babylon, in Revelation 18:

> Alas, alas, that great city Babylon, that mighty city! for in one hour is thy judgment come.
>
> And the merchants of the earth shall weep and mourn over her; for no man buyeth their merchandise any more:
>
> The merchandise of gold, and silver, and precious stones, and of pearls, and fine linen, and purple, and silk, and scarlet, and all thyine wood, and all manner vessels of ivory, and all manner vessels of most precious wood, and of brass, and iron, and marble,
>
> And cinnamon, and odours, and ointments, and frankincense, and wine, and oil, and fine flour, and wheat, and beasts, and sheep, and horses, and chariots, and slaves, and souls of men. (10–13)

Much of the context of this passage is reproduced in Bunyan's story, even if the reader does not recognize the ultimate biblical source. The early Christian churches in Revelation both scorned and feared their worldly persecutors. Similarly, the pilgrims refuse to trade with the Fair and are fiercely punished by its rulers. In Revelation, God's wrath has visited Babylon, and the prospect of a repetition of this event remains in the background of the new narrative.

Still taking his cue from Isaiah's identification of "all nations" with "vanity," Bunyan assigns them all to particular streets in the Fair. A parenthetical note makes certain that his meaning is clear:

> And as in other Fairs of less moment, there are several Rows and Streets under their proper names, where such and such Wares are vended: So here likewise, you have the proper Places, Rows, Streets (*viz.* Countreys, and Kingdoms) where the Wares of this Fair are soonest to be found: Here is the *Britain* Row, the *French* Row, the *Italian* Row, the *Spanish* Row, the *German* Row, where several sorts of Vanities are to be sold. (88–89)

The biblical citations now begin to relate this portrait to earlier satiric passages in the narrative, since "the world" is now mentioned directly: "Now, as I said, the way to the Coelestial City lyes just thorow *this Town,* where this lusty Fair is kept; and he that will go to the City, and yet not go thorow this Town, must needs *go out of the World.*" These words are an adroit combination of the idea of the journey of life with Paul's admission that some contact with other "lusty" sinners is unavoidable:

> I wrote unto you in an epistle not to company with fornicators:
> Yet not altogether with the fornicators of this world, or with the covetous, or extortioners, or with idolators; for then must ye needs go out of the world. (1 Corinthians 5.9–10)

In the final paragraph of his general description of Vanity, Bunyan makes one of the temptations of Christ a part of the town's history, taking advantage of the statement in the New Testament that the devil "shewed unto him all the kingdoms of the world" (Luke 4.5):

> The Prince of Princes himself, when here, went through *this Town* to his own Countrey, and that upon a *Fair-day* too: Yea, and as I think it was *Beelzebub,* the chief Lord of this *Fair,* that invited him to buy of his *Vanities;* yea, would have made him Lord of the *Fair,* would he but have done him Reverence as he went thorow the *Town.* Yea, because he was such a person of Honour, *Beelzebub* had him from *Street* to *Street,* and shewed him all the Kingdoms of

the World in a little time, that he might, if possible alure that Blessed One, to *cheapen* and *buy* some of his *Vanities.* But he had no mind to the Merchandize, and therefore left the *Town;* without laying out so much as one Farthing upon these *Vanities.* (89)

Satire by diminution of stature is finely handled in this portrait of the great devil Beelzebub as a kind of petty merchant, hawking his worthless, worldly wares.

The beginning of the Vanity Fair episode satirizes the world's principal lusts—particularly its desire for riches—while the latter portion attacks its habit of persecuting Christians. Bunyan unites these two themes in the verdict of the last of the jurors, Mr. Implacable: "*Might I have all the World given me, I could not be reconciled to him, therefore let us forthwith bring him in guilty of death*" (97). His words are an ironic perversion of Christ's warning about the last judgment: "For what shall it profit a man, if he shall gain the whole world, and lose his own soul?" (Mark 8.36). Mr. Implacable could never be reconciled to a true pilgrim even if his "profit" could include the whole world (a possession that, in biblical terms, is not worth having); and there is an evident implication that he is fated to lose his own soul at the last judgment.

After this full-scale indictment of the present world, *The Pilgrim's Progress* returns to more specialized satiric portraits. Having shown one character being "faithful unto death" in the practice of the Christian religion,[11] Bunyan now presents a group that prefers another opinion on the matter. First to make his appearance is By-ends, who is walking in the Way as a pilgrim but is cautious about giving his name to Christian and Hopeful. This trait is the first indication of his devious religious practices, which are comically displayed when he describes his relatives in the town of Fair-speech:

> Chr. *Pray who are your Kindred there, if a man may be so bold;*
> By-ends. Almost the whole Town; and in particular my Lord *Turn-about,* my Lord *Time-server,* my Lord *Fair-speech,* (from whose Ancestors that Town first took its name:) Also Mr. *Smooth-man,* Mr. *Facing-bothways,* Mr. *Any-thing,* and the Parson of our Parish, Mr. *Two-tongues,* was my Mothers own Brother by Father's side: And to tell you the Truth, I am become a Gentleman of good Quality; yet my Great Grand-father was but a Water-man, looking one way, and Rowing another: and I got most of my estate by the same occupation. (99)[12]

His emphasis on Lords and Gentlemen suggests that social status is an important motive in the religion of his clan. Rank is, of course, part of the "pride of life" that Faithful rejected before his martyrdom.

Christian denounces By-ends' preference for a comfortable religion. Instead, By-ends is joined by three others who find his company congenial—Mr. Hold-the-World, Mr. Money-love, and Mr. Save-all. For the first time in his story, Bunyan sends all the godly characters offstage and satirizes representatives of the world by having them converse with one another. Like Adam the first, Shame, and Mr. Implacable, they prove to be adept at self-condemnation. Mr. Hold-the-World, for example, is obviously a good companion for his two miserly friends, since he finds that both nature and the Bible demonstrate the validity of the "profit" motive:

> Let us be wise *as Serpents,* 'tis best to make hay when the Sun shines; you see how the Bee lieth still all winter and bestirs her then only when she can have profit with pleasure. God sends sometimes Rain, and sometimes Sunshine; if they be such fools to go through the first, yet let us be content to take fair weather along with us. For my part I like that Religion best, that will stand with the security of Gods good blessings unto us; for who can imagin that is ruled by his reason, since God has bestowed upon us the good things of this life, but that he would have us keep them for his sake. *Abraham* and *Solomon* grew rich in Religion. And *Job* saies, that a good man *shall lay up gold as dust.* (102)[13]

The name of Mr. Hold-the-World sums up the commitments of all the worldly characters who have appeared thus far; all have desired to hold onto the lusts of their transitory earthly existence instead of becoming true pilgrims like Christian, who seeks the reward of eternal life. After Mr. Hold-the-World has argued that ministers and tradesmen may use religion to help their profits, the four decide to consult Christian on the subject. The answer they receive hits directly at the philosophy embodied in Mr. Hold-the-World: "Even a babe in Religion may answer ten thousand such questions. For if it be unlawful to follow Christ for loaves, as it is, *Joh.* 6. How much more abominable is it to make of him and *religion a stalking-horse* to get and enjoy the world" (105). Christian then stuns the four worldly representatives into silence with a barrage of scriptural citations.

By-ends and his fellows come to grief when they reach Demas's silver mine, in the following episode. The name of the proprietor is taken from a pertinent remark in one of Paul's epistles: "Demas hath forsaken me, having loved this present world" (2 Timothy 4.10). As his silver mine indicates, Demas's motivation is interpreted in Bunyan's story as the love of riches. He is denounced by Christian, who traces his biblical ancestry to Judas (the betrayer of Christ for thirty pieces of silver) and Gehazi (who in the Old Testament attempted to get silver by fraud and was stricken with leprosy). Since By-ends, Hold-the-World, and the others tried to combine religion and the pursuit of wealth, they end their pilgrimage appropriately by falling into the mine. Christian's song links their fate to the point of the previous satiric portraits:

> By-ends, *and Silver-*Demas, *both agree;*
> *One calls, the other runs, that he may be*
> *A sharer in his Lucre: so these two*
> *Take up in this World, and no further go.* (108)

The scenes considered thus far show Bunyan directing his Bible-based satire with telling consistency. Nearly all the world's vices are summed up in the three daughters of Adam the first: the sins of the flesh, the love of riches, and the desire for rank and ease. The world, in turn, regards Christians as foolish, dangerous, or mad.

Mr. Ignorance

In the episodes involving Mr. Ignorance, something is missing from the sure touch that Bunyan has exhibited elsewhere in the First Part. The problem is not that he has failed to create an interesting character, for the portrait of Ignorance—a kind of early Candide—is vivid and memorable; as an exercise in satire, though, it almost certainly misses its mark.

The first interview with Ignorance occurs shortly before the encounter with Atheist. Like the latter, he is under suspicion as soon as he appears. Bearing an unflattering name, he walks into the Way from the country of Conceit and is described as "a very brisk Lad" (123). Some of his first words indicate that he will condemn himself by speaking scriptural quotations, as did Adam the first when he told the names of his daughters to Faithful. Listing his qualifications for entering the Celestial City, he gives this description of himself: "I know my Lords will, and I have been a good Liver, I pay every man his own; I Pray, Fast, pay Tithes, and give Alms, and have left my Countrey, for whither I am going" (123–24). His remark recalls the parable of the Pharisee in the temple, whose posturing contrasted with the publican's humility:

> The Pharisee stood and prayed thus with himself, God, I thank thee, that I am not as other men are, extortioners, unjust, adulterers, or even as this publican.
> I fast twice in the week, I give tithes of all that I possess.
> And the publican, standing afar off, would not lift up so much as his eyes unto heaven, but smote upon his breast, saying, God be merciful to me a sinner. (Luke 18.11–13)

The Pharisees are a promising source of allusions for Bunyan's satire on worldly folk, but he does not develop the reference in this scene. Instead, Christian ends the first meeting by quoting texts from Proverbs and Ecclesiastes: "When *Christian* saw that the man was wise in his own conceit; he said to *Hopeful*, whisperingly. *There is more hopes of a fool then of him*. And said moreover, *When he that is a fool walketh by the way, his wisdom faileth him, and he saith to every one that he is a fool*" (Proverbs 26.12; Ecclesiastes 10.3). Unlike the great majority of such citations in *The Pilgrim's Progress,* these do not seem wholly applicable to the character who illustrates them. Ignorance has shown that he possesses courtesy and modesty—qualities not usually associated with conceited fools. When Christian calls him a potential "*Thief and a Robber*" for not coming in at the Gate, he responds, "Gentlemen, ye be utter strangers to me, I know you not, be content to follow the Religion of your Countrey, and I will follow the Religion of mine. I hope all will be well." He has at least demonstrated an understanding of another text from Proverbs: "A soft answer turneth away wrath."

After several adventures, Christian and Hopeful hold another debate with Ignorance. Their talk ranges over a number of theological issues, and on every point Ignorance takes a stand that has been condemned in previous discussions throughout the First Part. Yet, although the weight of the argument is wholly against him, Ignorance does not cut a poor figure in the interview. He continues to answer his overbearing companions respectfully, asking enough questions to obtain a full awareness of their opinions. Then, unlike most of their previous opponents, he shows real skill in debate. Against Christian's views on justification, he raises the issue of antinomianism and receives only invective in reply:

> *Ignor.* What! would you have us trust to what Christ in his own person has done without us? This conceit would loosen the reines of our lust, and tollerate us to live as we list: For what matter how we live if we may be Justified by Christs personal righteousness from all, when we believe it?
> Chr. Ignorance *is thy name, and as thy name is, so art thou; even this thy answer demonstrateth what I say.* Ignorant *thou art of what Justifying righteousness is, and, as* Ignorant *how to secure thy Soul through the faith of it from the heavy wrath of God.* (148)

Eventually, Ignorance also decides that Christian and Hopeful must be mad. But, in contrast to previous representatives of the world, he reaches this conclusion after a lengthy inquiry, and he maintains an attitude of moderation in the face of their increasing petulance:

> *Hope.* Ask him if ever he had Christ revealed to him from Heaven?
> Ignor. *What! you are a man for revelations! I believe that what both you, and all the rest of you say about that matter, is but the fruit of distracted braines.*
> *Hope.* Why man! Christ is so hid in God from the natural apprehensions of all flesh, that he cannot by any man be savingly known, unless God the Father reveals him to them.
> Ignor. *That is your faith, but not mine; yet mine I doubt not, is as good as yours: though I have not in my head so many whimzies as you.* (148–49)

Though Christian is ready with texts about the necessity of revelation for knowledge of God, the biblical application of Bunyan's scene has been severely weakened. The sinful representative of the world is persistently turning the other cheek, while the godly pilgrims have become sourly self-righteous. Bunyan has in fact reversed the roles of the participants in the parable to which he alluded in the earlier scene. Having acquired the publican's humility, his Pharisee makes the pilgrims beat their breasts to assert their own superiority.

In the final appearance of Ignorance, at the very end of the First Part, Bunyan returns briefly to the technique with which he began the first encounter. After crossing the River of Death, Ignorance approaches the

Celestial City: "But he was asked by the men that lookt over the top of the Gate, Whence came you? and what would you have? He answered, I have eat and drank in the presence of the King, and he has taught in our Streets" (162–63). His words are taken from an earlier parable in Luke that also attacks the Pharisees (13.25–27). The King of the Celestial City orders Ignorance carried off to hell—a response that is similar to that of the master of the house in the parable: "depart from me, all ye workers of iniquity." More of these allusions might have salvaged a victory for Bunyan's attack on Ignorance, but his last appearance is too brief to erase the impression made in the two previous episodes.

Alone among Bunyan's worldly portraits, this one does little to further his satiric aims. Ignorance does not exhibit the right reactions, since he hears Christian and Hopeful out with patience instead of making fun of them. Furthermore, he shows little interest in any of the daughters of Adam the first, so the biblical texts that they represent do not appear to apply to him. Ignorance indeed fails to enter the Way through the Wicket Gate, and he hires the services of "Vain-Hope, a Ferry-man" to negotiate the River of Death. At these points the Bible is against him, for Bunyan's Wicket Gate is the "strait gate" of Matthew 7.13–14, and the children of Israel did not float across the Red Sea or the Jordan; yet at other moments, as we have seen, he seems to have Scripture on his side. Not surprisingly, Ignorance is the only false pilgrim who has won the sympathy of numerous readers.[14] We should not, however, allow the comparative failure of this one attempt to obscure our appreciation for Bunyan's overall achievement as a satirist in the First Part of *The Pilgrim's Progress*. Most of the way, his book is working in smooth partnership with *the* Book, holding worldly folk up to ridicule by making them behave exactly as the Bible says they do.

Biblical Satire in the Second Part

Two episodes in Bunyan's sequel continue to develop the satiric themes of the First Part. Before Christiana leaves for the Celestial City, she is visited by Mrs. Timorous, who repeats some of Mr. Worldly-Wiseman's warnings about the dangers of becoming a pilgrim. When Christiana rebuffs her, Mrs. Timorous goes to seek comfort with her worldly friends, "Mrs. *Bats-eyes*, Mrs. *Inconsiderate*, Mrs. *Light-mind*, and

Mrs. *Know-nothing*" (184).[15] Bunyan handles the scene in the same manner as he did the one involving By-ends and his friends (100–05). With no godly characters present, these townspeople condemn themselves out of their own mouths in a dialogue that is summed up in the remark of Mrs. Inconsiderate: " 'twas never a good World since these whimsical Fools dwelt in it" (185). Mrs. Light-mind adds a coda that extends Bunyan's satire on the lusts of the flesh by inventing several new characters:

> Come put this kind of Talk away. I was Yesterday at Madam *Wantons,* where we were as merry as the Maids. For who do you think should be there, but I, and Mrs. *Love-the-flesh,* and three or four more, with Mr. *Lechery,* Mrs. *Filth,* and some others. So there we had Musick and dancing, and what else was meet to fill up the pleasure. And I dare say my Lady her self is an admirably well-bred Gentlewoman, and Mr. *Lechery* is as pretty a Fellow.

The portrait of Madam Bubble, included near the end of the Second Part (300–03), also develops satiric material from the earlier narrative. Like the merchants at Vanity Fair, Madam Bubble ministers to the world's interests and pleasures: "I am the Mistriss of the world."[16] She is presented as a temptation of Mr. Stand-fast, who says he met her as "one in very pleasant Attire, *but old,* that presented her self unto me, and offered me three things, to wit, her *Body,* her *Purse,* and her *Bed.*" Her proposal is the same as the one made by Adam the first when he offered to Faithful the lust of the flesh, the lust of the eyes, and the pride of life. Bunyan intends the bed to suggest worldly ease, rather than lust—as Mr. Stand-fast makes clear: "I was both a weary, and sleepy, I am also as poor as a *Howlet,* and that, perhaps, the *Witch* knew."

Madam Bubble possesses the traits of many worldly figures who have appeared in both parts of *The Pilgrim's Progress.* Since she wears "*a great Purse by her side,*" with "*her Hand often in it fingering her Mony, as if that was her Hearts delight,*" she is evidently kin to the citizens of Vanity Fair, and to Mr. Money-love and Demas. Madam Bubble's sociability is similar to that of Mrs. Timorous and her friends: "She is a great *Gossiper,* she is always, both she and her Daughters, at one Pilgrim's Heels or other, now Commending, and then preferring the excellencies of this Life." She also shares the attitudes of Shame: "She always laugheth Poor Pilgrims to scorn, but highly commends the Rich." The biblical citations for this portrait include 1 John 2.15, the verse (already quoted) just before the one that contains the names of the daughters of Adam the first.

The scenes involving Mrs. Timorous and Madam Bubble appear somewhat out of place in the Second Part, largely because the typical actions of Bunyan's characters no longer conform to the ideas that are affirmed by the satire of the earlier story. At the beginning of the Second Part, we learn that the world in general has changed its mind about Christian: "For though when he was here, he was *Fool* in every mans mouth, yet now he is gone, he is highly commended of all. For 'tis said he lives bravely where he is: Yea, many of them that are resolved never to run his hazzards, yet have their mouths water at his gains" (175). When they reach the town of Vanity, the second group of pilgrims remembers the sufferings of their predecessors. Mr. Contrite informs them that religion is now esteemed in certain neighborhoods: "In *those* days we were afraid to walk the Streets, but *now* we can shew our Heads. *Then* the Name of a Professor was odious, *now,* specially in some parts of our Town (for you know our Town is large) Religion is counted Honourable" (275).

For their part, the pilgrims exhibit a greater affection for the world. Although in his preface Bunyan says that his new party will show "*how they still / Refuse this World, to do their Fathers will*" (167), the leisurely pace of the second journey makes their refusal seem less wholehearted. Instead of passing a night at the House Beautiful, as did Christian, they stay "about a Month or above" (224). They spend over ten days at the house of Gaius, and "a great while" at Mr. Mnason's in the town of Vanity (269; 277). The names of these hosts recall those of early Christians who provided lodging for Paul (Romans 16.23; Acts 21.16). They remind us that, even in New Testament times, Christians were able to find a measure of comfort and hospitality in the world.[17]

In the friendlier atmosphere of the Second Part, there is much less emphasis on the dreadful prospect of God's wrath. Instead, Bunyan invents new characters in order to stress a completely different side of the divine nature—God's mercy and love. His method continues to imitate the sermon *exemplum,* since he regularly presents an individual and then turns to the scriptures that describe him. He still has a satirist's attitude toward his characters, for their behavior also appears ridiculous when it is compared to the ideas that are affirmed by the narrative. However, the result is satire of a much milder sort. In the author's eyes, the sins of this new group are far less vicious than those which he assailed in the portraits of the First Part.

The new theme for Bunyan's satire is announced in the opening dialogue of the Second Part, where the topic of conversation is not the day of judgment but the warm reception given Christian at the Celestial City. A young woman named Mercy is an important member of the second group of pilgrims, and the pattern for the satiric portraits of the Second Part is presented in the scene when this new character is fearful of being rejected at the Wicket Gate. After knocking loudly, she falls down in a faint; the Keeper—gradually identified as Christ himself— then goes out and brings her in. Christiana, who was already inside, tells Mercy that "*When he heard your lumbring noise, he gave a wonderful Innocent smile. I believe what you did pleas'd him well enough, for he shewed no sign to the contrary*" (192). The Keeper's smile indicates that there is something faintly comic about Mercy's anxiety over her acceptance. In this part of *The Pilgrim's Progress,* a more merciful God is hardly likely to reject anyone who bears such a name.

Mercy's needless anxiety is shared by several other characters who appear later. The first of these is Mr. Fearing, who also fainted at the Wicket Gate (250). Great-heart emphasizes that his anxieties were not about the dangers of the present world: "When we came to the Hill *Difficulty,* he made no stick at that, nor did he much fear the Lyons. For you must know that his Trouble *was not about such things as those,* his Fear was about his Acceptance at last" (251). The citations at the end of the portrait make plain that Mr. Fearing's condition was not unusual in biblical times. Psalm 88 is particularly applicable: "For my soul is full of troubles: and my life draweth nigh unto the grave. . . . I am afflicted and ready to die from my youth up: while I suffer thy terrors I am distracted" (3.15).

During their stay with Gaius, the Pilgrims rescue Mr. Feeble-mind, a friend of Fearing's who "would, if I could, tho I can but *craul,* spend my Life in the Pilgrims way" (267). Because of his many infirmities, he objects to joining the group—until he is finally comforted with a quotation from one of Paul's epistles: "But Brother, said Mr. *Great-heart.* I have it in Commission, to comfort the *feeble minded,* and to support the weak" (270; 1 Thessalonians 5.14). He is soon joined by a man on crutches, Mr. Ready-to-halt, whose name is explained by a citation from Psalm 38: "For I am ready to halt, and my sorrow is continually before me" (17).

Part of the quiet comedy of the dancing scene near Doubting Castle is at the expense of the participants. These "chicken-hearted" pilgrims can only attain a degree of Christian joy after they have actually looked on the severed head of Giant Depair:

> Now when *Feeble-mind*, and *Ready-to-halt* saw that it was the Head of *Gyant-Dispair* indeed, they were very jocond and merry. Now *Christiana*, if need was, could play upon the *Vial*, and her Daughter *Mercie* upon the *Lute*: So, since they were so merry disposed, she plaid them a Lesson, and *Ready-to-halt* would Dance. So he took *Dispondencie*'s Daughter, named *Much-afraid*, by the Hand, and to dancing they went in the Road. True, he could not Dance without one Crutch in his Hand, but I promise you, he footed it well; also the Girl was to be commended, for she answered the Musick handsomely. (283)

Biblical inspiration for this episode probably comes from a passage in Jeremiah that looks forward to a joyful reunion of the scattered children of Israel: "Then shall the virgin rejoice in the dance, both young men and old men together: for I will turn their mourning into joy, and will comfort them, and make them rejoice from their sorrow" (31.13). We feel that these timid Christians might have embraced the joys and comforts of their religion a little earlier.

In the portraits of both parts of *The Pilgrim's Progress*, Bunyan's satiric methods are never far removed from their origins in the art of the sermon. Like a good homilist, he produces *exempla* in which character and action convey the spirit and often the exact language of particular biblical texts. Apart from this point-by-point correspondence between his narrative and Scripture, there is also a larger, more general resemblance between the satire in the two parts of his book and the conceptions that dominate the two principal portions of the Christian Bible. In each part, Bunyan's portraits stress the same attributes of the Deity that are emphasized in each of the two testaments. Thus, although many passages in the Old Testament testify to God's mercy, the dominant impression is that of a stern and angry Jehovah, who punishes wickedness by sending fires and floods, and who will judge Israel and all other nations. This is the God whose wrath occasions Christian's flight from the world and causes him to try to persuade its sinful inhabitants to join him. Similarly, while the idea of judgment is reaffirmed from Matthew through Revelation, the most important doctrine in the New Testament is the affirmation that a merciful God has sent his son to redeem the world. Much of Bunyan's satire in the Second Part of *The Pilgrim's Progress* suggests that this redemption can extend even to the most faint-hearted of believers.

Consideration of Bunyan-as-satirist has the effect of altering to some degree his place in literary history and even our impression of his personality. We tend to think of him as a holdover from the earlier seventeenth century, having little in common with the more secular writers who fill our anthologies of Restoration literature. At least one of the latter group agreed with this verdict. During act III, scene 4 of *The Way of the World*, Lady Wishfort sends Mrs. Marwood offstage to overhear an intrigue: "There are books over the chimney—Quarles and Prynne, and the *Short View of the Stage*, with Bunyan's works to entertain you." The suggestion is that, along with the other dour moralists on her closet shelf, the author of *The Pilgrim's Progress* would have been horrified by the lusts of Lady Wishfort's friends.

Nevertheless, Bunyan's methods do have something in common with those of more celebrated satirists of the Restoration period, and perhaps Congreve's image of him—like our own—lays too much stress on the stern and sober Puritan. Unlike the anxious younger man who wrote *Grace Abounding*, the later Bunyan had a self-assurance that enabled him to make merry with his opponents and to encourage his less confident friends. What is really unusual about his satire is that its premises are so firmly on the Lord's side rather than on the devil's. Skeptics have produced countless travesties, lampoons, and other assaults on the ridiculous behavior of dedicated Christians. It is rare indeed, though, to find a believer using the Bible to roast the complacent foes of Christianity or to laugh away the fears of the faint-hearted faithful. We would do well to remember the painting that hangs in London's National Portrait Gallery: while John Bunyan is shown holding the Bible firmly, there is a half-smile on his face.

DAYTON HASKIN

Bunyan's Scriptural Acts

In a sermon before the Commons in 1647, Ralph Cudworth spoke about the enormous energy lately unleashed in enthusiastic attempts to achieve a further reformation. He was not particularly sanguine about the rise of the sects. He said:

> We make a great deal of noise and raise a great deal of dust with our feet, but we do not move from off the ground on which we stood, we do not go forward at all: or if we do sometimes make a little progresse, we quickly loose again, the ground which we had gained. . . . As if Religion were nothing else, but a *Dancing* up and down, upon the same piece of ground and . . . not a sober Journying, and Travelling onwards toward some certain place.[1]

Cudworth's metaphors anticipated another, more indirect attempt, made some thirty years later, to channel the enthusiasm for "new lights" and further revelations. The phrase "Travelling onwards toward some certain place" points toward the full title of Bunyan's book: *The Pilgrim's Progress from this World to that which is to come; delivered under the Similitude of a Dream: wherein is discovered the manner of his setting out, his dangerous Journey, and safe arrival at the desired Country.*[2] When he identified the "certain place" toward which the pilgrimage was headed as "the world to come" and presented the Celestial City as "the desired Country," Bunyan was drawing upon what he understood to be a particular strand of writings within the New Testament. He was using the companion volumes of St. Luke and the Epistle to the Hebrews to take his stand on one of the major interpretive issues of the era: the goal of further reformation. For Bunyan the goal, both as *eschaton* and as *telos,* was beyond time and space—and not, as many radical sectarians were urging, a personal, interior enlightenment in this world.

Given the harsh treatment accorded them under the Clarendon Code, we might expect the prison literature of dissenters to be directed principally against the persecuting establishment, the Erastian Church of England. Recently, in his richly revisionary study of the literary culture of Restoration Noncomformity, N. H. Keeble has illuminated Bunyan's position within this historical milieu.[3] But *The Pilgrim's Progress,* for all its acknowledgment of the sufferings of dissenters and its debts to biblical texts that envisage persecution as the lot of the faithful Christians, suggests that there may be even more subtle dangers for its heroes in the "progressive" views being articulated by more radical dissenters.[4] As a fellow Nonconformist and sectary, Bunyan had enough in common with these radicals to take their position seriously. For the most part he shared their social and political attitudes; it was their theology to which he objected.[5] From his perspective, the radicals' insistence upon their personal authority, while it helped to inspire resistance against the unjust exercise of political authority, severely compromised the basis of its own inspiration: the power of God's grace as it continued to break forth out of the Scriptures.

In this essay it is not my business to explore the complex issues involved in judging to what extent Bunyan's perspective on his radical opponents was valid. Nor is it to take up questions that my argument may raise for a new study of the reception-history of *The Pilgrim's Progress,* a history that includes the induction of that self-designated "Novelty" into the larger history of English fiction.[6] My concern here is chiefly with Bunyan's discovery of playful reading and of writerly authority in the midst of his dialogue with the radicals. He came to see in the Scriptures a playing field for his own scriptural acts and to present his authority as so continuous with the purposes of the scriptural authors as not to rival their productions. This discovery is encoded in *The Pilgrim's Progress,* a book which, by distilling in a fictional representation what its author took to be the Bible's essential story, invites readers to make similar discoveries for themselves. In writing *The Pilgrim's Progress,* Bunyan found a way to leave behind reading the Bible primarily as a storehouse of promises and threats.[7] He transformed his Bible into a book that offered deferred endings and open spaces; he made it into a story that had foreseen his very retelling of it as an authentic part of the further reformation.

Bunyan and the Goal of Further Reformation

Disputes about the goal of further reformation had been at their most intense when Bunyan first got religion.[8] With the rise of the sects the notion that "new lights" were available had become a commonplace. Some radicals, to justify leaving behind a merely "traditional" understanding of the historic revelation enshrined in the Bible, extended Calvin's insistence that readers of the Bible need to be illumined by the Holy Spirit. They worked variations on widely accepted procedures of typological reading to project themselves into a historical narrative. Invoking an analogy with the dawning of day and its progress toward noon, they told the history of their times as a progressive enlightenment beyond the period of the first Reformers.[9] In a sermon of 1643, for example, William Seigwich (Sedgwick) acknowledged that the spirit of God must have been with Luther and Calvin and the Marian martyrs, at the same time dismissing these hallowed predecessors as unlucky victims of a historical era when only a limited amount of light had been available: "We may without arrogance think the Gospel hath gotten something in these fourescore yeeres, there is some more cleare light. They lived in the dawning of the day, we enjoy more light, that which succeeds us will be greater: and therefore it is no dishonour to them for us to proceed in a further reformation."[10]

This was "progresse" indeed, the "new light" necessary to usher in the millennium. A new outpouring of God's Spirit created the conditions not only for a "liberty of prophesying," but also for the idea that a final dispensation, eclipsing even that of the New Testament, had been inaugurated within history. The Apostles "have declared," wrote Winstanley, "that the same spirit that ruled in Christ, should in the latter dayes be poured out upon sonnes and daughters."[11] He was referring to the quotation from the prophet Joel (2.28) which, according to the Book of Acts (2.16ff.), Peter had enlisted on Pentecost to explain his companions' enthusiastic outburst. Taking this as a prophecy that was at last being fulfilled among God's Englishmen, various radicals saw in Peter's prediction that "young men shall see visions" and "old men shall dream dreams" the pretext for regarding even the New Testament as an old dispensation.[12] By the 1650s, as the "Postscript" in Henry Hammond's popular New Testament *Paraphrase* attests, this had become the text par excellence to which appeal was made by those who were bidding good-bye to the practice of appealing to a text.[13] For the Familists and other radicals, it was one of the texts that showed how the Bible itself pointed to the fact that it was to be superseded. According to George Fox, Christ was now come to "teach his people himself," and the knowledge enshrined in the Scriptures would at best confirm what could now be got through "pure openings of Light without the help of any man." Quaker "openings" were not so much insights into texts as they were sudden understandings of experience that might or might not be validated by scriptural precedents. When a priest at Aldingham "told me Matthew, Mark, Luke, and John were the Gospel," says Fox, "I told him the Gospel was the power of God."[14]

Bunyan had none of Fox's confidence that the power of God could operate independently of the Scriptures. He tells in *Grace Abounding* of the texts that chased him round and tugged on him as on a rope, especially certain passages from Hebrews which, he says, were enough to keep him out of heaven. Feeling certain that the verse about the exclusion of Esau, who had sold his birthright (Heb. 12.17), was meant to describe his own state, and unable to free himself from what Basil Willey once denominated "that last infirmity of noble Protestants—subservience to holy writ,"[15] Bunyan had gone on, "travailling" through the pages of the Bible as an outsider, seeing and not perceiving any promise addressed to him, hearing and not understanding any means for counting himself among the elect. He was sure that the day of grace had come and gone, and he had been left behind. Unable to make his way into the visionary company, he indulged a fantasy in which the passages that damned him had been expunged from the book. This sinful fantasy, as it turns out, clarified for him the nature of his problem. "Then methought I should see," he narrates, "as if both *Peter,* and *Paul,* and *John,* and all the Writers did look with scorn upon me, and hold me in derision; and as if they said unto me, All our words are truth, one of as much force as another. . . . [*T*]*he Scriptures cannot be broken, 2 Pet. 2.21.*"[16]

Although he felt he had to reconcile himself to the impossibility of ever producing a text to rival those of his great precursors, Bunyan got through his spiritual crisis, as the experience of the burdened Christian at the House of the Interpreter suggests, by continuing to read and by learning to interpret the sacred texts and to apply the promises for himself. He found room within which to write by presenting himself as a methodically humble interpreter; and he accepted his secondary and belated position vis-à-vis the Bible.[17] In casting *The Pilgrim's Progress* in the form of a dream-vision he avoided, rather than exploited, the opportunity to associate his book with the popular interpretation of the passage from Joel and Acts. And while it was his most audaciously original book, he insisted that it only *"seems a Novelty"*: it actually *"contains / Nothing but sound and honest Gospel-strains"* (*PP*, 7). From the time he had first entered the lists as an interpreter, in fact, Bunyan had been trying to come down squarely on the side of those who looked to the Bible not as a constraining or inhibiting force, but as an enabling power.[18] Until he wrote *The Pilgrim's Progress*, in which he also took seriously what a burden it was to work out a consoling interpretation of the Scriptures, his theory was naively optimistic. (Even in *Grace Abounding* the narrator does not see clearly the intimate relation between inhibition and enablement in the dialectic of the rival texts that tear at his soul. This makes for much of the poignancy of his story.) Writing against the Quakers, Bunyan titled his first book *Some Gospel-truths Opened*, evincing a conviction that the truths of the Bible are to be "opened" and applied in each generation anew. From the initial pages it is clear that Bunyan was arguing for a religion oriented toward a "certain place," the heaven into which, according to the Book of Acts, Christ had ascended bodily. The book was published in the year in which James Nayler rode into Bristol on an ass amidst shouts of "Hosanna to the Son of David!"

For the next twenty years and more, as Bunyan got to know his Bible better and learned somewhat more pleasurable ways to interpret it, he sustained a concern to chasten the self-centered activities of those who presented themselves as superior to the scriptural writers. He regularly sought to rule out the hope that all the promises were to be fulfilled within this world and this life. He was adamant in urging the importance of looking to "the world to come," and his principal writings show him attempting to work out the implications of a thoroughgoing belief in divine transcendence. The function, if not the form, of *The Pilgrim's Progress* was continuous with the efforts its author had been making ever since he began writing.

Finding a Place: Calvin's Commentaries on Acts and the Challenge of the Radicals

Bunyan's steady orientation toward a "heaven without," that is, a paradise that could not be reduced to a psychological state of consciousness within an individual believer, was tied to a particular understanding of the nature of God's Word in the Calvinist tradition. Although Bunyan is not simply to be called a "Calvinist," he "customarily agreed with Calvinists," as Richard Greaves has argued, "on the issues most basic to their theological system."[19] It is not likely that he read much of Calvin firsthand; but much of Bunyan's interpretive writing, including *The Pilgrim's Progress*, represents an attempt to work out a sound understanding of Calvin's idea of the Word and to challenge various developments among the radicals. Before taking up the creative uses to which Bunyan put the Scriptures in his imaginative narratives, therefore, it will be useful to attend to Calvin's commentaries on the book that became central to Bunyan's conception of the Christian's progress and to a few seventeenth-century departures from Calvin's doctrines about the Word and Spirit.

Calvin's interpretation of the Acts of the Apostles was crucial to his doctrine that the Holy Spirit illuminates the reader of the Bible, "opening" the true meaning and application of the text.[20] Dramatizing at its outset the ascension of Christ and the descent of the Spirit, Acts shows, says Calvin, that "distance of place doeth no whit hinder Christ from being present with those that be his, at all times."[21] For Calvin, Christ's "flesh" is not integral to his mediatorial office, for the Spirit is the true mediator. Commenting specifically on the passage about Christ's removal to heaven, he takes occasion to refute the papists' understanding of the abiding presence of Christ in the eucharistic elements. He argues that Christ is "absent from us bodilie" (13) and that "the heaven whereinto Christ was received, is opposite to the frame of this worlde" (14). It is the Spirit who bridges the gap between this heaven and earth, so that Christ may be said to be present in the world "by the power of his spirit, not by the substance of his flesh" (14). Where Calvin thus enlisted the doctrine of the ascension against the papists, Bunyan would appeal to it against the radicals, to disallow their propensity to look for fulfillment within themselves, apart from any external means, even apart from the body of the historical Christ.

The difficulties of Calvin's general tendency to depreciate a thoroughgoing belief in the Incarnation have a way of showing up here in the commentaries on Acts.[22] Calvin admits that "this word *heaven,* is interpreted divers waies, sometime for the ayre, sometime for the whole connexion of the spheres, sometimes for the glorious kingdome of God" (13). But he makes certain, when treating of the ascension and later of Stephen's vision of the "heavens opened" (Acts 7.56), to insist on Christ's bodily absence from the world. Acts depicts Stephen, just before his death, as enjoying a vision of "the Son of man standing on the right hand of God." This passage might, given Calvin's notion of a heaven "above the clouds," pose something of a problem for him, and he admits that "mans eye would never reach so farre." He preserves his ideas about a physical heaven and about Christ's bodily ascension by positing a "myracle," one "not wrought in heaven, but in [Stephen's] eyes" (177). Then, characteristically, Calvin draws a practical application for his readers: "Therefore if wee bee desirous to feele him present by the working of his grace, we must seeke him in heaven" (178).

For all his urging of Christ's bodily presence in a physical heaven above the clouds, Calvin breaks down, finally, in the course of treating Stephen's vision, and acknowledges further difficulties entailed by his doctrine. Here he writes with a recognition that the Scriptures often use language accommodated to our limited human perception.[23] "I confesse in deed," he writes, "that properly speaking, that is philosophically, there is no place above the heavens" (178). But instead of abandoning his doctrine, or proposing a merely figurative interpretation of the idea of heaven, Calvin sticks with the explicit statement of Scripture and retreats into a pious refusal to explain away the difficulties: "But this is sufficient for mee," he attests, "that it is pervers doting to place Christe any where els, save only in heaven, and above the elements of the world" (178).

When he moves into his commentary on the following chapter of the Acts, although he does not explicitly make the connection, Calvin provides a model on the basis of which we may understand this reticence.

The latter half of chapter 8 concerns the Ethiopian eunuch who, as he is reading from the prophet Isaiah without much understanding, is suddenly joined by Philip the deacon. Philip explains to him a text that he did not, says Calvin, "light . . . uppon . . . by chaunce but . . . it came to passe by the wonderfull providence of God, that Philip shoulde have a proposition or principle, from which the whole summe of Christianitie might be set" (203). In the eunuch's desire to have Philip explain this text Calvin discovers a model of the humility required of believers. He also proposes an application for modern readers that might apply also to his own experience in the face of texts that speak of a physical heaven: "as for those things which are yet hid from us, we must passe them over, untill we see greater light" (201–02). The principle might be illustrated from any number of places in Bunyan's writing as well. The song of Christiana and her party as they leave the House of the Interpreter aptly suggests that, with proper help, readers can discover "Gospel-truths" that have long been unavailable:

> *Here we have heard and seen*
> *Those good things that from Age to Age,*
> *To others hid have been.* (208)

For his part, Calvin goes on to praise the eunuch as that rare reader who acknowledges his ignorance and attends upon "a revelation of the Spirit" to open the meaning of the Scriptures. He also takes occasion to chastize those who require "inspirations and revelations from heaven," apart from the natural means that the Spirit employs, namely, ministers of the Word and commentators on the Bible. Discussing another instance of such receptivity to God's ministers at Acts 2.37–38, Calvin asserts that "those do never go away empty, which ask at the mouth of the Lord, & do offer themselves unto him to be ruled and taught: for that promise must needs be true, Knocke, and it shalbe opened unto you."[24]

Beyond this, Calvin expresses his confidence that the eunuch's experience is exemplary in another sense: it shows that when readers are patient and persistent, "the Lord will illuminate [them] by his Spirite, and will cause that reading which being barren and voide of frute . . . to have plaine light of understanding."[25] It is in fact the Spirit's especial task not only to illuminate passages but to bring readers into contact with personally appropriate texts. Although Calvin does not mention it,

Luther's experience with Romans 1.17 is the great paradigm; and Augustine's experience with Romans 13.13 is equally relevant.[26] But the story in Acts is sufficient to illustrate "the wonderfull providence of God" in bringing Philip, "by the secret direction of the Spirit," just the right text from which to open for the eunuch "the whole summe of Christianitie" (203).

The principal work of Calvin's Holy Spirit is then to bridge the gap between two worlds. This is accomplished chiefly by illuminating patient readers of the Word, who then experience the presence of Christ "by the power of his spirit, not by the substance of his flesh." The ordinary means is through the preaching and writing of God's ministers, not by special "inspirations and revelations from heaven," for heaven remains beyond human experience.

In the middle decades of the seventeenth century in England, when those arguing for further reformation drew heavily upon the idea of enlightenment by the Spirit, often with a view to instituting heaven on earth, more methodically humble interpreters spoke up to defend the idea that a reader is responsible to the meaning already encoded in the scriptural text. Cudworth, in his sermon before the Commons in 1647, for instance, sought to restrain the exuberance of those who were confident that the present light (in the sense of the state of knowledge) was vastly superior to that of times past. He cautioned against too facile an appeal to analogies between modern experience and biblical precedents. Those who suppose, he warned, that all the biblical promises are now fulfilled in their experience, though they regard themselves as true spiritual Israelites, "have nothing but Egyptian darknesse upon [their] hearts."[27] Already in *Areopagitica* (1644), though he anticipated the fulfillment of the prophecy of Joel 2.28, when God's Spirit would be poured out on all men, Milton urged the need to discriminate in using the bright light, newly available, to advantage. "We boast our light," he observed, "but if we look not wisely on the Sun it self, it smites us into darkness. . . . The light which we have gain'd, was giv'n us, not to be ever staring on, but by it to discover onward things more remote from our knowledge."[28]

While the writer of *Areopagitica* found it useful for his argument to interpret the rise of the sects as a sign of vitality, other interpreters of contemporary events documented the ways in which appeals to a "liberty of prophesying" often served the purposes of those hostile to Christianity. Two years after that notorious handbook of heresies, *Gangraena,* appeared in 1646, Samuel Rutherford sought, in *A Survey of the Spirituall Antichrist,* to catalogue the "errours" or a host of "Familists" and "Antinomians." He isolated the main currents of thought in the radical doctrines about a light within. Among these were the denial that the first Adam and the second (Christ) were real historical figures and the envisaging of a third Dispensation, that of the Spirit, which supersedes the gospel.[29] These radicals were no longer projecting "more light" and a "further reformation" into the future. They were seeking to spiritualize the Bible and to find its "fulfillment" in their interior religious experience. In the face of this attempt to render the New Testament a relatively old Testament, Rutherford sought to expose the presumptuousness of those who set up a dichotomy between text and interpretation:

[T]he light of Scripture & the light of the Spirit may, and must necessarily be together, and are no more contrary . . . then the light of the Sunne without, in the aire is contrary to the visible faculty of seeing within, in the eyes; the *Spirit* is by a metaphor called the *day-starre,* for the Spirit is not *formally* light, but *effectually* only; for it is that faculty by which the eyes of the understanding are strengthened to perceive the things of *God.* (1: 320)

The principal issue then was whether further light was to break forth out of the Scriptures or in addition to them. Quaker doctrine, with its notion of "pure openings of the Light," returned Christ to the earth as a spiritual presence that made the Scriptures dispensable, even as it promoted the possibility of extraordinary spiritual vision. Although particular openings were temporary, they could provide a vision of what Fox and the Quakers believed to be the essential nature of things, a universe renewed by Christ and a paradise regained. Like Calvin, Fox was eager to ascribe such a vision to the power of God. But the early Quakers part company from the Calvinist tradition in their unwillingness to speak of the bondage of the will and the depravity of human nature. According to the Quakers' message, no one inherits Adam's guilt. Through Christ, understood not as a person physically present in a distant heaven but as the power of the inward light, one might actually be restored to the Edenic condition and experience full "unity with the creation."[30] With this radical theology there was no need to feel separated in space from the risen body of the Savior, nor in time from the era of Christ and the apostles. Such views are quite contrary to the imaginative conception that informs *The Pilgrim's Progress,* where the "manner of . . . setting out" is the bearing of a guilty burden, and where paradise may be regained only with a "safe arrival at the desired Country" that lies on the other side of death. Bunyan's book proposes, first, that coping with guilt is a major problem in the course of the human pilgrimage and, second, that strategies for denying the reality of guilt—whether they take the form of Worldly Wisdom or of Ignorance—compound the burden that a sensitive person feels. Beyond this, it suggests that guilt is best dealt with by learning to interpret its significance for oneself.[31]

Bunyan and the Work of Interpretation: The Importance of Luke, Acts, and Hebrews

Bunyan's own work as an interpreter has not commanded much in the way of systematic attention.[32] From the vantage point of modern biblical scholars, he stands squarely within the company of precritical interpreters who lived before the rise of the Higher Criticism. *The Pilgrim's Progress* has been of interest to historians of interpretation only as an anachronistic curiosity, a Protestant throwback to the extravagances of medieval allegorists. Otherwise, Bunyan's interpretive activity has been supposed to share the uncritical assumptions of its era. The very attempt to weave together various biblical sources into a unified narrative seems sufficient to confirm that Bunyan accepted the prevailing notion that the numerous stories contained in the Bible comprise an interrelated world with a unified temporal sequence.[33] He also accepted the correlative idea that the Bible embraces in principle the experience of every generation. In view of these assumptions it is unremarkable that he should have taken it as the interpreter's task to discover a single cumulative story in the Bible as a whole and to fit the individual Christian's experience to an authorized paradigm.[34] The "outside" of the dream might seem a *"Novelty."* But the book was meant to serve as an elaborate model for opening *"Nothing but sound and honest Gospel-strains,"* which it hides under the cover of "Similitudes."[35]

To approach Bunyan's interpretive activity without the modern prejudice that values a conscious historical purpose and a pose of scientific detachment in the work of exegesis will enable us, first, to advert to

the fact that these modern canons are themselves historically condi-
tioned and, second, to appreciate that in *Grace Abounding* and *The Pilgrim's
Progress* Bunyan achieved a remarkable degree of originality as a biblical
interpreter. He grasped intuitively that the Epistle to the Hebrews and
the two volumes ascribed to St. Luke (the Third Gospel and the Book of
Acts) comprise a group of closely related texts. These three works share
an interest in the ascension of Christ and in the completeness of his
work; and they seek to explore the implications of that completeness for
those who come afterwards. Hebrews, Luke, and Acts share a common
Christology and eschatology; and they have this soteriological view in
common, that suffering comes from God's paternal care and is salutary
for Christian disciples, but it is not per se redemptive.[36] Because these
books depict the Christian life not as a series of deaths and resurrections
but as a progress to an other-worldly objective, they can be said to have
served Bunyan as a privileged center in the light of which he interpreted
the other biblical books. They were for him what Galatians and Romans
were for Luther and what the Johannine writings, with their emphasis
on interior illumination, were for the Quakers: the key for opening the
enduring meaning of the Text.

It is no doubt true that Bunyan's debts to a whole variety of individual
biblical books could be isolated and described. Coleridge aptly suggested how much the conception of earthly life as a wilderness owes to
the Book of Revelation.[37] And Brainerd Stranahan, besides uncovering
the debt to Hebrews for the conception of human experience as a pilgrimage, has demonstrated how Bunyan found in the Song of Solomon a language with which to depict human joys and pleasures.[38] But
N. H. Keeble, in a brilliant analysis of Bunyan's literary debts and
achievements, has shown how deftly he selected and arranged the diversity of biblical materials available to him to tell the fundamental "Puritan story."[39] It was this ability to fuse various sources into a rich config-
uration that made Bunyan a powerful interpreter. My concern in these
pages is to chart the ways in which Bunyan constituted as his principal
inspiration for recounting the typical Christian's exploits the Book of
Acts. According to the Geneva Bible, this book provides a unique "historie in a maner . . . sufficient to instruct a man in all true doctrine and
religion."[40] To this fundamental precedent and its near neighbors, the
third gospel and the Epistle to the Hebrews, Bunyan affiliated his own
scriptural acts.

This is not to say that Bunyan was a skillful interpreter from the start. But already in *Some Gospel-truths Opened* he was set on a course "toward some certain place." In his first pamphlet Bunyan had objected strenuously to an exclusive emphasis on the figurative meaning of biblical images. He sought to find meaning in an interplay between external physical senses and internal spiritual ones. In particular, he argued for a notion of heaven and of the ascended body of Christ, against a "new and false Christ . . . crucified within, dead within, risen againe within, and ascended within."[41] Like Calvin, he admitted that Scripture sometimes speaks of heaven metaphorically, "taken for the Church and people of God" (1: 77). But he kept insisting that Jesus' actual risen body is "*absent*" from the world and "must needs be above the clouds." When Christ ascended, Bunyan wrote, "he went AWAY from his Disciples." He "did not go into a heaven within them in his person, and humane nature" (1: 78). Therefore, anyone "that cries up a Christ within, in opposition to a Christ without, that man, instead of having the spirit of Christ in him, is possessed with a spirit of delusion." The essential problem with the radicals' attack on the scriptural picture of the Christ who had left the physical world was, in Bunyan's view, that it entailed a presumptuous self-centeredness. One who has the Spirit of Christ "is led out of himself by it" (1: 109–10).

Grace Abounding, published ten years later, attests to Bunyan's sense that he had won this interpretation at a great price. It shows him long imprisoned in self-centeredness, reading the Bible with an intensely introspective concern, before he was led out of himself into an active care for others. The narrative displays his overeagerness to apply Scripture texts to himself. It is to a large extent the record of his attempts to find the place in the Bible which most clearly resembled his own situation. The search for an apt biblical passage in which to rest involved making elaborate comparisons between his situation and the lives of various biblical figures, including Judas and David and Esau. This propensity to compare himself to an authorized biblical paradigm shows up not merely locally, as when he says that he once felt like Judas who "burst asunder" (Acts 1.18) or, alluding to Simon Magus (Acts 8.18–24), when he says he would have bought a calling for gold if it could be got that way (50, 24). It informs the shaping of the entire narrative. The narrating voice who tells the story from a position of assurance has displaced the Esau-figure who felt for so long that he had converted "too late,"

after the "day of grace" was "*past and gone*" (22). He is a Jacob who only
seemed belated for a time and has managed to secure the blessing at last.
In *The Pilgrim's Progress* his dreaming will take place in a den, if not at
Bethel; and he will be one of the "old men" who "dream dreams" in
"*this our Gospel-Day.*"[42] Beyond this, the writer of *Grace Abounding* is also
a *Paulus redivivus*. He says in his Preface, citing two examples from the
Book of Acts, that he is following "Pauls *accustomed manner* . . . *even to
open before his Judges, the manner of his Conversion*" (2). He then goes on to
write a modern version of the Pauline epistle, addressing the work to his
spiritual children.[43]

  Grace Abounding refers often to the Book of Acts.[44] Close examination
of these references reveals that they nearly all concern placement, or
displacement, that is, they have to do with a sense of belonging or fitting
in. None of them provides Bunyan with a secure resting place. This
turns out to be just the point. For the lesson that he learns at last is that
there is no fixed abode this side of what *Some Gospel-truths Opened* had
defined as "heaven" spoken of "properly," which is "the same place
where all the deceased Saints are in their Spirits."[45] Three of the nine
references to Acts in *Grace Abounding* occur in a single place, a list of
passages that ties Luke's book firmly to Hebrews. Hebrews itself is cited
twice in the list, which comes at the end of a paragraph about the implications of Jesus' bodily resurrection. "I have," writes Bunyan, "seen
him a man on the right hand of God the Father for me, and have seen the
manner of his comming from Heaven to judge the world" (38). The
concatenation of texts that he then cites as confirming evidence begins
with Acts 1.9–10, the account of Jesus' bodily ascension. The other
references—to Acts 7.56; Acts 10.42; Hebrews 7.24; and Hebrews
8.38—locate Jesus bodily in a "Heaven without," apart from the world.
In short, Acts and Hebrews establish for Bunyan a distinctive Christology and eschatology that entail, in the terms of his later book, the notion
that the Lord of the Hill will remain absent from the wilderness
throughout the course of Christian's journey. Although he may still
make himself known on earth in the breaking of bread, he is bodily
present in the holy place which is the goal of the earthly pilgrimage; and
he drives and draws pilgrims forward.

  In the Acts of the Apostles Bunyan found the original pilgrims'
progress. The Book of Acts recounts the exploits of the early Christians
as travelers making their way out from the literal, historical Jerusalem

to "the uttermost part of the earth" (1.8). It does not build to a climax, and it does not offer a sense of closure. Stopping short of an account of Paul's martyrdom, it is the most open-ended of the works that make up the New Testament. As Richard Baxter observed, "this History . . . is not to be supposed to contain all the Miracles, Preaching and Success of all the Apostles; but only the History of *Peter* and *Paul,* and some few others their Companions, and that for a short space of time. . . . And though this Historie of *Luke,*" he continues, "have more infallibility than other Histories of Church affairs since written, yet all other credible notice of mater of Fact and Church Practice . . . is of great use to us, and not to be despised."[46] While Acts breaks off suddenly and simply, saying only that Paul kept on preaching for two years from his Roman prison, a seventeenth-century prisoner, using data from all the biblical books and from the history of the church, took up the story and extended it through dark valleys and new pastures to the "certain place" depicted at the end of the Book of Revelation. Leaving out an account of the lost paradise of Genesis, he began his retelling of Acts with its original, the exodus from the City of Destruction. He propelled his hero through a series of narrow "passages," punctuated by leisurely sojourns in pleasant "places," until he reaches a personal apocalyptic consummation. In order to turn the Christian's journey into a pilgrimage, Bunyan drew not only on the Book of Revelation, with its climactic image of the heavenly Jerusalem, but also upon Hebrews.

Bunyan was indebted to Hebrews both as a repository of texts in relation to which he contemplated his own life's story and as a source for the allegorical pilgrimage.[47] Of all the biblical books, Hebrews spoke to him most frequently and most tellingly through the period that his conversion narrative seeks to retrace. He quotes it in *Grace Abounding* more than twice as often as any other book.[48] These citations generally involve passages that became personified in his imagination and played an active role in the course of his spiritual struggles. The most prominent was the nagging reference to Esau, from Hebrews 12.16–17, where he is said to have lost his birthright and to have found "no place of repentance."[49] It seems to have been precisely Hebrews' concern with places that most fascinated Bunyan.[50] The Epistle presents, first, the place of Jesus: he is positioned higher than the angels, now seated permanently in the heavenly sanctuary on the right hand of God, having "entered into his rest" (4.10). Second, it presents the place—or rather

the lack of a fixed position—of the earthly pilgrims, who have been
displaced from their respective cities of destruction and have therefore
to make their way through the wilderness of the world.

Bunyan's own reading, then, had isolated a distinctive strand within
the New Testament; it recognized the uniqueness of the vision shared by
Luke and the author of Hebrews. Matthew's gospel ends with the risen
Lord's promise to be with his disciples "alway, even to the end of the
world." John's gospel foreshortens the historical process that had been
depicted in the apocalyptic portions of the synoptics: it has the Second
Coming take place on Easter. But Luke's gospel ends with an image of
Jesus' absence: "he was parted from them, and carried up into heaven."
The episode at the beginning of the Acts, with Jesus ascending just at the
moment when the disciples expected the restoration of a literal earthly
kingdom, reiterates Luke's sense of Jesus' physical absence. It also puts
the image of the ascension into an ironic context. It shows Jesus leaving
at the time when the temptation to explain his teaching all over again
must have been greatest, as if to suggest that the teacher's removal has
become necessary for the disciples' growth in comprehension. The irony
thus directed at the literal-minded gives way later in the book, after the
descent of the Spirit, to experiences of Jesus' presence in other, non-
bodily ways; he communicates to them by voice and by vision from the
remove of his position in what Hebrews calls the heavenly sanctuary.

When Bunyan tells of the prompting that he received while playing
tip-cat, he draws upon two such episodes from the Acts as models:

> [A] voice did suddenly dart from Heaven into my Soul, which said, *Wilt thou
> leave thy sins, and go to Heaven? or have thy sins, and go to Hell?* At this I was put
> into an exceeding maze; wherefore, leaving my Cat upon the ground, I
> looked up to Heaven, and was as if I had with the eyes of my understanding,
> seen the Lord Jesus looking down upon me, as being very hotly displeased
> with me, and as if he did severely threaten me with some grievous punish-
> ment. . . . (*GA*, 10)

Behind this vision stand Stephen's vision of the Son of man at the right
hand of God and Paul's dramatic calling along the road to Damascus.
The prominence of Acts in *Grace Abounding* consists especially in this
shared emphasis on the idea that Jesus calls his disciples from afar. Bunyan not only refers to his following "Pauls *accustomed manner*" in narrat-

ing his story; he shapes the story to show himself passing through a period of works-righteousness before he comes to accept God's abundant grace. The relatively assured position that he enjoys as narrator is but an anticipation of a permanent place in the heavenly realm above and "without," a realm glimpsed by Stephen but more fully described in Hebrews.

The Pilgrim's Progress and the Book of Acts

Bunyan's debts to the Book of Acts in *The Pilgrim's Progress* make a large subject; and from the outset it should be said that some of these debts may be merely superficial. For instance, the author has taken the name "Beautiful" from the Gate referred to in Acts 3 and conferred it upon the Palace where the daughters of Philip the Evangelist (himself a character from Acts 8) entertain the pilgrim. Still, even if some of the references are trivial, the very idea of referring contemporary experience to Acts had important political consequences. There was in England a longstanding tradition, dating especially to Thomas Cartwright's lectures in Cambridge in the 1570s, of looking to Acts for an authorized vehicle for political criticism.[51] The possibility of drawing on Acts to provide a critique of the persecuting Establishment was obviously attractive to Bunyan; but, as indicated above, he also used Acts to counter the radicals' attempts to leave the Scriptures behind. The connections between Acts and Bunyan's book are often rather complex.

The first reference to the Acts in *The Pilgrim's Progress* appears in the margin alongside the opening paragraph of the narrative: Acts 16.31. A careful reader may be puzzled by this. The pilgrim's "Out-cry"—"*what shall I do?*"—derives from the Book of Acts; but there are more obvious places than chapter 16. In the account of events of Pentecost, Luke assigns the question to the crowd assembled to hear Peter's speech: "what shall we do?" (2.37). In the story of Saul's calling, when he is blinded by a "light from heaven," Luke again puts the question in the mouth of a character who is about to alter the course of his life: "he trembling and astonished said, Lord what wilt thou have me to do?" (9.6). When the marginal reference in *The Pilgrim's Progress* refers the reader to Acts 16.31, it points not to the question but to an answer to it. In the preceding verse, after "a great earthquake," the keeper of the prison asks Paul and

Silas, "what must I do to be saved?" They reply, "Believe on the Lord
Jesus Christ, and thou shalt be saved, and thy house" (16.31). The extended form of the question—"what shall I do to be saved?"—occurs in
the fourth paragraph of Bunyan's narrative, as the pilgrim is walking in
the fields just before he encounters the Evangelist. By this point it seems
rather unlikely that his "house," the members of which have been applying "Carnal Physick" to him, will be interested in being saved.

It is possible that the reference to 16.31 is a mistake for 16.30. But
assuming that it is correct, it points the reader toward the sort of complex intertextual activity that will be necessary for interpreting the
dream aright. The Book of Acts, after all, insists throughout that the
basic Christian message demands decision. The "last days" foretold by
"all the prophets from Samuel" onward (3.24) have arrived, and the
messianic era has been inaugurated by the outpouring of the Holy
Spirit.[52] Therefore the pressure of choice confronts each person who
hears the Word. The crowd assembled on Pentecost, Saul the persecutor of Christians, and the keeper of the prison all provide examples of
people at a critical moment of choice. The reference to what seems like
an answer, "Believe on the Lord Jesus Christ . . . ," suggests that
Bunyan's reader, who is setting out on an interpretive journey, is also
being offered the opportunity to hear the Word—and to raise the question anew.

Bunyan understands that this question has a privileged position in the
course of the spiritual life; it signals a turning point. Later in the dream,
when Hopeful is telling Christian about the early stages of his experience, Bunyan draws upon Acts 16.31 again, fusing it with an allusion to
Stephen's vision of the Son of Man looking down from heaven. (The
passage is of course reminiscent of Bunyan's account of his experience in
Grace Abounding.) In reply to Christian's question about how Christ was
revealed to him, Hopeful replies in language that is close to Calvin's
commentary on Stephen's vision:

> I did *not* see him with my bodily eyes, but with the eyes of mine understand-
> ing; and thus it was. One day I was very sad, I think sader then at any one
> time in my life; and this sadness was through a fresh sight of the greatness and
> vileness of my sins: And as I was then looking for nothing but *Hell,* and the
> everlasting damnation of my Soul, suddenly, as I thought, I saw the Lord

Jesus look down from Heaven upon me, and saying, *Believe on the Lord Jesus Christ, and thou shalt be saved.* (*PP*, 142–43)

The pressure to decide about one's relation to the Lord Jesus in heaven impinges, both in Acts and in Bunyan's book, because the "last days" have arrived and awakened an awareness of mortality. More than any other evangelist, Luke suggests a personal afterlife as an answer to the fear of death. Only Luke reports the parable of Dives and Lazarus, characters who go respectively to a physical hell and heaven after their deaths (Luke 16.19–31); the story had a particular fascination for Bunyan, who had made it the subject of *A Few Sighs from Hell* (1658). Only Luke reports the exchange between Jesus and the robber on the cross, where the last judgment is suggested to be something immediate and individual when Jesus makes the promise, "To day shalt thou be with me in paradise" (23.43). And then in the book of Acts Luke depicts a Stephen who, when he has his heavenly vision, feels that he is a martyr about to be welcomed into heavenly glory. That Luke should report such a vision is quite unusual, since in the synoptic tradition talk about the opening of the heavens and the Son of man coming in glory is otherwise reserved to the futurist eschatology that posits a Second Coming at the end of history. When Luke assigned this vision to a faithful individual on the point of dying, he radically reinterpreted the primitive Christian eschatology. He suggested that the univeral *eschaton* could be epitomized as a personal and private *telos,* that the whole biblical story could be experienced in miniature by the individual.[53] In concentrating the Bible's narrative into the experience of a typical Christian, Bunyan was developing this hint from Luke. As Gaius frames it in the Second Part, the tradition began with Stephen, James, Peter and Paul, characters from the Acts. It extended through Ignatius and Policarp, and has continued down to modern times, so that " 'Twould be impossible, utterly to count up all of that Family that have suffered Injuries and Death, for the love a Pilgrims Life" (260). And the story continues beyond the hero of the First Part: "wherefore," concludes Gaius after hearing of the virtues of the four boys, "*Christians* Family is like still to spread abroad upon the face of the Ground, and yet to be numerous upon the Face of the Earth" (260).

Bunyan was also in some measure following a lead from John; and this brought his message close to that of the radicals. On this basis, he was able to maintain something of a dialogue with his longstanding adversaries. Still, he seems also to have taken great pains to insist upon his differences from them, interpreting the Johannine figures in the light of Luke's idea of historical process. Since the early Christian centuries it had been generally recognized, though variously explained, that John's version spiritualizes the portrait of Jesus given in the synoptic Gospels. The Geneva commentators explained this in the argument that they prefixed to the four Gospels; Matthew, Mark, and Luke, they said, offer historical narration, or "the bodie," while John is concerned to present Christ's doctrine, or "the soule." John's gospel is therefore said to be "the keye which openeth the dore to the understanding of the others."[54]

In John's version, Christ is "the door," or "the gate," and this is the figure that Bunyan represents visually near the outset of the progress.[55] Christ is, moreover, "the living bread" and "the vine" and "the light of the world," whom the Quakers, carrying the spiritualizing tendency further, found "within" each individual. The most important Johannine figure for Bunyan was Christ as "the way." Jesus says, "I am the way, the truth, and the life: no man cometh unto the Father, but by me" (John 14.6). This, says Stanley Fish, is the "absolute and unqualified assertion which defines both the obligations and the dangers of the pilgrimage" embarked upon by Christian and the reader.[56]

But Bunyan qualified his use of the Johannine figure of the way with another "key" which he got from the Book of Acts. Both Luke, with his concentration of futurist eschatology into the experience of the individual Christian, and John, with his tendency to read the synoptics' historical narration figuratively, extracting "doctrine," suggested to Bunyan that every Christian's story is a progress to the world on the other side of death. There remains in Luke a strain of futurist eschatology that is not reduced from temporal to spatial terms, and this served Bunyan well in his polemics against those who claimed that complete fulfillment of the biblical promises was to be realized in this life. Luke was more interested in the period of the church than any other evangelist. By telling of Christ's bodily ascension both in the gospel and again in the Acts, he was careful to place Christ beyond time and history. This created the possibility of taking a more active interest in Christ's followers than other New Testament writers did. It was Luke who deemed the stories of Peter and Stephen and Saul to be worthy of a separate report in their own right. This was the decisive biblical precedent for the author of *The Pilgrim's Progress.*

It has long been recognized that in Bunyan's narrative the houses of resort, where pilgrims enjoy hospitality en route to the Heavenly City, have been modeled on precedents in the Book of Acts. In the twelfth chapter of the Acts, for instance, the apostle Peter is miraculously released from prison, and he straightaway repairs to the house of a woman named Mary and describes to her household his recent adventures and "how the Lord had brought him out of the prison" (12.17). The Second Part makes Bunyan's connection of his narrative with the Acts explicit: Great-heart brings the travelers to the house of "one Mr. *Mnason*, a *Cyprusian*" before they journey through Vanity Fair (*PP*, 273). It was Mnason who, according to Acts 21.16, had once given lodging to Paul and his companions. The connection is not simply a matter of providing biblical precedents for the separatist congregation that takes in a mechanick preacher.[57] Bunyan suggests a relation between his book and the biblical text that might have pleased his memory of the young man who had felt he could never rival the biblical writers. He defines the essential relation between his book and the precursor text when the dreamer tells of the "Rareties" that Christian sees at the Palace Beautiful. He is entertained by the daughters of Philip the Evangelist, a character out of the Book of Acts; and the entertainment consists of timely reading, such as Philip had helped the Ethiopian eunuch to learn to interpret (Acts 8.30–35):

> And first they had him into the Study, where they shewed him Records of the greatest Antiquity; in which, as I remember my Dream, they shewed him first the Pedigree of the Lord of the Hill, that he was the Son of the Ancient of Days, and came by an eternal Generation. Here also was more fully Recorded the Acts that he had done. (53)

Already there is a suggestion here that Christian was shown a kind of supplement to the canonical Gospels, a more extensive account of the life of Christ. The invitation to remember that one of the evangelists went on to write a second volume becomes more overt: "Then they read to him some of the worthy Acts that some of his servants had done" (53). And the sisters go on to show him something quite like Foxe's *Acts and Monuments,* amidst "several other Histories of many other famous

things" (54), such as Baxter pronounced to be "of great use . . . and
not to be despised." In the Second Part the Shepherds also display "some
Rarities" and then take the pilgrims on to "some new places," where
they meet "the Son of one *Great-grace,* of whom you read in the first part
of the Records of the *Pilgrims Progress*" (285). Again, just before Christiana crosses the water, it is disclosed that the proper place of the Records
of such Acts is the land of Beulah: "In this place there was a Record kept
of the Names of them that had been Pilgrims of old, and a History of all
the famous Acts that they had done" (304). If these books of Acts are
Beulah books, however, it is not because they describe experiences that
take place in the married land. Much of the biblical Book of Acts, as
John Foxe understood, concerns suffering and persecution. More of it
concerns journeying. Bunyan exploited both these features of his original for his own polemical purposes.

The most significant of the journey-narratives that comprise the
Book of Acts is the story of the conversion of Saul, which is told three
times. In the ninth chapter, Saul is travelling along a literal way when he
is overwhelmed by a blinding light "without" him. He has an experience that he associates with the risen Christ, and he turns away from
persecuting Christians and goes to "the street which is called Straight"
(9.11).

The term "way" (Greek, *hodos*) is a characteristic feature of the vocabulary of Acts. The first Christians' movement and their teaching are
defined reciprocally in terms of one another, and both are called "the
Way."[58] In fact, when "the way" is used to refer to teaching, it regularly appears in contexts that distinguish proper from incomplete and
misused varieties. Apollos, a learned Jew from Alexandria, was
"mighty in the scriptures" and had been "instructed in the way of the
Lord." But he knew only the baptism of John, and "Aquila and Priscil-
la . . . expounded unto him the way of God more perfectly"
(18.24–26). In the accounts of Saul's persecutions the word refers to the
company of believers: "I persecuted this way unto the death" (22.4).
Sometimes the term is a virtual synonym for what later became known
as Christianity.[59]

Already in the Third Gospel there were signs that Luke would be
interested in the possibility of seeing Jesus' path as a paradigm for his
followers.[60] The journey to Jerusalem becomes an image of Jesus' life's
work; the public career is an uphill struggle, culminating in death, for the

salvation of humanity. At Jerusalem even Christ's enemies admit that he teaches "the way of God" (20.21). An early evidence of the prominence that Luke assigns to the journey motif lies in the prophecy, uniquely recorded in his gospel, made by Zacharias to his son John: "thou shalt go before the face of the Lord to prepare his ways" (1.76). At the beginning of the report on Jesus' public life, moreover, Luke quotes the prophet Isaiah, just as Matthew and Mark do. But he makes a point of extending the quotation by another clause:

> Prepare ye the way of the Lord,
> Make his paths straight.
> Every valley shall be filled,
> And every mountain and hill shall be brought low;
> And the crooked shall be made straight,
> And the rough ways shall be made smooth.
> And all flesh shall see the salvation of God.

It is only Luke among the synoptic evangelists who quotes Isaiah's prediction that "all flesh shall see the salvation of God" (Luke 3.6; quoting Isaiah 40.5). In this way he includes the idea that will dominate the story that he goes on to tell in the Acts about the extension of the Way to "the uttermost part of the earth." (It is another index of Bunyan's reluctance to accept the idea that the biblical prophecies have already been fully realized that the topography of his hero's journey includes unfilled valleys, difficult hills, and rough and crooked ways.)

If Luke's gospel tells of the journey up to Jerusalem, Acts reverses the movement, showing the disciples going out to Samaria, Asia Minor, Greece, and Rome, with a message for "all flesh."[61] The sequel shows the disciples repeating in their lives and in their preaching the gestures and words of their teacher; they cure the sick, preach the good news, and suffer persecution at the hands of their opponents. A symbolic sense of journeying lies at the heart of this reiteration; they make literal journeys, but they do so as followers of Christ. They are called "Christians" for the first time at Antioch (11.26) and they become, as Gaius explains in the Second Part, the "Progenitors" of Bunyan's Christian (260). For many of them their way entails an imitation of Christ's sufferings.

The parallels between the stories of persecution in the Acts and in *The Pilgrim's Progress* are conspicuous, and it will be sufficient to attend only to the most prominent one. Acts depicts Stephen as the first Christian martyr and describes his stoning after the pattern of Jesus' crucifixion. Stephen's death, in its turn, came to be looked upon, as Bunyan's Gaius intimates, as the pattern for martyrs generally; and Bunyan likewise presents Faithful's death as an epitome of all faithful deaths. The passage suggests a thrice-painted canvas, with Bunyan painting over Luke's portrait of the death of Stephen, which had been painted over the portrait of the crucifixion:

> They therefore brought him out, to do with him according to their Law; and first they Scourged him, then they Buffeted him, then they Lanced his flesh with Knives; after that they Stoned him with Stones, then prickt him with their Swords, and last of all they burned him to Ashes at the Stake. Thus came *Faithful* to his end. (97)

Then as Saul replaced Stephen in the Book of Acts, so Hopeful replaces Faithful in *The Pilgrim's Progress*.

What is more significant than the existence of the parallels between the two books in their depicting of persecutions is the interpretation that Bunyan, following good reformed precedents, places on these parallels. Already in the sixteenth century it had been common to maintain that it was the mark of a true Christian to be persecuted. Luther had urged this view, and Foxe's *Book of Martyrs* purveyed the belief in England. The makers of the Geneva Bible, themselves exiled during the Marian persecutions, helped to disseminate this idea with their gloss on the word "witness" (Greek, *martyres*) at Acts 1.8: "To stand in the face of the whole worlde which signifieth that they must entre into heaven by afflictions, & therefore must fight before thei get the victorie." More significantly still, the argument prefixed to the Book of Acts counsels readers to look for evidence that "from the beginning of the Church" Satan has raised "conspiracies, tumultes, commotions, persecutions, sclanders and all kind of crueltie," so "that the crosse is so joyned with the Gospel, that they are fellowes inseparable."[62] A century later, when the dissenting ministers were silenced and ejected from their livings following the Restoration, they found therefore a biblical model for their sufferings in the experience of the early Christians. John the Divine had written a Revelation for people whose faith located them outside the political establishment and brought persecution upon them. The apostles had been driven out of Jerusalem by persecutors like Saul. Paul himself wrote from prison, and he had been tried before civil magistrates and had suffered false reports. English Nonconformists labeled the laws of the Clarendon Code the "persecuting acts" and looked upon their sufferings as fully in keeping with their Lord's prediction: "If they have persecuted me, they will also persecute you" (John 15.20).[63]

But seventeenth-century Englishmen were not greatly interested in all features of the early Christians' experience as it was depicted in the Book of Acts. One problem that weighed heavily upon Peter and Paul and Luke—the admission of the Gentiles to the Way—was no longer directly relevant to Bunyan and his Gentile readers. It is true that as a boy Bunyan had felt disappointment when he learned from his father that they were not "of the *Israelites,*" since the Scriptures said "they were once the peculiar People of God" (*GA,* 9). But as he grew older Bunyan came to accept the common explanation, whereby Gentile Christians were "true spiritual Israelites"; and with Luther and virtually all of Protestantism he read Acts and Galatians and Romans figuratively, as if they concerned general questions of legalism that were relevant to every age.[64] Christian's encounter with Mr. Worldly-Wiseman and his experience at the Village of Legality are products of this figurative reading, whereby the Judaizers of the Book of Acts are taken to be analogous to papists and other "Pelagians" who live by a righteousness based on works. The less obvious point is that Luke's treatment of the relations between Jews and Gentiles offered Bunyan a model for dealing with his own most persistent worry, the feeling that latter-day Christians might have been converted "too late," after the "day of grace" was "past and gone."

According to the Acts, the Gentiles began to be admitted to the Christian community after the apostle Peter had a vision. He saw all manner of beasts gathered together, as if in a great sheet hanging from the four corners of the heavens (chapter 10). A voice commanded him to "kill, and eat." Against all his sensibilities, he came eventually to interpret the vision as a divine revelation offering him new light: "God hath shewed me that I should not call any man common or unclean" (10.28). Thereafter he no longer scrupled to admit Cornelius and his household, though as pagans they ate unclean flesh, to the company of believers. The Book of Acts thus allows that Peter established the decisive precedent for what the Judaizers counted a heresy: he freed Gentile converts from the

necessity of following the Law. But Luke depicts Paul as the chief dis-
seminator of the conviction that he puts into Peter's mouth: "To him
[Jesus] give all the prophets witness" (10.43). According to the Acts, it
was Paul who made a highway out of the simple path that Peter had
opened.

The Book of Acts represents the first Christians as making a thoroughgoing reinterpretation of the Law and the Prophets, relating them
to Jesus wherever possible. The speeches of Peter and Stephen, no less
than those ascribed to Paul, make the Hebrew Scriptures precisely an
Old Testament.[65] Peter, as the seventeenth-century radicals were well
aware, had said that there was "new light" in his day, that the prophecy
of Joel had been fulfilled, and that the "last days" had arrived. In claiming that still more "new light" had come in their day, issuing in a Dispensation of the Spirit, they made also of the New Testament an "old
testament" now fulfilled "within," spiritually. Given the biblical
precedents, their position had a decided attraction even to those who did
not wish to leave the Text behind. But Bunyan began *The Pilgrim's
Progress* by insisting upon the importance of a light without, "yonder
shining light," which the marginal gloss identifies as "the Word." He
devised his own strategies for connecting his "Gospel-Day" to the privileged era when Christ had been bodily present on earth. Just as Bunyan
was persuaded at last that he was like Jacob rather than Esau, so he
created a hero who "came of the Race of *Japhet,*" the father of the
Gentiles, whom God had planned from of old to install in "the Tents of
Shem" (*PP,* 46).

The concern to deny the belatedness of the truly elect runs throughout both parts of *The Pilgrim's Progress* and forms, in fact, the motive for
the journey in the Second Part, where the entire narrative illustrates,
through its leisurely pace, that it was not too late for Christian's household to be saved.[66] But it is Mercy who is most anxious about late-
coming. From her first exchange with Christiana, Mercy worries that
she lacks the special personal invitation that her companion received.
While Christian had been able to persuade the Porter at the Palace
Beautiful that he was not too late because he "came of the Race of
Japhet," Mercy explains to the Keeper of the Gate that she does not
really belong: "I am come, for *that,* unto which I was never invited, as
my Friend *Christiana* was. *Hers* was from the King, and *mine* was but from
her: Wherefore I fear I presume" (190).

To "presume" is to usurp, or take possession of without right. Literally, it is "to take beforehand." According to the *Oxford English Dictionary* it also means, in accord with the progress motif here, "to advance or make one's way over-confidently into an unwarranted position or place." Mercy's worry that she is out of place in the way, reminiscent of several features of Bunyan's own experience, does not preclude her being admitted. When the Keeper takes her in, he seems aware that she is not capable of being a battlefield on which competing texts pull and tug; and he gently assures her that faith is the sole criterion for admission. This is just the lesson that, according to the Acts, the early Christians had worked out when they agreed not to require the Gentiles to follow the Law. As Luther explained it, the Gentiles were included in the promise given to the Jews, "for we have been foreordained to the communion of the saints. . . . All this has been recorded, not for the sake of Shem and Japheth but for the sake of their descendants."[67]

The lesson that it is never too late had been taught to Christian by two negative *exempla* at the House of the Interpreter, the climactic scenes in his education there. Eager as he was to return to his literal progress, Christian was detained to learn that real progress entails rooting out bad interpretations. The Man of Despair, like the Bunyan who for so long identified his situation with Esau's, remains stuck in the desperate surmise that, having betrayed Christ, there is no second chance.[68] Ironically, although Christian is learning to serve as an interpreter himself, he cannot help this man to escape from the Iron Cage in which he is trapped by his excessive introspection. Nor can Christian help the man with the obverse of this problem; the other man he meets does not think that he has come too late but that the Judgment has already come, catching him unprepared. He is a victim of an eschatology realized too soon and, like the Man of Despair, also a victim of a self-fulfilling prophecy. Both are weighed down in their faulty interpretations of their situation. Christian, by contrast, is just about to lose his burden. He has been schooled in the House of the Interpreter.

According to Luke, interpretation was also essential to the first Christians whom he depicted in Acts—interpretation and reinterpretation. But again it is Christ as depicted in Luke's gospel who sets the pattern. In the last chapter of Luke, the risen Christ appears first to two disciples on a journey to Emmaus and teaches them, though they do not recognize him immediately, to reinterpret the Scriptures in light of what

they had known about his life and death (24.13–35). This "opening" is
followed by another, this one made to the awestruck disciples in Jerusalem: "Then opened he their understanding, that they might understand
the Scriptures" (24.45). One story involves opening the Scriptures themselves, the other the understanding of readers; in both cases the teacher
then disappears, and the disciples are left to carry on for themselves.

That such reinterpretation entails the work of memory is emphasized
in John's gospel. There, "the Comforter" is promised to the disciples as
one who will lead them into "all truth" after Jesus has left the world.
The gap between an immediate interpretation of a fresh experience and
a reinterpretation, mediated by the Comforter, of a remembered experience suggests how much the Gospels themselves owe to an imaginative
re-creation, through memory, of previous events.[69] The decisive importance of memory as an agent of reinterpretation emerges most dramatically in *The Pilgrim's Progress* near the end of the First Part. As Christian is
overwhelmed by a "great darkness and horror" at the prospect of death,
Hopeful comforts him with a fitting reference to Psalm 73: "Then said
Hopeful, My Brother, you have quite forgot the Text. . . . These
troubles and distresses that you go through in these Waters, are no sign
that God hath forsaken you, but are sent to try you, whether you will
call to mind that which heretofore you have received of his goodness"
(158).

Stanley Fish has called the power of memory here, using the phrase
rather more casually than technically, the "source of the inner light."
He maintains that every crisis in the book "is a crisis of memory."[70] The
Gospels themselves evince this recognition that creative memory in
moments of distress can be of the utmost importance. It is under the
pressure of disappointment at the death of Jesus, and of their own hopes
for him, that the disciples en route to Emmaus had to learn first to
remember the apt text and second to reinterpret it in a hopeful fashion.

In Bunyan's allegory the sequence of experience-followed-by-
interpretation appears most conspicuously in the scenes at the House of
the Interpreter. The sequence is operative throughout the book, and
Christian regularly pauses in his journey to remember and reinterpret
his experience. In fact, by stopping to remember he continues to make
progress. The sequence occurs as well in the dreamer's experience; the
whole book is supposed to be his memory of a dream. It also occurs in the

experience of the reader, whom the Conclusion bids makes a proper interpretation after the reading has ended.

The incident in the Book of Acts that best dramatizes the workings of this reinterpretive process involves Philip the Evangelist and the Ethiopian eunuch. It serves as a model behind various episodes in Bunyan's book, including Christian's encounters with the Evangelist and the Interpreter. In the Acts the disciples learn to reinterpret exile, which in the Hebrew Scriptures had generally been understood as a form of punishment; they come to see their exile from Jerusalem as a divinely authorized opportunity. Having been "scattered abroad," they go their various ways. Philip, for his part, chances upon a neophyte along a literal road; and "by the wonderfull providence of God," as Calvin says, the eunuch happens to be reading an apposite text. It comes from the fifty-third chapter of Isaiah, one of the Servant Songs. This affords Philip the opportunity to imitate the interpretive activity of the figure who had appeared along the road to Emmaus. The relevant portion of the text reads, "He was led as a sheep to the slaughter; and like a lamb dumb before his shearer, so opened he not his mouth" (Acts 8.32; quoting Isaiah 53.7).

Luke's story goes on to compare the dumb lamb to Jesus before his executioners. It also hints at a profound reason for Jesus' silence and for his absence from the Book of Acts generally: "Then Philip opened his mouth, and began at the same Scripture, and preached unto him Jesus" (8.35). The incident thus epitomizes what Bunyan saw in Acts; it is a book about what happened when Jesus was silent, when he ascended into a Heaven without, "AWAY from his Disciples." The good teacher in due course hands over the work of interpretation to the students. But the canonical text remains as the starting point in relation to which new scriptural acts are performed.

The Reader's Progress

If Bunyan's early biographers gloried in calling attention to his patient endurance of his imprisonment, they also celebrated his semi-illiteracy, the better to delight in his extraordinary inspiration. They regularly remarked on the meagerness of his library, repeating the story that he had with him in prison only a Bible and Foxe's *Book of Martyrs*.[71]

The significance of Bunyan's prison library, however, lies not in its having been scant but in its having been complete. Foxe's lengthy folio volumes in the expanded edition of 1641 are rooted squarely in the biblical Book of Acts, and they extend the story down through the ages, beyond the Tudor era, into the seventeenth century. Bunyan regarded this work as a privileged supplement to the Book by which alone all who were to be saved would be saved. In *Grace Abounding* he cites it along with various biblical passages as a proof-text, allowing that this "Ancient Historie" had a power to encourage him in his work equal to that of the Holy Scriptures themselves.[72] That is, of course, just what the first Christians had done when they ascribed to "the Acts [Jesus] had done" an efficacy previously reserved for the Hebrew Scriptures; and it is what Luke had done when he extended the story of Jesus into the Acts of the next generation, depicting the apostles' lives as a reiteration of the journey, though headed out from Jerusalem. Given such precedents, it was virtually inevitable that *The Pilgrim's Progress* should have spawned sequels from various pens, even before Bunyan himself took up the story of Christiana and the boys. For Bunyan's basic understanding of the Bible, as he had built it into the first part, was that it was in principle always ready to be opened, and that it was susceptible to extension and supplementation, as modes of application and confirmation, when history progressed. Where Bunyan differed from more radical interpreters lay chiefly in the status that he claimed for his interpretations; it was only the surface of his book, he proposed, that accommodated the modern's taste for "Novelty," while the essential message was *"Nothing but sound and honest Gospel-strains."* The song of Christiana and her party as they leave the House of the Interpreter drags the theory of the "Author's Apology" into the realm of the narrative: *"Here we have heard and seen / Those good things that from Age to Age, / To other hid have been"* (208).

Drawing upon the authority he had by virtue of his knowledge of all the biblical books, the author of *The Pilgrim's Progress* presumed to treat the truths of the unbroken Scriptures like so many scattered pieces of the body of Osiris and to reassemble them into a unique personal synthesis. Unlike the scissors-and-paste work of the authors of theological compendia like Ames or Wolleb or even Milton, Bunyan used as his model the Book of Acts, with its narrative structure and its interpolated sermons. And instead of supposing that doctrine is the last word, to be fixed in the systematic form of a treatise of divinity, he conceived his role on the model of the risen Jesus en route to Emmaus or of Philip in the company of the eunuch. He cast the teacher as an opener of the Scriptures who, at the right moment, had the good sense to disappear:

> *NOW Reader, I have told my Dream to thee:*
> *See if thou canst Interpret it to me;*
> *Or to thy self, or Neighbour: but take heed*
> *Of mis-interpreting: for that, instead*
> *Of doing good, will but thy self abuse:*
> *By mis-interpreting evil insues.* (164)

Bunyan had found in Luke and Acts and Hebrews what he took to be ample warrant for believing that Christ's work is complete but that each earthly pilgrim, in order to arrive at the rest which the risen Christ enjoys, must make a journey of interpretation. The "Author's Apology" for *The Pilgrim's Progress* assigns the reader the "travail" of interpretation as a means of "travel" to the Celestial City, thereby implicating others in the work into which Luke, as he presents himself at the outset of his gospel, had been drawn, namely, going over others' versions of the story and attempting to reconceive the pattern of those materials "in order" (Luke 1.3).

All this is to say something about the way that, in *The Pilgrim's Progress,* Bunyan displayed his ingenuity as an interpreter to provide an alternative to the radicals' solution to the characteristic Protestant problem of belatedness. Against the "realized" eschatology of the Quakers, who said that the resurrection and day of judgment had already taken place in the hearts of the children of the light, Bunyan pitted the "final" eschatology of Luke and Acts and Hebrews to deny that paradise was to be regained in this life. In Bunyan's view, if paradise was to be found, this would be achieved by the reader entering into the story and conceiving of life as another chapter in the progress along the Way to a transcendent realm of completion and everlasting rest. But Bunyan's decisive innovation was to develop Luke's insistence on historical process: Bunyan cast as his central character an unskilled reader, burdened by his book and only beginning to learn the rudiments of discipleship. Where Luke had made Peter and Paul (who once seemed to Bunyan intimidating precursors) his principal characters, Bunyan reduced the teachers in his story—Evangelist, the Interpreter, and Help, for instance—to merely auxiliary, methodically humble, roles.[73] This aided him in making it clear that for every Christian journeying and interpreting were to be defined in terms of one another. If this equation were to be valid, it must also be clear to every wayfaring interpreter that, short of entrance into that "certain place," there would be no settling down in a single moment of interpretation.

This perspective at once took seriously the Lutheran insistence that every reader is ultimately his own interpreter and the cardinal assumption of classic Protestantism that the Scriptures alone are sufficient for salvation. And while it imposed upon each reader the awesome duty of learning to read for himself, it held out the promise that the interpretive journey offered large scope to the imaginative pleasures involved in reconstituting the fundamental biblical story. In short, *The Pilgrim's Progress,* by the demands that it placed upon its readers to discover connections among discrete biblical passages, transferred to the reader of the Bible the sense that he was participating in the essential scriptural act defined by the theory and practice of Luke's companion volumes: retracing earlier versions of the story to discover a trajectory that embraces every future reader and propels each person whom it implicates toward a closure yet to come.

JAMES F. FORREST

Allegory as Sacred Sport: Manipulation of the Reader in Spenser and Bunyan

For the Puritan writer the danger of the allegoric mode lies in its way-ward tendency to imaginative excess. While recognizing that "x" may be represented by "y," he is also aware that the resultant "y" means much more than "x," because the mysterious alchemical power of the imagination has transmuted the given fact into something beyond the artist's controllable intent. So it is that the writer finds himself in sympathy with the typical seventeenth-century preacher, to whom vanity of vanities is the undisciplined cogitation that breaks from the mind's orderly ranks to pursue a will-o'-the-wisp; that rebel thought's true range, the divine believes, is indeed the world of shadow, the fragmentary sphere of time, a universe of seeming in which reason is left behind and the quarry of the fanciful run to earth. Consequently, he is opposed to giving the imagination free rein. Like Richard Baxter, he sees the moment of meditation preceding the first outrage as a grim illustration of how the mind may move without the will's command, just so long as the will does not forbid; and he is led to wonder "whether Reason be not given man, as the Rider to the Horse, not to *enable* him to *move,* but to *Rule* his *motion:* so that the Horse can go if the Rider hinder not, so the sensitive appetite can cause the actions of eating, drinking, thinking, speaking sensually, if *Reason* do but drop asleep, or not hinder."[1] Or with Thomas Goodwin he agrees that this disorder is the mark of Cain that stamps the mind as vagabond and sets man's eyes in the far corners of the earth: "[O]ur thoughts, at best, are as wanton Spaniels, who though indeed they goe with and accompany their Master, and come to their journeys end with him in the end, yet doe runne after every Bird, and wildly pursue every flock of sheepe they see."[2]

Driven thus to insist on the primacy of reason and on the urgent bridling of the fancy through continual exercise of the will, the seventeenth-century divine finds congenial a view of art which regards the linguistically simple and straightforward as the most beneficial; in the literary theory of the seventeenth century a similar orientation becomes apparent in the emphasis on memory, reason, and judgment. In spite of his rooted materialism, therefore, Thomas Hobbes is actually applying a critical concept shared by Puritan writers when he asserts his mistrust of "wit" and the need for government of the imagination; indeed, one of the figures he employs to describe the imaginative hunt— "as a spaniel ranges the field till he find a scent"—is very close to Goodwin's analogy, although Hobbes's spaniel seems a hound of a different breed, since it follows a recognizable trail.[3] But Hobbes also realizes that the unguided "fancy," like the riderless horse, is prone to gallop recklessly off; and very much like the Puritan, he paradoxically insists, despite his apparent determinism, on the efficacy of the will operating through the "judgment" to restrain it. This opposition of "wit" and "judgment" becomes after Hobbes almost axiomatic in literary criticism. It appears in Thomas Rymer, in Dryden, who also uses the popular metaphor of the nimble spaniel to image the restless quest of the searching fancy, and in Pope, who gives the antithesis its most precise expression in the line, "For wit and judgment often are at strife."[4] In critical theory of the later seventeenth century, then, we find increasingly reflected a grave concern with the extraneous whimsy that is brought in by artifice, and with the voluntary employment of reason to counter it.

Even earlier than this, however, toward the end of the sixteenth century, a comparable interest is evinced in the deliberate and controlled use of imagination to lay hold upon truth. Thus Arthur Golding, in the "Address to the Reader" which prefaces his translation of Ovid's *Metamorphoses* (1587), apologetically argues that it is the proper office of the poet to raise virtues and vices interestingly and purposively before us; we do the maker of fictions no justice, he claims, nor do we edify ourselves, if we decline to entertain his specious notions. But the definitive statement comes from Sir Philip Sidney, who in *The Defence of Poesy* (published 1595) opposes the view that regards poetry as a triviality pandering to the weakness of the mind and claims that the poet does not simply record the dismembered jottings of a diseased brain, the detritus of a sick soul, but imaginatively imposes a divine and salutary unity on things previously disconnected. Taking up Aristotle's shrewd remark that poetry is more philosophical than history, that the essence of the artistic vision is the relationship of the particular and the design, Sidney likens the highest reaches of the poetic mind to the creative force of Nature, and finds that the "golden world" which this arcane alchemy delivers asseverates the existence of a state of perfection humanity once enjoyed but now has lost; for poetry, he believes, can momentarily recapture that original excellence with all its pristine freshness, even if we are so depraved that we cannot live up to the beauty of the vision apprehended. The great virtue of poetry indeed lies in its educative function, inasmuch as its "final end is to lead and draw us to as high a perfection as our degenerate souls, made worse by their clayey lodgings, can be capable of."[5] Poetry is thus to be valued primarily for the help it affords, in Milton's words, "to repair the ruins of our first parents"; and the degree of success (depending, of course, largely on the delight involved) that attends this desirable end becomes the touchstone of poetry's greatness.[6] Far from fostering wild illusions, poetry in fact serves a noble ethical purpose, because the poet, through the managed use of his imagination, evokes in man inspiriting thoughts of true virtue. And poetry (or fiction) teaches this virtue "not only by delivering forth his very being, his causes, and effects, but also by making known his enemy, vice, which must be destroyed, and his cumbersome servant, passion, which must be mastered . . ." (105).

There is much in Sidney that derives from the pressure of traditional analogy. The key to this argument is actually the ancient parallel he develops between God as creator and the poet who, he maintains, can make "things either better than Nature bringeth forth, or, quite anew, forms such as never were in Nature" (100). The same analogue of God as Creator and the poet as maker is employed in the fourteenth century in *Piers Plowman* (Passus IX - B text), where Langland makes the point that, just as God must work with His Word and show His wit, so must the poet work with his words and wit. Consequently, it is essential that Wit not waste time nor squander words:

> since to waste speech that germ is of grace,
> And God's gleeman and a game of heaven;

> Would never the faithful Father his fiddle were
> un-tuned,
> Nor his gleeman a vagabond a goer to taverns![7]

Now this idea of Langland's that speech is God's "gleeman" or minstrel, the offshoot of grace and "a game of heaven," has vast ramifications for the Renaissance as well as for the Middle Ages. In the medieval period, of course, the word "game" has significant connotations; and the conception of the theater as a game, of drama as meaningful play, in the sense in which the Proclamation to the *Ludus Coventriae* employs the notion, has been well described by V. A. Kolve, who refers to the game as "a lie, designed to tell the truth about reality" in an exploration of the nature of medieval drama in the context of Johan Huizinga's *Homo Ludens*.[8] But while, on the evidence of such a document as William Prynne's *Histriomastix* (1633) and the whole thrust of the seventeenth-century attack on the stage, it might be thought that the Puritans never fully understood or believed in this meaning of "game," the reverse seems wholly true. For this concept of the heavenly game, particularly when allegory becomes its name, and characters like Truth and Despair and Melancholy are brought forth, fully grown (as it were) from nothing, actually finds its peculiar warrant in God's creation of the world *ex nihilo,* and it consequently culminates in a most interesting relationship between the writer and his audience. If speech is "God's gleeman" and the holy play the sprout or "germ" of grace, the medium is indissolubly conjoined with the message by an act of divine dispensation, and the creative artist himself, God's surrogate, has become responsible for directing his imagination to the mediation of his Creator's will to all humanity.

Already highly conscious of his inescapable share of the burden of general corruption and of the deadly nature of the common ground whereon he stands, the post-Reformation artist is led by this conception of his function to an even closer awareness of his reader. In exploring truth he must now take cognizance of an awakened introspection, but because the means to this enterprise lie embedded in a community of interest he shares with his readers, he can readily adapt his technique. Thus for the Renaissance and seventeenth-century writer the whole concept of vision itself is fraught with fascinating artistic possibilities. According to St. Paul, the inner perception that enables one to under-

stand vision is entirely a matter of grace. Writing to the Corinthians of
the ineffable nature of the divine vision (1 Corinthians 2.10), Paul remarks that God's true wisdom is transmitted only by the Spirit, which
"searcheth all things, yea, the deep things of God." When such things
are communicated to others, the words used are not those of human
wisdom, but those conveyed by the Spirit; the natural human is therefore quite incapable of understanding this peculiar language which can
be only "spiritually discerned." St. Paul's comment is illuminated by
Christ's remark in Matthew 13.9–11, which in turn makes reference to
the prophecy in Isaiah 6.9–10; and all these citations are crucially significant for those who seek to appreciate Puritan literature. For Isaiah and
Christ and Paul enunciate a truth that contains within itself the seeds of
prodigious artistic potential, insofar as it can imaginatively distinguish
the sheep from the goats, the elect from the reprobates. As has been
pointed out, Shakespeare wittily exploits the doctrine in *A Midsummer
Night's Dream,* in Bottom's delicious and unconscious parody of 1 Corinthians 2.9, while describing his bottomless dream (IV.i.210ff.), to make
the serious point that "it is the bestial or natural man who is unable to see
to the bottom of things; he is the fool or ass who cannot expound the
dream."[9] Milton, too, employs the idea in *Comus,* where the Lady finally
puts down her tempter by insisting that Comus lacks the spiritual insight
that would enable him to penetrate "The sublime notion, and high mystery" that enfolds "the sage / And serious doctrine of Virginity."[10] But
since neither Shakespeare nor Milton dares deny his readers the power
to grasp the meaning of things, the relevance of the doctrine clearly
reaches to a consideration of each of the works mentioned as a whole.
Precisely because the poet's attitude is let him see and hear who can, his
vision searches and investigates us: from this point of view his art becomes in the fullest sense a mirror held up to nature, a looking-glass that
can reflect the image of our selves and reveal thoughts both good and ill
lodging in the mind, thus manifesting the soul's state.

Similarly inspired to influence the mind of the reader, Spenser and
Bunyan exercise their art with due deliberation. Spenser's avowed intention in *The Faerie Queene* is to fashion a gentleman, and there is no
evidence to suggest that he deviates in any way from the view of his
friend, Sir Philip Sidney, on the value of poetry in achieving this objective. Bunyan's conception of his art is likewise utilitarian, if somewhat
more narrowly so. That both are alive, as they write, to the continuing

presence of their readers, and that both are sometimes motivated in their art by this intimacy alone, are no doubt universally acknowledged; but the extent to which their technique is at the same time bent to the service of that great cooperative enterprise between artist and reader is not perhaps so fully realized. Yet no matter how vaguely worked out or apprehended the aesthetic appears, the allegory each engages in becomes a sacred sport in which the mind is managed through exposure to certain suggestions and situations to which the reader is induced to respond.

After a new look had been designed for Spenser half a century ago, it became fashionable for a while for students to assume that Spenser was never clothed before. But the Romantic critics in general felt that Spenser was actually overdressed, and much of their criticism was devoted to trimming the peacock-feathers of his ostentatious singing-robes. Readers were accordingly invited to forget Spenser's allegory and to concentrate on his poetry as they would on pictures in an art gallery. Wordsworth inclined to that view, and the essential quality he found in Spenser he distilled into the celebrated lines, "Sweet Spenser moving through his clouded heaven / With the moon's beauty and the moon's soft pace."[11] No doubt the time was ripe, the moon's phase right, for C. S. Lewis to produce a counterblast by demonstrating that Spenser's quiddity is not simply saccharinity, nor his meaning merely moonshine.[12] Yet it would be a mistake to suppose that the Romantics spoke with one voice on the matter. Guided by the sanity of his own true genius, Charles Lamb discerned what gave value to *The Faerie Queene*. Pointing out that the allegory gives the poem its thoughtful content and a sanity which the novels of his own day do not have, Lamb remarks that it is not the human element which lends value to an episode like the Cave of Mammon, but the allegorical meaning behind it.

Now it is certainly true of the characters and events of *The Faerie Queene* that in their "inner nature, and the law of their speech and actions, we are at home and upon acquainted ground."[13] Although Spenser's tale is one of chivalry and the land of faerie, of knights and giants, of hags and fair ladies, beneath the element of narrative are the fundamental ideas, the moral pitfalls, and lessons of real life. This in itself posits the closest kind of liaison between reader and writer, but lest it be thought that *The*

Faerie Queene makes no ulterior demands upon our common humanity, it must be added that no poem ever required more from the average reader.[14] The theological terms that Spenser uses rarely call for an automatic response which the modern reader fails to give, but occasionally they demand the recreation of a system of association which is very nearly alien to the popular mind at the present time. And the only solution to this problem would seem to lie in an awareness of it.

But even the reader who is alive to the demands of the allegory often finds a curious complexity of vision within the poem. The Cave of Mammon episode (II.vii.) is really a test-case of the subtlety of Spenser's allegorical method, for here the allegory is revealed in a manner that is purely descriptive and pictorial; there is no hint of a dramatic conflict within Guyon's breast, and he is tempted only insofar as he is inquisitive. What human interest exists in the scene is not aroused by the characters involved, but by the human values which are expressed in the allegory operating through them. We are shown in turn the various emblems that typify the love of hoarding, the avarice of profiteering, and the scramble for honor founded on the possession of worldly goods; then, in the Garden of Proserpina, we are confronted with the most refined type of worldliness, that of the cultured Epicurean and Cynic, represented by Tantalus and Pilate, who know the truth but have no willpower or faith to resist temptation. The uniqueness of the scene, however, is that its focal point is constantly the reader's mind. As soon as Mammon makes his offer of "grace," the perceptive reader recognizes the level on which the narrative is moving and the assumptions underlying enactment of the temptation. As acceptance of Mammon's "offred grace" would constitute a rejection and denial of all heavenly grace, it is by no means accidental that Mammon's tantalizing remark to Guyon becomes, rather like Bottom's speech, somewhat of an ironic parody of part of the famous passage in Corinthians already mentioned.

> Perdy (quoth he) yet neuer eye did vew,
> Ne toung did tell, ne hand these handled not,
> But safe I haue them kept in secret mew,
> From heauens sight, and powre of all which them pursew. (II.vii.19.6–9)[15]

And precisely insofar as this is true, the allegory at this moment boldly inverts the common universe of values, subverts the spiritual by the

material, and leaves it all up to the reader to distinguish the real from the
apparent.[16] Guyon at this point is actually no more than the agent
through whom the reader is himself, as in a game, brought face to face
with the world, the flesh, and the devil, and compelled to make the
choice that teaches self-knowledge. Those things with which "th' Elfin
knight with wonder all the way / Did feed his eyes, and fild his inner
thought" (II.vii.24.3–4) are indeed imaginatively recreated within the
compass of the reader's own thought so that he has the opportunity to
stand firm with Guyon and keep his mind inviolate. Guyon's three-day
defiance constitutes, of course, a reliance on prevenient grace (not unlike Christ's in the wilderness) that is symbolized in the appearance of
the angel who attends him during his swoon; his ordeal else would have
been unavailing, for the intense strain of resistance, though undra-
matized, totally absorbs the physical resources of the spiritual individual. The point is underscored by the complete isolation of Guyon from
the Palmer: Guyon recognizes these as sins by himself, and all his effort
lies in the voluntary endurance.

As Guyon continues, in Milton's phrase, to "see and know, and yet
abstain," the challenge to the reader's mind offered by the thought of
evil becomes the basis of Book II of *The Faerie Queene*.[17] Knowing about
sin is clearly essential to Guyon's role, and his series of confrontations
represents the facing of allurements which he immediately knows to be
evil. The Bower of Bliss episode only emphasizes this capacity for in-
stantaneous recognition, for his single hesitation is dramatically revealed as only a temporary error about the true nature of the "two
naked Damzelles." While Guyon focuses his eyes in incipient glee,
Spenser soberly and significantly compares the ladies with the morning
star rising from the sea and with Venus born of the foam:

> As that faire Starre, the messenger of morne,
> His deawy face out of the sea doth reare:
> Or as the *Cyprian* goddesse, newly borne
> Of th' Oceans fruitfull froth, did first appeare:
> Such seemed they. . . . (II.xii.65.1–5)

Since such indeed they seem, the mistake is genuine, not willful, and it
therefore requires but the Palmer's stern rebuke to turn Guyon's wandering eyes, as he is about to succumb to *peccatum delectationis morosae*,

when he "gan relent his earnest pace," and "His stubborne brest gan secret pleasaunce to embrace" (lines 8–9). The experience is really no more than a mere toying with the notion, because the outcome is happy, the flicker of newly kindled lust being promptly quenched. Guyon's mind remains unsullied or at least so thoroughly cleansed that Guyon is not deflected from his course, but rather intensifies the hunt for "lustfull game," until with the fowler's snare he nets the biggest catch of all.

But while on this allegorical plane Spenser vividly portrays mastery of the sinful thought in the dramatic presentation of Temperance, on another level he provokes his reader's reaction to that stimulus. Lest initially there be any doubt, the ground is well prepared for an educated response. The narrative of II.xii is conceived within the context of moral thought and feeling that for the Elizabethans had come to be closely identified with Greek mythology, for Guyon's voyage parallels that of Odysseus, and the identification of Acrasia with Circe is plain. Far from being an eminently desirable, sensuous woman, Acrasia is thus actually established as being inimical to life. As C. S. Lewis long ago demonstrated, Acrasia's bower, which cunningly contrives to imitate Nature, only pretends to actuality, while the elaborate gate depicting the story of Jason and Medea merely counterfeits it; and throughout, the emphasis on veils and half-concealments bespeaks life unfulfilled or thwarted.[18] The entire conception, in short, accords with the long tradition of *delectatio morosa,* because concern with the seductive power of the artefact and the factitious is a familiar motif, not only among contemporary moralists, but also among the early Fathers. And when Spenser's vision of voluptuousness is at length perfected in the siren song about the rose, evoking emotionally ambivalent memories of literary antecedents that are profoundly significant, the reader experiences the trying nature of the situation to the full. So it is that in the fluxes and refluxes of his agitated mind the reader comes to know himself, for who is not so base as would not dally with the beguiling thought of being Acrasia's bondman?

This testing of the soul's quality is not confined by Spenser to the limits of Guyon's quest. At the very start of *The Faerie Queene,* in fact, Spenser introduces us to the proper way of reading the poem, to the rules of the allegorical game, as it were, when he dramatizes for us the dangerous delectation of the eye and the fatal susceptibility of the mind to the seductive suggestion. The poem indeed opens with an ironical situation, in which Una and the Red Cross Knight, having taken shelter from a storm in a labyrinthine wood (in medieval literature, the great symbol of covert danger), are thereafter "with pleasure forward led" to "beguile the way" with excessive joy in the song of birds and extravagant admiration for a whole catalogue of trees (I.i.8–10). Since the characters dally with these delights, it comes as no surprise to learn that they have transgressed; but in case we are uncertain, Spenser actually names the situation for us; they find themselves lost, and wandering in Wandering Wood, soon they meet the monster, Error. The Red Cross Knight vanquishes Error, yet shortly afterwards he commits an even more heinous trespass, when in the evil dream, brought at Archimago's behest from the house of Morpheus, he is seduced into mistaking the nature of the lady to whom he owes fidelity. Spenser, then, makes us fully aware at the outset that even the purest of hearts is in constant jeopardy of losing its steadfastness and melting in a bath of "wanton blis and wicked ioy" (I.i.47.6).

And so we proceed. The dragon of sin against which the Red Cross Knight battles for two whole days to emerge victoriously only on the third is the objective measure of the old Adam with which every Christian has to deal, while the machinations of Duessa provide a mental fret-work of seeming that can readily befuddle the human psyche. Nor is there any question that the Garden of Adonis betrays a similar interest in the reader's mind. On one level Spenser is here concerned to realize poetically a complex emotional subtlety that will eventually lead toward a conclusion that provides the motive-force of his own work, namely, that it is only under a veil of imperfect matter that the perfect form of the Divine can be perceived. No doubt Sidney enthusiastically approved of the idea, especially of the mode of its presentation, for Spenser's poetry ostensibly gives a local habitation and a name to a vision of Paradise. Nevertheless, the portrayal of this perfect state is not so emotionally satisfying to the reader as ideally it ought to be, for Spenser has circumvented him. The "immortal blis" which the "felicity" of the Garden supposedly embodies is to the reader's discomfiture ultimately felt as no more than a pale shadow of heavenly bliss, a series of mortal longings for earthly joys; in this way it gradually dawns on the reader that it is not within his power to apprehend the ideal world except in terms of the actual. And it is to bring him to such an awareness, to stimulate in him such a tension as will discover to him something about the state of his own nature, that Spenser playfully but reverently directs his art, using the poetic vision to search and disclose the true character of his reader's innermost desires.

Spenser's holy game culminates in the poetic resolution of the perplexing problem of time and change, wherein we have the allegorist's most personal statement about the awesome power of vision to affect the mind. In the Mutability Cantos, Nature rejects Mutability's claim to omnipotence and goes on to explain, by a most ingenious paradox, that Mutability in seeking to control everything in reality seeks nothing less than her own ruin, since after "all shall changed bee" by the supreme conquest of time, Mutability shall own no more her sway, but fade away into the changelessness of eternity:

> Cease therefore daughter further to aspire,
> And thee content thus to be rul'd by me:
> For thy decay thou seekst by thy desire;
> But time shall come that all shall changed bee,
> And from thenceforth, none no more change shall see. (VII.vii.59)

The point, of course, is unanswerable, and Mutability is silenced and made obedient. In this way Spenser reveals that the "cruell sports" of "the ever-whirling wheel / Of Change" are neither wanton nor illogical tricks of fortune, but are completely comprehensible as the operation of Providence in the outworking of the divine will and purpose. Here is a consideration, which, running parallel to the ulterior notion of the Garden of Adonis, includes within itself the justification of Spenser's art. If fallen humanity is unable to image perfection in other than finite terms, it is purely because mere mortals cannot look upon perfection directly, or see the majesty of God in all its nakedness; instead, we must behold his glory under a veil, as in a glass darkly. For this reason Dame Nature appears as veiled; she is Unchanging Perfection partially reduced to the level of human understanding under the guise of mutable matter, an indeterminate incarnation caught in an eternal moment of transfiguration; and therefore part at least of her allegorical function is to embody the truth that the temporal is the divinely ordained means by which we can attain to a knowledge of the eternal. From this point of view, just as change is no mere device to encompass humanity's destruction, but a unique and mysterious instrument to accomplish its salvation, so the contemplation of mutability and corruption is not the human mind's surrender to baseness, but a supreme moral imperative for gaining its knowledge of virtue.

Spenser's thought thus presupposes that all tends toward perfection, and it is to bring about this devoutly wished-for consummation that he believes it important to fashion his perfect gentleman. Concerned as he is with virtues and vices that are written large in the human consciousness itself, Spenser has infinite faith in the capacity of his reader to enter into his moral ploy. His allegory is of the human condition a grand and timeless metaphor that never speaks about anything other than life, and only, perhaps, when our own natures are perverted, and our thoughts a culpable chaos, does it seem to talk a strange language and the sport with the sacred purpose leaves us then profitably admonished.

Bunyan's relationship to his reader is likewise closely bound up with the material of his allegorical subject matter. *The Pilgrim's Progress* may be defined, from one point of view, as a Puritan saga of predestination wherein certain problems of election and reprobation, mutually significant to writer and reader, are treated dramatically. In the conceptual scheme of the work, the play element is indeed pervasive, because Bunyan continuously closes with the reader in sacred sport, the stakes of which are ethically vital, involving no less for the participant than the guerdon of salvation or the doom of perdition. But although Bunyan makes this quite plain in the "Apology" prefacing his work, he has not always been adequately heeded. This is a pity, for paradoxical as it may seem, the inheritors of the Puritan tradition, even the unlettered such as Bunyan, were probably more truly in touch with the imagination than others of greater learning or of different allegiance, and Bunyan's preface really deserves extremely close attention.

Most of the "Apology" is devoted to defending *The Pilgrim's Progress* against the allegation that it is all mere play or fiction; that having no correlative within the known world, it is frivolous and impractical at best, and at worst, a collection of morally corrupting lies. With avuncular good humor Bunyan states the various objections, then rejects them all:

> *Why, what's the matter? It is dark, what tho?*
> But it is feigned, *what of that I tro?*
> *Some men by feigning words as dark as mine,*
> *Make truth to spangle, and its rayes to shine.*
> But they want solidness: *Speak man thy mind:*
> They drown'd the weak; Metaphors make us blind.
> *Solidity, indeed becomes the Pen*
> *Of him that writeth things Divine to men:*
> *But must I needs want solidness, because*
> *By Metaphors I speak; was not Gods Laws,*
> *His Gospel-laws in olden time held forth*
> *By Types, Shadows and Metaphors?*[19]

Bunyan in this way accepts the charge of darkness imputed to allegory (Spenser's "dark conceit"), but he immediately transforms the darkness of metaphor to light, comprehends the darkness by light, when he claims that it can be made to "spangle." God's "gleeman" may be dark, but the truth he sings is clear enough: "*My dark and cloudy words they do but hold /* *The Truth, as Cabinets inclose the Gold*" (4). What Bunyan plainly sees is that to expound truth in sermons is simply not enough. The fallen mind must learn to seek the sunshine with a torch; it must be invited to grasp something, put aside the veil, turn up the metaphor, unlock the riddle; indeed, it must work for what it gets, but the grail is held worth the questing. And having thus placed his prize and goal wholly outside the circumscription of quotidian life, Bunyan can then legitimately assert the hallowed value of his frolic, which involves a higher reality, against the worth of mere play, which (so Huizinga informs us) is "not serious" and has no function beyond the world in which it occurs.[20]

The object of the stratagem, then, is to engage the reader's wits, to immerse him thoroughly in the work. As a fisher of men, a snarer of souls, Bunyan uses all the devices appropriate to the fisherman and the fowler (the traditional images he restates), but he recognizes that even these may not suffice, that there will yet remain from here to eternity eyes closed against all seeing, ears dulled against all hearing. His vision consequently summons the reader to find out who he is and whither he is bound: "*Would'st read thy self, and read thou know'st not what / And yet know whether thou art blest or not, / By reading the same lines?*" (7). So the reader must come, not in any otiose spirit, nor with divided mind, but *ad utrumque paratus,* ready for either event, good or ill; nor is it possible for him to ignore such a peremptory challenge, when all the imaginative elements do the same tale repeat in dream and symbol, riddle and emblem, and even anagram.

In his career Bunyan becomes more and more fully alive to this wonderful wizardry of art. In particular, vision takes on for him the most profound meaning as a source of human action. In *The Pilgrim's Progress* of 1678 he exploits one dramatic advantage of the Pauline definition, by using the passage in Corinthians as the ground-plan of Vanity Fair, in which the eyes, ears, and heart of the world are so full of earthly vanities that they cannot comprehend God's mystery as it is embodied in Christian and Faithful, who speak a strange tongue and dress and act peculiarly; far more than simple xenophobia occasions there the commotion and arrest (89ff.). The doctrine is likewise artistically exploited on those occasions, most notably in Gaius's house, when the pilgrims are asked to expound riddles, or when, as in *The Holy War* (1682), the inhabitants of Mansoul find themselves able to open many previously insoluble riddles, whenever Emmanuel occupies the town.[21] But in the Second Part of *The Pilgrim's Progress* (1684) the true value of vision is appraised anew, with the allegorist acknowledging afresh the role his reader must play as a participant in the sport. Bunyan's odd choice of form at the start of this allegory, dream-within-dream, is not based on sheer authorial ineptitude, as some critics have supposed, but rather on the premise (excitedly expressed) that the reader's mind be first prepared for a correct response. If Sagacity at the outset has indeed this educative function, the form of the work can thus be viewed as the writer's vindication of his own practice.[22]

An intense awareness of the reader and the need to stimulate his mind adequately underlie the artistic procedure of all Bunyan's imaginative works. No doubt this is determined to some extent by the nature of the allegorical subject matter itself, in which the human soul is invariably the protagonist and problems of election and reprobation are treated in such a way as to prompt a desired reaction; but it is also the result of Bunyan's own exploitative technique of involving the reader in the work and forcing him to sift the action of symbolic content. While this remains true of Bunyan's allegories in general, the effect is particularly pervasive in *The Pilgrim's Progress,* which confronts the problem of pre-destination directly and which consequently raises most acutely the gravest question concerning the treatment of that doctrine in literature: the arousing and the maintaining of interest in an action the end of which is predestined, for such fore-ordination might seem to deprive the action of all interest as to what will happen next. The issue is of some moment because most readers of *The Pilgrim's Progress* would surely agree that the miracle of the book consists precisely in the persuasive power of its narrative and in its ability to arouse suspense so that the wonder is not that the doctrine of predestination is felt, but that it is not more keenly felt.

To consider why this should be so is to come close to the heart of Bunyan's manipulative art. First, Bunyan's choice of visionary form is itself significant, and in assessing its consequences for the allegory as a whole, we might find it enlightening to contrast the prose work with a great poem of predestination, Chaucer's *Troilus and Criseyde.* The form of the latter is objective; Chaucer takes himself off to a sphere where he can become a commentator on his story and he quite conspicuously in-terposes himself between the actors and the reader until the end of the action. Chaucer thus sees the action whole and he sees it as inevitable; consequently, he makes us see and feel the operation of predestination in the events depicted. With Bunyan the case is very different. His dream-form is so subjective that his influence almost ceases to be felt as the narrative progresses. True, he intrudes early when at the Slough of Despond the author/narrator self-consciously asks Help a question, but the curious artistic effect of this episode is merely to contribute to the impression of reality, since our readiness to believe in the actuality of the vision is confirmed in Bunyan's accepting here the dream as truth (14–16). Thereafter, the presence of the author is indicated only by the occasional reiteration of "I saw in my dream. . . ." Such remarks ful-fill the artistic function of creating a time-sense and are not felt to de-tract from the reality of the dream-world in which we are immersed. Even when the dreamer awakes only to dream again, there is no loss of reality or continuity. In short, nowhere is the truth of Bunyan's dream challenged, so that his vision is unified in the mind of the protagonist himself, and Christian's vision becomes our vision, the only dream of the book. How, then, can we doubt the reality of the unhappy chance that lands both Christian and Faithful in the dungeon of Doubting Castle? The misery and the danger are for us at that moment as actual as the pilgrims experience them. Nor are those feelings so readily dissipated when Christian suddenly remembers the Key of Promise he has carried with him all the time; the facile escape from damnation causes the story at this point to creak and jolt every bit as much as the lock on the dungeon door that goes *"damnable* hard" (118). The episode merely illustrates the general truth that although on the long view we know that Christian will win, the issue is often in doubt; and looking through Christian's eyes, we are constantly reminded that all our present happiness hangs, like the Damoclean sword, by a slender thread.

But this explanation is hardly adequate to account for the quality of fearful suspense the tale arouses. There is a sense in which we never wholly identify ourselves with Christian at all; indeed, sometimes our emotions are so far at variance with his that our fear may be greatest when his is least. Certainly this is the case throughout the Apollyon episode, where Christian takes his stand upon the terms of the covenant, confident of eventual success; he despairs later only momentarily, when Apollyon temporarily gets the better of him in the fight:

> This sore Combat lasted for above half a day, even till *Christian* was almost quite spent. For you must know, that *Christian,* by reason of his wounds, must needs grow weaker and weaker.
>
> Then *Apollyon* espying his opportunity, began to gather up close to *Christian,* and wrestling with him, gave him a dreadful fall; and with that *Christian*'s Sword flew out of his hand. Then said *Apollion, I am sure of thee now;* and with that, he had almost prest him to death; so that *Christian* began to despair of life. (59)

There may be no ultimate danger for Christian here, but we feel most strongly that there is. What has happened is that our minds have been directed from confident anticipation of the future to anxious contemplation of the present; Bunyan has manipulated our attention by vivifying and emotionalizing the uncertainties and exigencies of the immediate. And this he does through the medium of language that is at once simple, homely, vivid, and concrete. "[W]ords easy to be understood," he reminds the "Learned Reader" in an epistle at the beginning of *The Holy City,* "do often hit the mark, when high and learned ones do only

pierce the air."[23] Bunyan can hit the mark. In Apollyon, to George
Bernard Shaw's delight,[24] Bunyan scores a bull's-eye of terror with
dramatic raging, but he knows the value of silence too, and can daringly
paint a speaking picture with the greatest of ease: "Then *Christian* and
Hopeful looked one upon another, with tears gushing out; but yet said
nothing to the Shepherds" (121). Such drama of phrase denotes a power
that can completely involve us. It is the measure of the artist that he can
so thoroughly absorb us that we are temporarily cut off from assurance
to be made aware that there is always a chance of things going wrong.
And this awareness moves us.

If the impact of form and style helps to sustain the interest of the
allegory, so also does the structure. As Wolfgang Iser has pointed out,
the Calvinist scheme of salvation which forms the theological ground-
plan of *The Pilgrim's Progress* of necessity accentuates, as against the design of Deguileville's *Le Pèlerinage de la Vie Humaine,* "the importance of
the individual soul, giving it precedence over means of grace, the institution and the hierarchy" and makes "the attainment of *certitudo salutis*"
something that is "objectively unattainable."[25] That this inevitably
leads to the uncertainty of relationships within the story, to introspection, the probing of motives and nervous searching for identity, merely
affords greater challenge and opportunity to the allegorist. Christian is
not Everyman, but he is every man's paradigm; and Bunyan takes care to
make him recognizably human in his transparent fallibility. Throughout
the various episodes in which Christian falls to rise, is baffled only to
fight better, there is constantly maintained a tight structural unity. Thus
we cannot fail to notice, as we travel along the pilgrim highway, the
many signposts that invite our attention to what lies ahead. Since much
counsel is given to Christian during his journey (did ever mortal man
receive more advice about where to go and what to do?), we become
interested to discover his future conduct. Not infrequently what
happens to him anticipates his vicissitudes, as when he receives his roll at
the Cross or is clad in armor by the damsels of the House Beautiful; the
ritual associated with the presentation of these awakens us to the probability that the roll will later be lost and the armor eventually proved.
Hopes and fears are created also by the numerous recapitulations of
spiritual progress to date and by the vivid vignettes that introduce such
villains as Talkative, By-ends, Demas, or the Flatterer. Sometimes great
expectations are aroused only to be delayed in fulfillment, as when our

acquaintance with Ignorance is twice interrupted or when Christian glimpses the Delectable Mountains from the House Beautiful or descries the gates of the Celestial City from the summit of Hill Clear. Such delays enhance the suspense by producing impatience and are entirely legitimate tactics of the allegorist's playful art.

There is ultimately a rhythm in pilgrim affairs that imposes itself on the mind. It is a structural pattern that leads us to anticipate a moment of calm following a period of tumult, a time of activity succeeding an interval of rest. This is often derived from the ironical juxtapositioning of contrasting episodes, as when, after his violent combat with Apollyon, Christian is restored to physical and spiritual health and strength in an atmosphere of peace. The progress makes evident also the human failings and potentialities that lead us to suppose that Christian will indeed "catch a slip" in the Valley of Humiliation and will dare to venture into the Valley of the Shadow of Death despite the warnings of the two terrified men. But although our minds become thus attuned to following the line of probability, Christian is still capable of surprising: witness his astonishing display of vanity shortly after his humiliation, when just outside the valley he overtakes Faithful "and did also over-run him, so the *last was first*. Then did *Christian* vain-gloriously smile, because he had gotten the start of his Brother: but not taking good heed to his feet, he suddenly stumbled and fell, and could not rise again, until *Faithful* came up to help him" (66). In such a way is anticipation suddenly satisfied by surprise and surprise instantly subverted by the realization of anticipation. With regard to this incident, Stanley E. Fish comments that we

> have here two complementary and interdependent experiences. The reader is forced to give up a premature interpretation just when Christian is forced to give up the self-confidence and self-reliance of his vainglorious smile. Not only do hero and reader stumble together, they are picked up together, and in the same way, by an agent from without. Christian could not have risen, we are told, "until *Faithful* came up to help him," and without the second, and *revelatory,* stage of the episode, we would have remained the captives of a literal and incorrect reading.[26]

The effect, according to this critic who makes the episode serve as a model of Bunyan's entire narrative procedure, is to humble the reader along with Christian by disparaging his intellect in favor of intuition through experience; that explanation, however, would seem not only to rob the situation of much of its ironic value, but also to depreciate the structural design which we have delineated and which is apprehended by the faculty of memory to which Fish afterwards very perceptively allots a significant role in the allegory (250ff.).

Even those seemingly static episodes, which superficially do nothing to advance the action, help to arouse our expectations for the future. Take, for instance, the visit Christian pays to the Interpreter's House, where he has shown to him a veritable museum of emblems. What is most interesting about this episode is that it is an example of allegory within allegory, for the emblems are themselves allegories in miniature; and there is a Langlandian subtlety and profundity about its depth. On one level, it teaches the insight that the elect receives into his state at a certain point in his career; on a second, it signifies that the soul may read the signs and seek the meaning of its own condition; on a third, it represents the meaning of meaning by demonstrating how we may interpret the allegory as a whole; and on a fourth, it postulates a system of values which sets up hopes that we long to see fulfilled in action. Here in *The Pilgrim's Progress,* generally regarded by critics as the supreme example of "simple" allegory, is allegory of such multiple significance and complexity that it even seems capable of yielding sense according to the fourfold system of medieval allegorical hermeneutics. Far from being inert, the episode is actually among the most dynamic of the book, for not only does it move the action by concentrating on the present (the state of the elect soul at the moment of vision), but it also motivates future action by revealing what is desirable (the evangelical consummation longed for) and what is to be avoided (the misery of the gross exemplars, particularly the Man in an Iron Cage). Its effect on our reading of the allegory is remarkable; it creates expectation, excites suspense, and prolongs anxiety for the outcome.

By all these means, then, as well as by others, Bunyan opposes the artistically stultifying tendency of predestination to produce a work of marked tension and vigor. His art is the art of management, and if its object is to bring the reader face-to-face with his own mind and enable him to know himself, its method is first to enmesh him in the magic web of the dream and thereafter to search and investigate him to the uttermost depths.

The joy of such allegoric captivity is nowhere more sweetly rendered than in Spenser and Bunyan, as each in his own way engages the mind in a holy game of words to bring his reader to a required stage of enhanced self-awareness. While it is no doubt true that this is the general end of all literature, the means to it are perhaps more overtly employed in the allegories examined, the aims of which are avowedly didactic. The intellect recognizes this as soon as it becomes alive to the opportunities afforded the writer by the nature of his task; but emotionally it is felt keenly, whenever the mind is actively engrossed in experiencing the works. For the sport issues from the conviction (as Bunyan expresses it) that the fish *"must be grop'd for, and be tickled too, / Or they will not be catcht, what e're you do"* (3), that *"base things"* may *"usher in Divine"* (6), that *"Ones fancie"* can be made to *"Checkle"* (170); and even the most tireless reader of treatises, the most confirmed lover of sermons will concede that what Spenser and Bunyan offer is something supremely desirable, which the moral philosopher, for all his power of reason, can never give: momentous exposure to the thing itself, "with all her baits and seeming pleasures" (as Milton puts it) intricately inwoven, the savory sauce with the hellebore judiciously compounded.[27] Small wonder, then, that as the spell of their sacred art is cast within him, the right reader finds himself bound always to be on the alert, continually vigilant, since he knows that the allegory is continuously reading him. He plays strenuously who plays in the field of the Lord.

BARBARA A. JOHNSON

Falling into Allegory:
The "Apology" to
The Pilgrim's Progress and
Bunyan's Scriptural Methodology

The first readers of John Bunyan's *The Pilgrim's Progress* must have been startled by the title page of the 1678 edition, for it both announces and attempts to conceal the true nature of the volume.[1] The first few lines are, of course, fairly straightforward: "THE / Pilgrim's Progress / FROM / THIS WORLD, / TO / That which is to come:"[2] but what follows is anything but predictable for a Puritan audience: "Delivered under the Similitude of a / DREAM." The word "dream" is in heavy black type, by far the largest lettering on the page. "Delivered under the Similitude of a," positioned above it, is in the smallest lettering and could almost be overlooked. A description of the dream's contents comes next, emphasizing that what will be revealed in the "DREAM" is the journey of a character: "Wherein is Discovered / The Manner of his setting out, / His Dangerous Journey; And safe / Arrival at the Desired Countrey." And finally this summary is followed, above the author's name, with what must have seemed an admission of guilt if not effrontery: "I have used Similitudes, Hos. 12.10." The dynamics of the title page thus underscore the surprise for the book's first audience; John Bunyan, the Dissenter, the mechanick preacher, has produced not a "plain tract," but a fictional work that depicts its subject through a similitude.

The skittishness reflected on the title page is played out in full in "The Author's *Apology* For His Book," prefixed to the first and all subsequent editions of *The Pilgrim's Progress*. The "Apology" is one of the most puzzling statements ever offered for a work of fiction. Far from a conven-

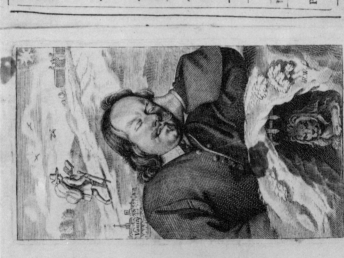

THE
Ann Palmer
Pilgrim's Progrefs
FROM
THIS WORLD,
TO
That which is to come:

Delivered under the Similitude of a

DREAM

Wherein is Difcovered,
The manner of his fetting out,
His Dangerous Journey; And fafe
Arrival at the Defired Countrey.

I have ufed Similitudes, Hof. 12. 10.

By *John Bunyan.*

Licenfed and Entred according to Dpder.

LONDON,
Printed for *Nath. Ponder* at the *Peacock*
in the *Poultrey* near *Cornhil,* 1678.

The title page from the first edition of *The Pilgrim's Progress*, 1678 (reproduced by permission of the Huntington Library, San Marino, California).

tional introduction, it is, rather, a strenuous defense. One measure of its contradictory nature appears as soon as we turn from the title page to the opening statement. For while the title page has used language that indicates intentionality, Bunyan begins by proclaiming that he didn't mean to make a fictional work at all; it just happened that he "Fell suddenly into an Allegory."[3] We notice also that he is falling into verse to introduce this "accidental" work. His denial of an original literary intention in writing and his presentation of the arguments of the "Apology" as mere retrospective reflections after the event provoke skepticism. After beginning by talking in simplistic terms about his work, he gradually changes his tone, moving finally to a comprehensive and radical statement about his fiction. His style in verse conspicuously lacks the simple clarity for which his prose style has always been admired; as a result, the sheer difficulty of following shifts in his argument has prevented due appreciation of how drastic a position he is taking and how sophisticated is his articulation of it.

Critical response to the "Apology" has, for the most part, accepted at face value the statements about origin and form put forth in the beginning of the preface. Henri Talon and Roger Sharrock use them to support their view of Bunyan as an unconscious artist, Talon stressing Bunyan's "instinctive art," while Sharrock notes his "supremely unsophisticated attitude to the literary product."[4] William York Tindall theorizes that for Bunyan and his original readers the book was a controversial pamphlet.[5] He does recognize, however, that the prefaces to all of Bunyan's fictional works are "essays in criticism," and that "these formal commentaries . . . testify to [Bunyan's] thorough consciousness of the arts which he employed" and to the "hostility of some readers to the use of those popular devices" (181–82). Tindall further notices two features of the "Apology" that tend to be overlooked— Bunyan's completely conscious command of aesthetic issues and his marked apprehensiveness about the reception of the book.

U. Milo Kaufmann, however, has given more extended attention to the "Apology" as an "aesthetic brief."[6] Pointing to the speaker's claims that the work had a will of its own, Kaufmann argues that this confession of intention is "the inadvertent witness to a radical irresolution on Bunyan's part" (4). Kaufmann sees a tension existing in Bunyan's aesthetic between "the didactic and literalist methods widespread in Puritanism and the imaginative methods native to the grand tradition in literature" (5).[7] I will argue that this "tension" is far from inadvertent, but that it is resolved in the "Apology" itself.

The Pilgrim's Progress is a fiction whose imaginative dimensions are at the core of the "Apology." In Puritan discussions of literature, as Lawrence Sasek notes, the word " 'feigned' appears regularly as a pejorative term" indicating simple falsehood.[8] Indeed, even Renaissance poetic theory used terms like "dissimulation" and "duplicity" in discussing the relationship of form and content, especially in metaphor and allegory. George Puttenham's *Arte of English Poesie* (1589) epitomizes the Renaissance definition of Allegoria: "which is when we speake one thing and thinke another, and that our wordes and our meanings meete not," thus amounting to "a kinde of dissimulation."[9] Puttenham finds allegory and metaphor to be closely allied:

> But properly and in his principall vertue *Allegoria* is when we do speake in sense translatiue and wrested from the owne signification, neuertheless applied to another not altogether contrary, but hauing much conueniencie with it as before we said of the metaphore . . . and this manner of inuersion extending to whole and large speaches, it maketh the figure *allegorie* to be called a long and perpetuall Metaphore. (186–87)

Puttenham thus emphasizes the gap between word and meaning: "for what els is your *Metaphor* but an inuersion of sense by transport; your *allegorie* by [but?] a duplicitie of meaning or dissimulation vnder couert and darke intendments . . ." (154). The defense offered by Renaissance theory was that truths unpalatable to those not yet attuned must be made attractive by pleasing language, that metaphor and allegory are a protection from the intrusion of those not morally or intellectually qualified, and that the difficulties in reading train the capacities of mind and heart so that the reader can understand more truth. These defenses, however, had not been accepted by Puritans.

One major charge the "Apology" attempts to forestall is the idea that a work "delivered under the similitude of a dream" is in some sense a lie. Bunyan is aware that "allegory" goes counter to a major principle of Puritan rhetorical practice, since "plain style" was the universal model for Puritans (Sasek, 55). *The Pilgrim's Progress,* however, is not "plain" and it does not "preach" or exhort; it shows a man getting to heaven rather than instructing how to get there. Bunyan must, therefore, go to great lengths to justify his fictive expression, and he must maneuver his reader into accepting it through a series of strategies whose implications become clear only upon careful examination.

The "Apology" begins at the point where his own conventional expectations and those of his readers most nearly converge. He, or rather the authorial guise he employs, functions as a kind of first reader of the work. He registers all the objections he believes he would encounter from his readers, first presenting then rejecting the usual Renaissance defense of imaginative works, and turning finally to a biblical defense of his "method." The "Apology" has four distinct units. The first section describes how the book came into being. The second explains how it came to be published. The third and longest is a defense of style and method and includes a debate with an unspecified but learned objector. The final section describes the relationship of author, book, and reader on which the method depends.

The first thirty-four lines present a wonderfully appealing picture. Denying outright that he ever meant to write what he has, Bunyan claims he was writing an altogether different book at the time:

> When at the first I took my Pen in hand,
> Thus for to write; I did not understand
> That I at all should make a little Book
> In such a mode; Nay, I had undertook
> To make another, which when almost done,
> Before I was aware, I this begun. (1.1–6)

Here he is underscoring the most significant objection he expects the work to encounter: its choice of mode. His second verse paragraph defines this mode; he tells us that while engaged in writing that other book, he "fell suddenly into an Allegory" (1.9), and describes this "falling" as a process with a will of its own, a spontaneous generation of ideas that multiply "Like sparks that from the coals of Fire do flie" (1.14). Ideas "breed" in him until he removes them and sets them apart for fear they will swallow up the book he was originally writing. Up to this point, Bunyan is disclaiming all authorial intention in the making of *The Pilgrim's Progress*. The next verse paragraph takes up the question of why, in that case, he continued to write the book: "I did it mine own self to gratifie" (1.24), and "I only thought to make / I knew not what . . ."

(1.21–22). He does not justify this kind of writing as anything but a diversion. Having offered this apology, Bunyan can then go on to describe how the book grew to its full length. In simple but, as we shall see, highly significant terms, he tells us his technique: "For having now my Method by the end; / Still as I pull'd, it came . . ." (2.1–2).

That Bunyan found it necessary to adopt so naive a persona is a measure of how strong the Puritan's distrust of imagination truly was; it was easier in the Puritan context to defend an intentionless activity. Indeed, this first section probably reflects a distrust on Bunyan's own part as well as an anticipation of it in his audience. His tactics are sound in beginning his defense at the point where he and his reader stand on common ground in their response to fictive expression. But these lines, far from revealing Bunyan to be an "unconscious" artist, are a measure of just how conscious he was of his status as a "mechanick" whose ability to write was as suspect as his enterprise was controversial.[10] We see him taking on a persona to confirm his image and to dispel any impression that he was trying to be something he was not.

In the second section, Bunyan turns to the book's fate as an independent creation. Even after the book was written, his doubts caused him to show it to friends, who disagreed heatedly about what should become of it:

> Well, when I had thus put mine ends together,
> I shew'd them others, that I might see whether
> They would condemn them, or them justifie:
> And some said, let them live; some, let them die:
> Some said, *John,* print it; others said, Not so:
> Some said, It might do good; others said, No. (2.5–10)

The first set of terms in which the book is assessed is moral: "condemn" or "justifie" (2.7); the second is judicial: "let them live" or "let them die" (2.8); the third is literary: to print or not to print (2.9); the last is didactic: will the book do good or not (2.10). This sequence of frames through which to view the book provides a paradigm of the Puritan response to the world. We begin with the ethical issue of whether the book can be justified intrinsically, apart from any good it might do. The didactic question is not the first issue of importance, but the last.

Throughout this second section Bunyan's naive persona remains. He has decided to publish the work, he says, only because his friends could not decide for him: "To prove then who advised for the best, / Thus I thought fit to put it to the test" (2.17–18). He hopes it may give delight to those who thought it should be printed; those who thought it should not be printed are asked to withhold judgment until they see what happens; those who don't like it do not have to read it: "If that thou wilt not read, let it alone; / Some love the meat, some love to pick the bone" (2.27–28). No other introduction to a fictional work offers quite such a defensive account of the steps leading to publication.

With the third and longest section of the "Apology," however, Bunyan's tone changes sharply. Gone is the naive persona. A significant shift in strategy occurs; a comparatively elaborate defense of style and method takes the form of a debate between the speaker and an unspecified objector. The speaker now addresses directly the two major Puritan objections to imaginative writings we noted earlier: that they are "dark," that is, hard to understand, and "feigned," i.e., untrue. Emphasis on the need for clarity in religious writing was as widespread in Puritan thought as strictures against lying. Since the charge that the work is "dark" because of its allegorical mode is a serious one, Bunyan's defense is that his work contains only *"sound and honest Gospel-strains"* and hence that his particular kind of allegory will be clear because of its scriptural underpinnings. But as his subsequent comments show, he is aware of complexities. The Puritan attitude toward the use of a simile or metaphor, Kenneth Murdock has noted, was fairly straightforward: "The method was dictated by the purpose. If a simile or metaphor made truth more intelligible and rationally more convincing, it was good; if it simply tickled the senses and gave pleasure, or if it distracted the reader's attention from doctrine, it was clearly bad."[11] Bunyan contends that the story will please the reader and direct him to doctrine rather than divert him from it. But before he can argue that point, he must develop an answer to charges of "darkness" and "feigning." Renaissance literary theory had, of course, developed standard justifications for the writing of literature, and Bunyan begins by asserting them. His objector, however, is presented as unconvinced; indeed, these defenses for literature provoke him into making two additional charges. These the speaker answers by shifting from a literary to a biblical defense and presenting three far more substantial justifications for the work.

Bunyan begins this section by taking up the question of what good the work can do a reader, the last question asked by Bunyan when discussing whether the work should be published. He focuses now specifically on the issue of whether the style and method chosen can legitimately be used to instruct as well as delight the reader: "May I not write in such a stile as this? / In such a method too, and yet not miss / Mine end, thy good? why may it not be done?" (2.31–33). His first answer is to repeat the standard Renaissance view of imaginative writings, the Horatian dictum of *dulce et utile,* which claims that literature instructs by delight, because it entices the reader and draws him toward truth through fictional means. Here Bunyan dwells upon entrapment; the way a fisherman catches fish, or a fowler snares game, is analogous to the way the writer must approach the reader:

> You see the ways the Fisher-man doth take
> To catch the Fish; what Engins doth he make?
> Behold! how he ingageth all his Wits;
> Also his Snares, Lines, Angles, Hooks and Nets:
> Yet Fish there be, that neither Hook, nor Line,
> Nor Snare, nor Net, Nor Engin can make thine;
> They must be grop'd for, and be tickled too,
> Or they will not be catcht, what e're you do. (3.7–14)

Just as the fisherman must "tickle" some fish in order to catch them, the writer must "tickle" with a decorative surface fiction in order to bring the reader to truth.

John Steadman has noted that the notion that poetry should delight through its fictions and instruct through its allegorical meaning was "a commonplace, if not an axiom, of both medieval and Renaissance criticism."[12] It is not an accident that Bunyan begins with this commonplace, even though, like Puritans in general, he then rejects it, except as an interim argument:

> If that a Pearl may in a Toads-head dwell,
> And may be found too in an Oister-shell;
> If things that promise nothing, do contain
> What better is then Gold; who will disdain,
> (That have an inkling of it,) there to look,
> That they may find it? Now my little Book,
> (Tho void of all those paintings that may make

It with this or the other man to take,)
Is not without those things that do excel,
What do in brave, but empty notions dwell. (3.23–32)

He would emphasize that his notions of truth are not empty, and that other works provide, only with careful qualifications, a model for his own. The references to the "pearl in an oyster," or, later, to "Truth within a Fable" (7.3), show Bunyan demonstrating a conscious knowledge of literary works. The fact that he himself ultimately calls these beautiful lies "empty notions" indicates how half-hearted this defense is. (One of the reasons the meaning is murky here is that Bunyan's guise as an unlettered preacher is being compromised; how does he know of these other works to which *his* work is an alternative?)

His learned objector answers this defense by shifting the grounds on which the book is to be judged. The central question, he argues, is not what good the work can do—the potentially good results of an act are no defense if the act is intrinsically immoral—but rather whether the book can "stand" in itself. Is it ethically justifiable to write a work of this kind? Speaking in the first person, this critic clearly signals Bunyan's profound concern for the reception of his book. But his creating a figure to declare objections distances the issue. The objections emerge as a debate:

> *Well, yet I am not fully satisfy'd,*
> *That this your Book will stand, when soundly try'd.*
>   Why, what's the matter? *It is dark, what tho?*
> *But it is feigned, what of that I tro?*
>   Some men by feigning words as dark as mine,
>   Make truth to spangle, and its rayes to shine.
> *But they want solidness:* Speak man thy mind:
> *They drown'd the weak; Metaphors make us blind.* (3.33–36; 4.1–4)[13]

All the major charges have here been brought together; the work is "dark," hard to understand; "feigned" because it is based on a lie, the dream; and, because of its allegorical mode, lacking in solidity. The standard Renaissance formulation that truth can be delivered through a decorative fiction, a lie, is not acceptable in the Puritan aesthetic precisely because the "feigned" nature of any given work cannot be ethically justified however benevolent its intention. "Metaphors make us

blind" because what the implied comparison adds to truth is a distrac-
tion from truth which should be delivered plainly.

To counter this objection, Bunyan replies that by "feigning" words
other writers have in fact revealed truth: "Some men by feigning words
as dark as mine, / Make truth to spangle, and its rayes to shine." But
against the more formidable charge that metaphoric language lacks
solidity and makes us blind, Bunyan has to counter by invoking a more
authoritative model than any mere work of literature:

> Solidity, indeed becomes the Pen
> Of him that writeth things Divine to men:
> But must I needs want solidness, because
> By Metaphors I speak; was not Gods Laws,
> His Gospel-laws in older time held forth
> By Types, Shadows and Metaphors? Yet loth
> Will any sober man be to find fault
> With them, lest he be found for to assault
> The highest Wisdom. No, he rather stoops,
> And seeks to find out what by pins and loops,
> By Calves, and Sheep; by Heifers, and by Rams;
> By Birds and Herbs, and by the blood of Lambs;
> God speaketh to him: and happy is he
> That finds the light, and grace that in them be.
>   Be not too forward therefore to conclude,
> That I want solidness; that I am rude:
> All things solid in shew, not solid be;
> All things in parables despise not we,
> Lest things most hurtful lightly we receive;
> And things that good are, of our souls bereave. (4.5–24)

With this statement, the whole tenor of the "Apology" changes; the
speaker becomes much more explicit about what he is doing and argues
more forcefully for the validity of his work. He offers here the first of
several descriptive phrases that define his work, and, more importantly,
he lays the groundwork for a defense that can withstand all the significant objections. He begins by agreeing with his critic that solidity is
necessary when writing "things Divine to men," thus announcing that
his purpose is to write of divine reality. The word "solidity" clearly
refers to the content of his work and implies that its vision will be sub-

stantial and meaningful. But can metaphoric language be "solid"? Can it encapsulate truth? The answer to that question is contained in the rest of the verse-paragraph; Scripture uses "Types, Shadows and Metaphors" to deliver divine truth to men. God himself speaks through symbols: "By Birds and Herbs, and by the blood of Lambs." Thus, metaphoric language is capable of delivering divine reality to men and Bunyan is justified in using it.

Because his allegory has very little in common with Renaissance allegories, Bunyan seeks a mode of discourse that has "solidness," not merely feigned words. In the rest of the "Apology," he achieves this by linking his mode of discourse to that of the Bible. Scripture's metaphors, unlike the ones the objector attacks, have "solidness" because God himself uses them. Bunyan thus transposes the very idea of metaphor from the realm in which Puttenham located it, the realm in which the tenor and the vehicle are in opposition, to the realm of scriptural truth; there tenor and vehicle are intrinsically connected, because God has made the world in such a way that these connections exist. In the Bible, word and meaning meet.

Bunyan explicitly classifies his metaphors with those of God himself: "By Metaphors I speak; was not Gods Laws, / His Gospel-laws in older time held forth / By Types, Shadows and Metaphors?" (4.8–10). Unlike the traditional rhetorician's metaphor which links disparate things, these "Types, Shadows and Metaphors" are available for discourse because they embody an intrinsic connection built into the creation itself. Even God has no more direct mode of discourse in which to speak of major truths. No words can convey divine truth as adequately as concrete things used metaphorically: "By Birds and Herbs, and by the blood of Lambs" (4.16). Bunyan's fictional strategy constructs a comparable mode of discourse in which tenor and vehicle are connected not by the incongruity and distance which fuel Renaissance allegory, but by an intrinsic resemblance which makes the true meaning an extension of the ostensible meaning.

The contrast between Bunyan and Spenser makes the difference clear. Book I of *The Faerie Queene* and *The Pilgrim's Progress* both depict a Christian moving toward salvation, but the terms in which Spenser conveys his meaning are markedly different. For instance, Red Cross is really Holiness, both more and less than Everyman; Christian is simply Christian. Faerie Land and what happens there depict a series of actions that in themselves do not directly reveal meaning; meaning is discoverable only by a constant and conscious process of translation from a chivalric to a Christian context. Signals, such as dislocation, riddles, and difficulties in the literal level itself, invite the reader's participation. The surface fiction of the Knight's adventures keeps the literal and allegorical levels distinguishable. By enlisting the reader in explicating the poem, Spenser forwards his purpose to "fashion" the reader.[14]

The Pilgrim's Progress requires no translation to a Christian context. Its terms are defined by Scripture; its landscape is created out of Scripture and its meaning is intrinsically inseparable from it.[15] Bunyan captures what the real world is like to someone whose perception of it is altered by grace. This is a much sparer strategy than Spenser's, producing a typically low-key style. For example, "Then *Christian* and *Hopeful* outwent them again, and went till they came at a delicate Plain, called *Ease,* where they went with much content; but the Plain was but *narrow,* so they were quickly got over it" (106). The term "delicate" is all that lifts the line from the colorless. But by means of it Bunyan can speak both figuratively and accurately about a Christian's experience in this world. His marginal note underscores what he means: "The ease that Pilgrims have is but little in this life" (106). Bunyan's metaphors do not deflect us toward a concept but rather embody an experiential truth. He offers the most direct mimesis possible of the way a Christian, as opposed to a non-Christian, experiences his life (Knott, 450, 461). Indeed, if Bunyan's defense of poetry resembles any other, it is Dante's explanation of the allegorical method of *The Divine Comedy* in the letter to Can Grande, which Bunyan cannot conceivably have known.[16] Bunyan, like Dante, offers a biblical model for his narrative—not fable, but parable, not truth wrapped in a beautiful lie, but similitudes that encapsulate truth: "My dark and cloudy words they do but hold / The Truth, as Cabinets inclose the Gold" (4.25–26). With this assertion the critic is heard from no more, although Bunyan clearly continues to address his remarks to him for the rest of the section.

The speaker next cites the actual practice of the prophets, the apostles, and Christ:

> The Prophets used much by Metaphors
> To set forth Truth; Yea, who so considers
> Christ, his Apostles too, shall plainly see,
> That Truths to this day in such Mantles be. (4.27–30)

He then reasserts that Scripture is full of allegories:

> Am I afraid to say that holy Writ,
> Which for its Stile, and Phrase, puts down all Wit,
> Is every where so full of all these things,
> (Dark Figures, Allegories,) yet there springs
> From that same Book that lustre, and those rayes
> Of light, that turns our darkest nights to days. (4.31–36)

Bunyan's appeal to the Bible's use of allegory counters the charge that his style is unacceptable because it is "dark." Light springs from the allegories of the Bible; truth is revealed through the use of "Dark Figures." The traditional secular model of writing asserts that truth can appropriately be concealed in decorative fictions which merely attract, without contributing to the truthfulness of the work, a model Bunyan's earlier remarks show he fully understood. Bunyan holds a different view of the relationship between form and content. Biblical allegorical modes intrinsically reveal truth. They are not tools for enticement; instead they offer the only possible means of apprehending what lies beyond man's usual experience.

Having qualified the charge of "darkness," Bunyan turns to the critic and asks him to look to his own life, "And find There darker Lines, then in my Book / He findeth any" (5.2–3). Bunyan is not just striking back at his critic but signaling an important way to view his book; to understand what Bunyan's portrayal of sainthood means, one must read *The Pilgrim's Progress* with one's own life in mind.

Bunyan next articulates the effect he expects his book to have on the reader, a theory of reading far more sophisticated than the argument for moral benefit with which the "Apology" began:

> Come, Truth, although in Swadling-clouts, I find
> Informs the Judgment, rectifies the Mind,
> Pleases the Understanding, makes the Will
> Submit; the Memory too it doth fill
> With what doth our Imagination please;
> Likewise, it tends our troubles to appease. (5.9–14)

The surface fiction is like "Swadling-clouts" that enclose divine truth. The term "Swadling-clouts" is a biblically based conception of form and content. In Luke 2.12, an angel tells the shepherds, "And this shall be

a sign unto you; Ye will find a babe wrapped in swaddling clothes, lying
in a manger."[17] Swaddling clothes are a sign by which to know Christ.
They do not conceal to reveal, nor are they like the surface "delight" of
Renaissance theory; they are not chaff or shell. They ready a living truth
to reveal itself and make recognition of it possible. Bunyan's metaphors,
like the "Swadling-clouts," contain divine truth that cannot be conveyed in any other way. The base things of this world become the means
of apprehending the divine. Judgment, mind, understanding, and will
are all exercised and informed. The vision of truth retained by the memory is one that has pleased the imagination. Finally, this reading experience tends to appease other troubles.

The speaker then evokes biblical authorities to differentiate his kind
of fiction from Puttenham's kind:

> Sound words I know *Timothy* is to use;
> And old Wives Fables he is to refuse,
> But yet grave *Paul* him no where doth forbid
> The use of Parables; in which lay hid
> That Gold, those Pearls, and precious stones that were
> Worth digging for; and that with greatest care. (5.15–20)

He acknowledges that Paul forbids old wives' tales, but Paul does not
forbid the use of parables. Fable and parable lie at distinguishable points
of the rhetorical spectrum.[18]

Yet not even biblical models, a sophisticated theory of reading, and
the explicit sanction of New Testament writers allay Bunyan's uneasi-
ness completely:

> Let me add one word more, O Man of God!
> Art thou offended? dost thou wish I had
> Put forth my matter in another dress,
> Or that I had in things been more express?
> Three things let me propound, then I submit
> To those that are my betters, (as is fit.) (5.21–26)

That Bunyan still feels the final judgment should be left to others reveals
how severe the strictures are against which he is ranging himself. He
asks himself yet again whether "another dress," another mode, might
still be preferable to the fictive and the allegorical. Would eliminating

the fictional frame, even if it is marginally licit, be more appropriate? Are "Dark Figures," even defensible ones, inferior to "more express" language?

The last part of this section recapitulates the foregoing argument under three headings. The first sets conditions for licit use of metaphorical language:

> 1. I find not that I am denied the use
> Of this my method, so I no abuse
> Put on the Words, Things, Readers, or be rude
> In handling Figure, or Similitude,
> In application; but, all that I may,
> Seek the advance of Truth, this or that way. . . . (5.27–32)

The writer may use allegorical methods so long as he does not "abuse / Put on the Words, Things, Readers" (5.29), that is, force more meanings than legitimately exist upon his contents or his audience. Nor must he do violence ("be rude") to figures and similitudes in their handling. Neither will happen as long as his principle is to "Seek the advance of Truth, this or that way" (5.32). Then Bunyan interjects a curiously cryptic passage claiming that his use of allegory is not merely allowed; writers he can legitimately take as models offer him actual examples to follow:

> Denied did I say? Nay, I have leave,
> (Example too, and that from them that have
> God better pleased by their words or ways,
> Then any Man that breatheth now adays,)
> Thus to express my mind, thus to declare
> Things unto thee that excellentest are. (5.33–36; 6.1–2)

Clearly Bunyan is referring to other imaginative works he has seen that seem to employ the same strategy as *The Pilgrim's Progress,* specific literary models in the past from which he derives either his method or support in using it. What models he had in mind, why he felt compelled to be so coy about them, and why, that being so, he brought them up at all is one of the most puzzling aspects of the "Apology," and one made even more baffling by Bunyan's scanty and scattered comments on his own reading. The matter is too complex to pursue here, though I address it elsewhere.[19] Clearly, however, he wants his reader to regard *The Pilgrim's Progress,* not as a "novelty," though it may appear that way to contemporary eyes, but as part of a larger tradition more pleasing to God than any discourse, Puritan or non-Puritan, being produced "now adays."

For wayside support he cites another kind of model, the dialogue, whose didactic purpose is widely accepted as justifying its fictitious character: "2. I find that men (as high as Trees) will write / Dialoguewise; yet no Man doth them slight / For writing . . ." (6.3–5). Presumably he is referring to works like Arthur Dent's *The Plaine Mans Path-way to Heauen* (1601), in which four characters debate Christian doctrine through the course of a day.[20] Bunyan's point is that writers of dialogues are not criticized for creating a fictional situation unless "they abuse / Truth" (6.5–6). Next, he harks back to the opening of the "Apology":

> . . . let Truth be free
> To make her Salleys upon Thee, and Me,
> Which way it pleases God. For who knows how,
> Better than he that taught us first to Plow,
> To guide our Mind and Pens for his Design?
> And he makes base things usher in Divine. (6.7–12)

Bunyan is saying that he did not willfully choose his mode of writing; the event was by divine will. Truth makes "Salleys" upon a writer, as well as a reader. Here, again, his model is the Bible and its author, the Holy Spirit who first taught us "to Plow." By the seventeenth century, plowing had become a common metaphor for preaching. A secondary meaning plays on the metaphorical possibilities for plowing: breaking open the "earth," the scriptural text, and turning it over to bring to the surface scriptural truth; such "plowing" is done with "Mind" and "Pens." God himself directs in working his "Design," whether the writer has one or not.

A third statement develops this idea by connecting Scripture with his own method:

> 3. I find that holy Writ in many places,
> Hath semblance with this method, where the cases
> Doth call for one thing to set forth another:

> Use it I may then, and yet nothing smother
> Truths golden Beams; Nay, by this method may
> Make it cast forth its rayes as light as day. (6.13–18)

That Bunyan feels the need to reiterate the point reflects a quite accurate sense that it is a revolutionary one for some readers, and that he respects and shares his objector's conviction that a literary language can only be justified if it is not really feigning at all, that is, if it reveals truth—and not just any truth, but truth of a particular kind.

The speaker has journeyed a long distance from the author's initial assertion that he had never intended to make a book in such a "mode"; that mode has now been identified as biblical practice. That he "fell suddenly into an Allegory" has now been traced to God's guiding his pen and mind. The specious excuse that he wrote only to divert himself from worse thoughts has been replaced by explaining Truth's "Salleys" upon both the writer and the reader. And finally, "Still as I pulled it came" has been superseded by aligning the method with that of holy purpose even where man has none: "He makes base things usher in Divine."

That some subjects by their very nature require allegorical treatment while others do not is confirmed by the contrast between *The Pilgrim's Progress* and another of Bunyan's works, *The Life and Death of Mr. Badman* (1680), the preface of which indicates that the two books are companion pieces:

> As I was considering with myself what I had written concerning the Progress of the Pilgrim from this world to glory, and how it had been acceptable to many in this nation, it came again into my mind to write, as then, of him that was going to heaven, so now, of the life and death of the ungodly, and of their travel from this world to hell.[21]

Use of the same metaphorical language about pilgrimage underlines the similarity:

> Here therefore, courteous reader, I present thee with the life and death of Mr. Badman indeed; yea, I do trace him in his life, from his childhood to his death; that thou mayest, as in a glass, behold with thine own eyes the steps that take hold of hell; and also discern, while thou art reading of Mr. Badman's death, whether thou thyself art treading in his path thereto. (590)

Here the invitation to watch Mr. Badman's "steps" leads the reader
to expect another allegorical journey. *Mr. Badman,* however, is not an
allegory. It adopts a different form, the dialogue, and has two figures,
Mr. Attentive and Mr. Wise, who discuss Mr. Badman's sins in realistic
detail. These include swearing and cursing in childhood, followed by
drunkenness, dishonest business practices, and cruelty toward his wife.
We can infer that Bunyan's choice of a narrative form rests on his belief
that the experience of a life without grace does not call for allegorical
representation. Allegorical representation is called for in *The Pilgrim's
Progress,* however, because the world it portrays has been altered by the
Christian's changed perspective, one no longer resembling the usual. As
John Knott observes,

> In the terms of Bunyan's narrative one can gain entrance to heaven only by
> learning to understand the visible world of ordinary experience in the meta-
> phoric terms established by the Word: as an alien, and ultimately unsubstan-
> tial country through which God's people must journey until they attain the
> ultimate satisfaction of communion with God.[22]

In short, Bunyan means exactly what he says when he argues that the
subject he was treating when the idea for *The Pilgrim's Progress* took hold
of him, "the Way / And Race of Saints in this our Gospel-Day" (1.7–8),
is one of a specific and limited group of subjects "where the cases / Doth
call for one thing to set forth another" (6.14–15) so that "similitudes"
are not just licit but necessary.

A fourth and last section of the "Apology" attempts to "shew the
profit" (6.20) of a book written in this way. Defining its contents more
precisely, the author delineates his purpose in a more practical way and
asks the reader questions to entice him into reading the work. It is
significant that, at this point, Bunyan abandons the unnamed critic he
has been addressing and turns his attention exclusively to the general
reader. The description now offered for his book is a broad one:

> This Book it chaulketh out before thine eyes,
> The man that seeks the everlasting Prize:
> It shews you whence he comes, whither he goes,
> What he leaves undone; also what he does:
> It also shews you how he runs, and runs,
> Till he unto the Gate of Glory comes.

> It shews too, who sets out for life amain,
> As if the lasting Crown they would attain:
> Here also you may see the reason why
> They loose their labour, and like fools do die. (6.23–32)

He will portray not just the history of one Christian soul but of many, some of whom will fail in the journey, thus setting the conversion experience of one man in a world peopled with other Christian seekers. His metaphor emphasizes the visual; the work "chaulketh" a winning runner. It then relies on a succession of images to tell a fundamental truth about human experience that requires revising established Puritan prejudice against imaginative writing. Because the book rests upon a commonplace—life as a journey and Christian as a traveller—Bunyan can dare to develop that metaphor to aid the reader's own life:

> This Book will make a Traveller of thee,
> If by its Counsel thou wilt ruled be;
> It will direct thee to the Holy Land,
> If thou wilt its Directions understand:
> Yea, it will make the sloathful, active be;
> The Blind also, delightful things to see. (6.33–37; 7.1)

The fictional representation can deliver doctrine and, perhaps, do this better for the slothful and the blind, because it contains "Truth within a Fable" (7.3). For a less learned audience, Bunyan needs no scruples about the word "fable," and can reincorporate standard Renaissance views on the connection between *utile* and *dulce*.

In a final summing up Bunyan terms *The Pilgrim's Progress* "rare, and profitable" (7.2), a "Truth within a Fable" (7.3), and full of "Riddles" (7.14). It is a book that can make one laugh and weep (7.19), a book where one can lose oneself and find oneself again (7.20–21), and finally a book in which one can dream and not be asleep (7.18). The speaker's audience has clearly changed. Emphasis has shifted back to the playful aspects of fiction, which, after the preceding wrenching exposition, can now be acknowledged.

Two of his phrases deserve particular attention:

> This Book is writ in such a Dialect,
> As may the minds of listless men affect:

> It seems a Novelty, and yet contains
> Nothing but sound and honest Gospel-strains. (7.8–11)

The allegorical mode is a "dialect," a variation of language used within
a sub-group. Its value for that group is its ability to affect the minds of
"listless men" who are unmoved by plain, exhortative language. Thus
its unusual mode can communicate to an audience that has not yet
awakened to religion. Though this strategy makes the book a "Novelty," it introduces no novel content. His final four lines stress another
"use" for his work:

> Would'st read thy self, and read thou know'st not what
> And yet know whether thou art blest or not,
> By reading the same lines? O then come hither,
> And lay my Book, thy Head and Heart together. (7.22–25)

To read the book will be to read oneself and learn whether one is of the
elect or not. In other words, Bunyan asks that the book be read like
Scripture, and the reader must take responsibility by gleaning doctrine
and applying it to the self: "my Book, thy Head and Heart" must come
together, so that the reader, not the writer, must perform the final step.
    It is worth noting what the "Apology" does not say. The title-page
word given the most emphasis is "DREAM." The most logical defense
of the book, given Puritan attitudes, would have been to claim that it
records an actual dream, as Bunyan himself had already done in *Grace
Abounding,* where he describes a "Vision" in which he sees the members
of the Bedford congregation on the sunny side of a mountain, cut off
from him by a wall. He then interprets the dream: "Now, this Mountain
and Wall, &c., was thus made out to me; the Mountain signified the
Church of the living God. . . . the wall was I thought the Word that
did make separation between the Christians and the world . . ."
(19–20). But Bunyan did not choose such a strategy for *The Pilgrim's
Progress.* Instead, he seems to have wished to describe what life within
that wall is like and to have felt that no usual mode of discourse was
adequate. To do justice to the world within the "wall," he must use the
wall itself, the Bible, and must also make his reader fully conscious that
he is doing so, even at the risk of incurring the disapproval of the very
people whose transformed mode of life he is depicting. He must call
attention to the book's status as a made thing, rather than gloss over it.

When Bunyan modifies traditional literary defenses of art, he is driven
to a much more radical claim; since it is God who guides the "Pen" and
"Mind," *The Pilgrim's Progress* not only resembles Scripture but is also an
extension of the very process which produced Scripture in the first
place.

Generations of readers of *The Pilgrim's Progress* have assumed that its
author worked outside the literary traditions of earlier ages, and was
influenced by other thinkers only enough to have absorbed the evangelical thought of his dissenting milieu. The "Apology" makes evident a
more sophisticated relationship. Bunyan is quite aware of traditional
Renaissance theories about imaginative literature. He insists that he had
literary models from an earlier time, models he defends while clearly
regarding them as either too provocative to be named directly, or too
incompatible with his "mechanick preacher" stance to be specified in
detail. In his aesthetic the Bible is seen not merely as a source of doctrine
or a catalyst for self-examination, but as a model for and example of
metaphorical discourse. Radical as this stance is, Bunyan did not intuitively stumble upon it. Rather, he is knowingly extending the implications of contemporary views of the Bible as asserted by Protestant
theorists in the Anglican/Puritan debate over the nature of a "plain"
style in preaching. In the seventeenth century, as Barbara K. Lewalski
has pointed out, the Bible was viewed not only in terms of salvational
history, but as a rhetorical work as well; poets and rhetoricians found in
the Bible "a literary model which [the Christian poet] can imitate in
such literary matters as genre, language, and symbolism, confident that
in this model at least the difficult problems of art and truth are perfectly
resolved."[23] Such a view of the Bible was pervasive enough to have laid
the groundwork for one of the most creative periods in English religious
poetry.

Four seventeenth-century treatises, in particular, seem pertinent for
Bunyan's "Apology." John Smith, in *The Mysterie of Rhetorique Unvailed*
(1657), presents a survey of traditional tropes and figures. His book
differs from other rhetorics, however, in that he illustrates his prescrip-
tions not only with literary examples in both English and Latin, but also
with examples from the Bible:

> Lastly, for that the holy Scripture is not barren of, but abounds with
> Tropes and figures of all sorts containing the most excellent and sublimist

eloquence, and is like a pleasant Garden, bedecked with flowers, or a fruitful
field, full of precious treasures, I apprehended it a work worthy the undertaking, to dig into those sacred Minerals for the better finding out the Metaphors, Metonymies, Synecdoches, &c. which lie hid there, and have given
Scriptural Examples pertinent to each of the Tropes and Figures. . . .[24]

His end is to redeem rhetoric by aligning it with right understanding of
Scripture:

> Rhetorique, where it is reduced to a blessed subordination and conformity
> to the teachings of the Spirit of Truth, is a good gift of God, proceeding from
> the Father of lights, and very conducent to the unfolding and right under-
> standing of the Figurative and Tropical Elegancies of that blessed Book,
> which abounds with the most excellent and divinest eloquence. . . . (sig.
> A6)

Similarly, John Prideaux's *Sacred Eloquence: Or, the Art of Rhetorick, as it is
layd down in Scripture* (1659) argues that study of the Bible can improve
rhetoric. For Prideaux, "*SACRED ELOQUENCE* is a Logicall kind of
Rhetorick, to be used in Prayer, Preaching, or Conference; to the glory
of God, and the convincing, instructing, and strengthening our
brethren."[25] Both men would redeem rhetoric from the charge that it
is an inherently amoral science.

A more radical defense can be seen in Robert Ferguson's essay, *The
Import and Use of Scripture-Metaphors* (1675), published only three years
before *The Pilgrim's Progress*. Ferguson proclaims that "God by his
unfolding himself and his Mind to us in several kinds of Metaphorical
Terms, hath not only allowed, but sanctified our Use of the like."[26] This
argument comes closest to Bunyan's. It is therefore important to note
that Ferguson, like Bunyan, was a Nonconformist, and that his tract is
intended as

> The vindication of the *Non-Conformists,* who are publickly charged for
> *turning Religion into unaccountable Phansies and Enthusiasm's, drest up with empty
> Schemes of speech; and for embracing a few gawdy Metaphors & Allegories instead of the
> substance of true and real Righteousness.* So that if you will believe a late Authour,
> herein lyes the *Material difference between the sober Christians of the Church of* En-
> gland, *and the Modern Sectaries, that while those express the precepts & Duties of the
> Gospel in plain and intelligible Terms, these trifle them away by childish Metaphors and
> Allegories, and will not talk of Religion but in barbarous and uncouth Similitudes.* (278)

For Ferguson, as for Bunyan, religious doctrine is inextricably wed to metaphoric expression: "Metaphors are not used to impregnate our Minds with gawdy Phantasms, but to adjust the Mysteries of Religion to the weakness of our Capacities" (342). When God speaks in metaphors "he condescends to lisp those Mysteries to us which would never be so well understood by any other way of expressing them" (281–82). Ferguson's language makes clear that the very features of Bunyan's title page which seem the most startling—his emphasis on presenting *The Pilgrim's Progress* as not just a dream but a feigned dream, and his choice of "I have used Similitudes" as an epigraph—are features which demand understanding in the context of a particular attitude to Scripture. In short, Bunyan's title page aligns him with those Nonconformists Ferguson's treatise was intended to defend.

On the other hand, we must remember that Ferguson means by "metaphors" only the verbal figures we encounter in the individual sentence. A tract by John Smith, "Of Prophecy" (1660), which contains a view of Scripture similar to Ferguson's, develops it in a direction more oriented toward narrative elements and therefore sheds further light on Bunyan's justification of narrative allegory. Smith, of course, is speaking exclusively about biblical prophecy. But his analysis of how biblical prophecy works resembles Ferguson's description of the function of biblical metaphor:

> *Truth* is content, when it comes into the world, to wear our mantles, to learn our language, to conform it self as it were to our dress and fashions: it affects not the State or *Fastus* which the disdainfull Rhetorician sets out his style withall, *Non Tarentinis aut Siculis haec scribimus;* but it speaks with the most *Idiotical* sort of men in the most *Idiotical* way, and becomes all things to all men, as every sonne of Truth should doe, for their good.[27]

Truth wears our "dress," and "learn[s] our language"; but Smith goes even further by widening the conception of metaphorical discourse from verbal trope to dramatic action:

> But for a more distinct understanding of this business, we must remember what hath been often suggested, *That the Prophetical scene* or *Stage upon which all apparitions were made to the Prophet, was his Imagination;* and that there all those things which God would have revealed unto him were acted over *Symbolical-lie,* as in a *Masque,* in which divers persons are brought in, amongst which the

> Prophet himself bears a part: And therefore he, according to the exigencie of this Dramatical *apparatus,* must, as the other Actors, perform his part, sometimes by speaking and reciting things done, propounding questions, sometimes by acting that part which in the *Drama* he was appointed to act by some others; and so not only by Speaking, but by Gestures and Actions come in in his due place among the rest; as it is in our ordinarie *Dreams.* . . . (222)

He even goes so far as to say that "it is no wonder to hear of those things done which indeed have no *Historical* or *Real* veritie; the scope of all being to represent something strongly to the Prophets Understanding . . ." (222). This description of prophecy bears considerable similarity to the action of *The Pilgrim's Progress,* especially Smith's understanding that such prophecy included a projection of the prophet-narrator himself acting a part among the other characters and offering commentary and explanation. If such strategies are inherent in biblical prophecy, they could offer a model for writers concerned to create a vision—or a revision—of the Bible from the point of view of the individual Christian.

Commentators like Ferguson, Prideaux, and John Smith in "Of Prophecy," however, are concerned strictly with improving the reader's grasp of the Bible itself and with using it as a rhetorical model for religious instruction at the level of the individual verbal trope or figure. Ultimately, their argument underlines the uniqueness of Bunyan's enterprise. Bunyan took the Bible as a model not just on the level of the sentence, but at the level of an entire plot, in which a complete narrative, generated out of whole cloth, is accorded the status of a biblical "Similitude."

The paradoxes of Bunyan's title page call attention to the central point his "Apology" defends discursively and his plot enacts in practice. Bunyan means exactly what he says when he asserts that Scripture was his model. In his view, the otherness of Christian experience demands a new mode of discourse that breaks with taboos on fictional narrative. In *Grace Abounding,* speaking of a time before his conversion experience, Bunyan describes his encounter with a community of radical Christians: "they were to me as if they had found a new world, as if they were people who dwelt alone, and were not to be reckoned among their Neighbors, Num. 23.9" (15). That new world is the subject of *The Pilgrim's Progress.* To portray it, and to describe how grace alters one's perception of the world, was to use allegory. But the allegory had to be derived from Scripture. Thus Christian is depicted in accordance with the biblical paradigms, and the landscape through which he walks is both a register of his internal stages and an allegorical/scriptural representation of the world. *The Pilgrim's Progress* is allegorical as a means of being mimetic, since its subject is a special kind of experience: the process of moving from one kind of reality to another and therefore simultaneously the discovery of that other reality and a rediscovery of this one.

RICHARD L. GREAVES

The Spirit and the Sword: Bunyan and the Stuart State

"*[O]ft I was* as if I was on the Ladder, with the Rope about my neck," Bunyan mused about his early months in the cold cell of a Bedford jail, comforted only by the thought that his last words on the scaffold might convert another sinner.[1] He was now face-to-face with the resurrected Stuart state, the earlier demise of which he had probably pondered very little. His military service had been confined to a county garrison at Newport Pagnell rather than the New Model Army, which bore the brunt of the fighting against the royalist forces. Only in the heady days of religious enthusiasm following his conversion did he begin to consider political issues, and then it was almost certainly through the eyes of the Fifth Monarchists, such as John Child, a fellow member of the Bedford gathered church.[2]

Not until 1660 did Bunyan have to confront a government openly hostile to his religious principles, Charles's promise of liberty to tender consciences notwithstanding. Uncertain of their future, the Bedford congregation set apart 12 December as a day of special prayer for the churches and the nation, in order that God "would direct our governors in their meeting together."[3] Bunyan himself was scheduled to preach on 12 November to a conventicle at Lower Samsell, though a warrant had already been issued for his arrest. "[H]ad I been minded to have played the coward, I could have escaped . . . ," he reminisced, but instead he rejected a friend's plea to flee. In a spirit that recalled William Strode's defiance when Charles I schemed to arrest leading members of Parliament, Bunyan proclaimed, "I will not stir. . . . Our cause is good. . . ."[4] He was, in fact, resolved to ascertain what the magistrates could say or do to him, inasmuch as he was convinced that he had done no wrong. Already, perhaps, John Foxe's *Acts and Monuments* was having an impact on him, for he was willing to suffer in God's cause in the expectation of a future reward. A sense of bravado and a determination not to provide a poor example to weaker saints were operative as well: "I had shewed myself hearty and couragious in my preaching, and had . . . made it my business to encourage others; therefore . . . if I should now run, and make an escape, it will be of a very ill savour in the country. . . ."[5] In short, fidelity to the gospel outweighed obedience to the state.

But what, precisely, was Bunyan's attitude toward the Stuart government? The answer to this question has been the subject of sharp disagreement among Bunyan specialists. On the one hand, Bunyan's prominent Evangelical disciple and editor, George Offor, was convinced that in his political views Bunyan was "a thorough loyalist" and a proponent of "high monarchial principles."[6] At the other extreme, William York Tindall has asserted that "Bunyan cherished a deep and natural hatred of both king and government, like any normal Baptist of the time. . . ."[7] While Bunyan proclaimed his loyalty to the monarchy and disavowed sedition, such statements, Tindall insisted, were required by both expediency and conformity to Baptist practice. Although Particular and General Baptist confessions of faith typically contained articles professing obedience to magistrates, Tindall has pointed to the treasonous activities of such Bunyan acquaintances as Vavasor Powell, Hanserd Knollys, Henry Jessey, and Henry Danvers.[8] To mask his own seditious sentiments, according to Tindall, Bunyan used the oblique techniques of allegory and biblical exegesis. Such "indirection relieved his feelings, communicated his ideas to the saints, and hid them from all but the closest scrutiny of the authorities" (139). Despite the practice of this "politic duplicity," Tindall argues, Bunyan was telling the truth when he professed his innocence of sedition, for in his mind those who were loyal to God's commands could not simultaneously be guilty of treason (142).

Most writers have avoided the extremes presented by Offor and Tindall, preferring to skirt the issue of Bunyan's attitude toward the magistrate. John Brown, in a biography that verges on making Bunyan heroic, contented himself with the observation that Bunyan was "a law-abiding subject," willing to demonstrate his loyalty to the government if given an opportunity.[9] Brown provides no hint of sedition or hostility toward monarchy on Bunyan's part, even when he discusses the critical posthumous works, *Of Antichrist and His Ruin* and *An Exposition of the First Ten Chapters of Genesis*.[10] The leading modern authority on Bunyan, Roger Sharrock, has said only that he "remained a staunch and consistent supporter of civil obedience."[11]

Bunyan's conscious decision to disobey statutory law by addressing a conventicle in November 1660 and consequent imprisonment resulted in a temporary fear of the gallows but no remorse for his defiance. On the contrary, incarceration reinforced his resolve to stand firm for his right to preach. To Justice Wingate's offer to release him if sureties would guarantee his silence, Bunyan retorted: "I should not leave speaking the word of God . . ." or do anything to "dishonour my God, and wound my conscience" (RI, 107, 109). For this recalcitrance, some two months after his arrest Sir John Keeling sentenced him to three more months in prison and threatened perpetual banishment if he remained obdurate. Under the law, should he be found in the realm without a royal license subsequent to being exiled, he faced the gallows (118).

In the months that followed, Bunyan commenced the legal studies that are reflected in such later works as *The Advocateship of Jesus Christ*. When Paul Cobb, a well-meaning clerk sent by justices of the peace, visited him in prison in a futile attempt to persuade him to capitulate, Bunyan lectured him on jurisprudence:

> I conceive that that law by which I am in prison at this time, doth not reach or condemn, either me, or the meetings which I do frequent: That law was made against those, that being designed to do evil in their meetings, make the exercise of religion their pretence to cover their wickedness. (119–20)[12]

The act in question, 35 Elizabeth I, c. 1, he insisted, did not ban private meetings solely for the purpose of worship. Nor would he accept Cobb's attempt to refute that argument by associating it with the recent abortive rising of Thomas Venner and his Fifth Monarchist allies. Bunyan's own earlier attraction to the Fifth Monarchists notwithstanding, he joined most religious radicals in prudently disavowing the insurrection. Moreover, he pointedly underscored his loyalty to the state: "I look upon it as my duty to behave myself under the King's government, both as becomes a man and a christian; and if an occasion was offered me, I should willingly manifest my loyalty to my Prince, both by word and deed" (RI, 120). But such a profession of loyalty did not bear the same meaning for Bunyan as it did for Cobb and his associates. To Bunyan, loyalty to the prince was predicated upon prior fidelity to God's precepts, which included the exercise of such divinely bestowed gifts as preaching (122).

In defending his position, Bunyan cited three authorities: Scripture, statute, and John Wyclif (as quoted in the *Acts and Monuments*). Willingly, he embraced the Pauline doctrine of obedience to the higher powers as divinely ordained (Romans 13.1–7), but he was also quick to point out that Jesus and Paul had suffered at the hands of magistrates even while accepting this "ordinance." The key was in distinguishing the two forms of obedience: "The one to do that which I in my conscience do believe that I am bound to do, actively; and where I cannot obey actively, there I am willing to lie down and to suffer what they shall do unto me" (RI, 124–25). Here, then, is a clear affirmation of the classic doctrine of passive resistance, as espoused, for example, by Martin Luther.[13]

Statute too was used by Bunyan in his defense. Displaying a remarkable degree of sophistication in a person of his educational background, he distinguished between the letter of the law and the intent of its makers: "I would not entertain so much uncharitableness of that parliament in the 35th of *Elizabeth*, or of the Queen herself, as to think they did by that law intend the oppressing of any of God's ordinances, or the interrupting [of] any in the way of God" (RI, 121). The statute itself, he pointed out, was concerned only with those who used religion to cloak incendiary designs. By way of substantiation, he deftly quoted the crucial clause of the Elizabethan act, which singled out meetings held "under colour or pretence of religion" (121).[14]

Finally, Bunyan turned to John Wyclif for support. Although there is no evidence that he had ever read Wyclif's writings or subsequent Lollard literature, he knew Wyclif's story from Foxe's account. To Cobb's plea that he forbear preaching at least for the immediate future, Bunyan responded, "*Wickliffe* saith, that he which leaveth off preaching and hearing of the word of God for fear of excommunication of men, he is already excommunicated of God, and shall in the day of judgment be counted a traitor to Christ" (RI, 122).

During the exchange with Cobb, Bunyan offered an insight into his views about the critical issue of the nature of government. As Christopher Hill has pointed out, the influence of the radical tradition was greater on Bunyan than was his impact on it, and one might therefore expect to find him espousing republican ideology.[15] After all, many soldiers who fought on the parliamentary side in the civil war, as Richard Baxter observed, were persuaded "sometimes for State Democracy. . . ."[16] The Presbyterian Robert Baillie generalized—inaccurately—that sectaries sought the liberty to overthrow all kings and parliaments, and in their place to "set up . . . the whole multitude, in the Throne of absolute Soveraignty. . . ."[17] The more extreme radicals did, in fact, oppose monarchy as the tool of the priests and the rich.[18] Within the Fifth Monarchy tradition there was also a pronounced anti-monarchical bent, as the saints called for action that would topple sovereigns preparatory to the rule of the godly. Thus John Tillinghast boldly proclaimed that "the overturning [of] the Thrones of the kings, is to be performed by the Saints," in whose hands both civilian and military power must reside.[19] Such was the ideological environment in which Bunyan began to formulate his concept of government.

Rather than embracing republican tenets, Bunyan steered an indifferent course. To Cobb he said, "I did look upon myself as bound in conscience to walk according to all righteous laws, *and that whether there was a King or no* . . ." (RI, 124; emphasis mine). In other words, the precise form of government was of no immediate consequence to Bunyan (though he later was critical of absolute monarchy). His basic indifference reflects the influence of certain strains of the radical tradition, though clearly not the republicans, Levellers, or Diggers. Like Baxter, Bunyan was convinced that all forms of governing power originated with God, and he would have likely embraced Baxter's thesis that God did not prescribe a single polity.[20] "The reason why God did not Universally by his Law tye all the World to One forme of Government," Baxter asserted, "is because the difference of persons, times, places, neighbours, &c. may make one forme best to one people, and at one time, and place, that is worst to another" (78). But whereas Bunyan was presumably content to let the matter rest at this point, Baxter proceeded to argue stringently that monarchy is the best form of polity because it corresponds the closest to nature (94–95). The leading Arminian Independent, John Goodwin, was another who postulated that monarchy, aristocracy, and democracy were all divinely bestowed, "not any of them determinately, or with exclusion of the rest."[21]

Despite their theological differences, a statement made by George Fox to Charles II might just as well have come from Bunyan:

> We, for our *selves* desire no greater *Liberty,* either in things *Religious,* or in things *Civil* . . . than we desire *all others might enjoy:* And if such a *Government* as this be set up, then if he that is *Chief* in taking care and seeing that Justice may be done to all without respect of persons, if he be called a *King,* a *Judge,* a *Protector,* or *General,* we shall not be against *either* or *any* of the *Names.* . . .[22]

While Bunyan did not embrace any single form of government, from the outset he insisted that a Christian must submit to duly constituted authority, bearing "patiently the penalty of the law" if in conscience he could not obey the dictates of the state (RI, 124).

During his early years in the Bedford county jail, Bunyan set aside strictly political questions in order to concentrate on the subjects of prayer and Christian suffering. In his apology for extempore prayer, *I Will Pray with the Spirit* (c. 1662), Bunyan lashed out not at the king or his magistrates but at those doctors of the established church who imposed the Book of Common Prayer, a human invention "neither commanded nor commended of God. . . ."[23] With obvious personal bitterness, he protested that one who lived peaceably could nevertheless be condemned as seditious simply for refusing, in good conscience, to accept a form of worship that had not been divinely mandated. Silencing ministers and threatening offenders with the gallows or exile was, he claimed, blatantly antichristian persecution (283–85).

Having established the context of righteous suffering in his prayer tract, Bunyan reinforced this theme in his *Prison Meditations* (1663). Jail became a school of Christ in which the elect prepared to die, victims of an ungodly regime.[24]

> *Just* thus it is, we suffer here
>   For him a little pain,
> Who, when he doth again appear
>   Will with him let us reign. (49)

Those who quailed before such suffering were exhorted to render the ultimate sacrifice:

> . . . make the *Tree* your stage
> For Christ *that* King potent. (50)

Bunyan was, in fact, less concerned with Charles II and his secular offi-
cials than with those propertied Puritans who had made their peace with
the Restoration state.

> When we did walk at liberty,
>   We were deceiv'd by them,
> Who we from hence do clearly see
>   Are vile deceitful Men.
> These Politicians that profest
>   For base and worldly ends,
> Do now appear to us at best
>   But Machivilian Friends. (47)

Hypocrisy had a worse sting than persecution. Betrayal was particularly
odious to those such as Bunyan who were embittered by the sudden
collapse of the Good Old Cause.

Between 1663 and 1665 Bunyan turned increasingly to millenarian
themes, reflecting perhaps his earlier attraction to the Fifth Monarchists. The promise that suffering saints would eventually reign with
King Jesus was expanded in *One Thing Is Needful* (1665) to include an
apocalyptic vision of the Last Judgment, replete with a Christ who

> . . . comes with Head as white as Snow;
> With Eyes like flames of fire;
> In Justice clad from top to toe,
> Most glorious in attire.[25]

Those who persecute the saints have cells reserved for them in the great

> . . . Prison with its locks and bars,
> Of Gods lasting decree. (93)

Having denied the saints liberty to worship in accord with the dictates
of their consciences, the condemned must suffer where

> . . . Conscience is the slaughter-shop,
> There hangs the Ax, and Knife,
> 'Tis there the worm makes all things hot. (94)

Although Bunyan clearly had his tormentors in mind when he penned this exercise in apocalyptic vengeance, he wisely refrained from making this explicit.

The millenarian themes are equally in evidence in *The Holy City,* a companion work to *One Thing Is Needful,* published the same year and certainly intended to be read in tandem. This time, however, the tone is quieter, the role of governors more explicit and positive. Bunyan is careful to assure traditional rulers that the holy city, the Gospel church, is not a revolutionary institution posing a threat to their sovereignty. "The governors of this world," he wrote, "need not at all to fear a disturbance from her, or a diminishing of ought they have." Because the church's interests are not material, "she will not meddle with their fields nor vineyards, neither will she drink of the water of their wells. . . ." Those who charge the church with treason lie, for it is not, nor has it ever been, "a rebellious city, and destructive to kings, and a diminisher of their revenues."[26]

Tindall's contention that Bunyan despised kings is roundly refuted in the pages of *The Holy City.* On the contrary, monarchs are accorded a clear measure of respect: "The people of the nations they are but like to single pence and halfpence, but their kings like gold angels and twenty-shilling pieces" (444). Yet Bunyan's own knowledge of Charles I and Charles II, coupled with the influence of a radical tradition that depicted kings as the root of tyranny,[27] led him to the provocative conclusion that most rulers were enamored with "mistress Babylon, the mother of harlots, the mistress of witchcrafts, and abominations of the earth." They not only fornicate with her but defend her from "the gun-shot that the saints continually will be making at her by the force of the Word and Spirit of God" (445). Bunyan, however, resisted the conclusion that monarchs should be toppled as aiders and abettors of supreme evil. It was simply a matter, he said, that kings were the last to come to Christ, the first being the poor. But their coming was a certainty: "The kings must come to Jerusalem . . ." (444, 445).

Victory over temporal sovereigns, however assured, would be a tumultuous business. Although some rulers will eventually succumb to grace, this would only happen after their unsuccessful war against the Son of God. Just as Darius, Cyrus, and Artaxerxes assisted Ezra and Nehemiah in reconstructing Jerusalem, so would some monarchs help build the holy city, but "the great conquest of the kings will be by the beauty and glory of this city, when she is built" (444–45, 446). Rulers who ultimately refuse to accept the church "must take what followeth" (410), a harsh fate vividly depicted in *One Thing Is Needful.*

In *The Holy City* Bunyan refused to attribute final responsibility for the church's persecution to temporal sovereigns. Instead he laid it at the foot of the Antichrist, the "mistress of iniquity," who used witchcraft to beguile rulers into vexing the saints (446). As his own incarceration stretched from months into years, Bunyan sought a deeper meaning for this suffering. The answer lay in the form of an earthly purgatory in which saints were readied for entry into God's presence: "The church in the fire of persecution is like Esther in the perfuming chamber, but making fit for the presence of the king . . . ," or like gold "on which the fire of persecution and temptation hath done its full and complete work" (431). Through the overarching work of providence, then, rulers who persecuted the church were, in Bunyan's mind, agents of the divine plan, more to be pitied than hated, but never to be violently resisted.

Bunyan's prison writings are straightforward in presenting a doctrine of passive resistance, and there is no evidence to indicate that they were intended as a mask to conceal covert support for insurrection. Between August 1661 and March 1662, Bunyan used the occasional liberty given to him by his jailer to travel to London. He may have gone solely to procure spiritual guidance from such friends as George Cokayne, John Owen, George Griffith, and Anthony Palmer, or he may have obtained legal advice. His enemies, however, were convinced that he went to the City to "plot and raise division, and make insurrection . . ." (RI, 130), but Bunyan denied the charge. Cokayne and his associate, Nathaniel Holmes, both avowed millenarians, were preaching to illegal conventicles in this period, and Cokayne was suspected of writing seditious tracts. Palmer, a recent convert to the Fifth Monarchists, was regarded in government circles as one of the "violent projecting men." In 1661 he was preaching against the Restoration court, and late the following year the state suspected him of participating in Ensign Thomas Tong's plot to assassinate the king and the dukes of York and Albemarle, seize Windsor Castle, and reinstitute the republic.[28] There is no proof that Bunyan knew of such activities.

In the years that followed, Bunyan's imprisonment must have become stricter. His name is not recorded in the *Church Book* between October 1661 and November 1668, but in the latter year the expiration of the 1664 Conventicle Act led to an increase of Nonconformist activity.[29] As a direct consequence, fears of new plots began to spread. From York, a customs collector warned Sir Joseph Williamson in October 1669 that unlawful meetings of Dissenters looked suspiciously like those which had preceded the recent rebellion, while from Coventry another of Williamson's correspondents expressed concern the following month about the growth of conventicles.[30] In May the secretary had been warned by Daniel Fleming, writing from Westmorland, that the Presbyterians were "now designing some mischeif. . . ." Fleming cautioned, "Faction will strike (notwithstanding all their fair & gilded pretences) at the crowne as well as at the miter. . . ."[31] While there was far more smoke than fire, the concerns were genuine enough. The Bedford church to which Bunyan belonged was itself caught up in these suspicions, particularly after brother Humphrey Merrill "began in an obscure way to charge the Church with rebellion. . . ." In an appearance before the quarter sessions no later than September 1669, Merrill recanted the profession of faith he had made to the Bedford church, but he went further by testifying "that they had their hands in the blood of the king: that they were disobedient to government, and that they were not a church. . . ."[32] These were probably the emotional reactions of an embittered member or the inventions of a timid soul afraid of the justices before whom he stood. It can hardly be more than coincidence that in the first year of Bunyan's renewed attendance at church meetings (1668–69), the congregation was accused of treasonable activity. The same year (1669) Bunyan's colleague, Samuel Fenn, was blamed for "intending to incite and move rebellion and sedition in this realm of England," but apparently only because he denied the royal governorship of the Church of England.[33]

The years 1669–72 were, in any case, the time when Bunyan and the Nonconformists who were imprisoned with him worked out the strategy by which they established a network of preachers in Bedfordshire and the surrounding counties that enabled the Dissenters to survive later attempts at suppression. Specifically, the Bedford congregation joined forces with dissenting churches at Stevington, Keysoe, Newport Pagnell, and Cranfield to provide a network of religious leaders and meetings throughout the region. When Bunyan and his colleagues sought licenses to preach in May 1672 under Charles's Declaration of Indulgence, their application contained the names of no less than twenty-seven men in twenty-six towns and villages in six counties.[34] Such careful planning helped to ensure the ultimate right of Nonconformists to freedom of worship.

Released at last in 1672, Bunyan became embroiled almost immediately in a controversy involving one of his favorite themes, church membership and communion. In his initial contribution, *A Confession of My Faith* (1672), which sparked the dispute, he was at pains to insist that there was nothing in his principles that savored of rebellion or heresy, or was in any way grounds for spending a dozen years in prison, threatened by perpetual exile or hanging. The *Confession* was intended as a vindication of his innocence, and for that reason he reiterated his doctrine of passive disobedience: "Neither can I in or by the superstitious inventions of this world, consent that my soul should be governed in any of my approaches to God, because commanded to the contrary, and commended for so refusing." On this point he would not relent, though professing himself "at all times a peaceable and an obedient subject."[35]

Most contemporary sectarian confessions of faith included an article on magistracy, which provided Bunyan with an obvious reason to include such a statement in his confession. A typical article is found in the 1656 Confession of the Western Association of Baptists, one of the leaders of which was Thomas Collier:

> That the ministry of civil justice (being for the praise of them that do well, and punishment of evil-doers) is an ordinance of God, and that it is the duty of the saints to be subject thereunto not only for fear, but for conscience sake . . . and that for such, prayers and supplications are to be made by the saints. . . .[36]

In a similar fashion Bunyan postulated that magistracy is a divine ordinance, adding that it is a judgment of God to be without magistrates. After quoting Romans 13.2–6, he returned to the theme of passive resistance: "Many are the mercies we receive, by a well qualified magistrate, and if any shall at any time be otherwise inclined, let us shew our Christianity in a patient suffering, for well doing, what it shall please God to inflict by them."[37]

An illustration of how Bunyan intended this doctrine to be practiced appeared in another work published the same year, *A Defence of the Doctrine of Justification by Faith,* a refutation of Edward Fowler's *The Design of Christianity* (1671). Bunyan had no use for the Latitudinarian Fowler, rector of Northill, Bedfordshire, whom he mercilessly castigated as one who could, "as to religion, turn and twist like an eel on the angle; or rather like the weather-cock that stands on the steeple." Because Fowler had turned his back on the Puritan principles he had espoused in the 1650s, Bunyan found it appropriate to lecture him that obedience to the state does not extend to the point of denying the fundamentals of the faith. The implicit lesson was sufficiently manifest: the turncoat rector should have stood his ground, rejected the demands of the Stuart state to conform, and suffered alongside Bunyan and his confederates.[38]

In the decade that ensued, not even a temporary return to prison in 1676–77 prompted Bunyan to deal with the issue of obedience to the state.[39] Only when Charles II dismissed three successive parliaments in the epic struggle over excluding the Duke of York from the line of succession did Bunyan choose to speak out once more on matters of state. This time he did so through the medium of a complex allegory with multiple levels of meaning. Critics who fault Bunyan for undertaking such a technically difficult and ambitious work ought to consider the need for such obliquity. Thanks to *The Pilgrim's Progress,* Bunyan was now an acclaimed author, with his first allegory reaching its eighth edition in the year *The Holy War* (1682) was published. The device of multiple allegory afforded him the opportunity to address several needs at once, ranging from the soul's struggle with evil to the contemporary political crises that boded ill for Nonconformists. The king and his agents had launched their scheme to remodel the corporations, thereby ensuring domination by men whose principles were staunchly Tory and Anglican. In August 1681, the state's decision to hang and quarter Stephen College for his intemperate advocacy of exclusion made him a Whig martyr. His declaration of innocence deliberately evoked memories of the Marian martyrs: "I earnestly pray mine may be the last Protestant blood that murdering Church of Rome may shed in Christendom and that my death may be a far greater blow to their bloody cause than I could have been by my life."[40] In these perilous times for the Nonconformists, Bunyan felt it was incumbent to address the major issues.

The political message of *The Holy War* was barely concealed. When Diabolus seized control of the town of Mansoul, he became not mayor but king—a pointed reference to Charles II. If that allusion slipped by, no reader could escape the obvious parallel when Diabolus remodeled the corporation, replacing Lord Understanding, the lord mayor, with

Lord Lustings, and Mr. Conscience, the recorder, with Forget-good. Among the new burgesses and aldermen were caricatures of those Tory-Anglicans who were assuming office around the country as Charles remodeled the corporations—Mr. Atheism, Mr. Whoring, Mr. False Peace, and Mr. Haughty. Command of the castles was placed in the hands of new governors, Spite-God, Love-no-light, and Love-flesh.[41] As a former jailhouse lawyer, Bunyan could not resist having Diabolus "make havock of all remains of the Laws and Statutes of *Shaddai,* that could be found in the Town of *Mansoul.* . . ." He "spoiled the old Law Books" (24, 26). Not only did Diabolus treat Gospel ministers with hostility, but he also allowed the town to be filled with atheistic pamphlets as well as obscene ballads and romances (30, 40). In short, Diabolus was a "rebellious Tyrant" (28).

The radical nature of *The Holy War* stems from this attack on the government of Charles II, not from a revolutionary social vision. While Christopher Hill correctly calls attention to the large number of Diabolonian lords and gentlemen in the allegory,[42] there is a contingent of aristocrats in Emanuel's service. In striking contrast to Gerrard Winstanley, who regarded Jesus as "the greatest, first, and truest Leveller that ever was spoke of in the world," Bunyan made Christ the greatest peer in the kingdom.[43]

Bunyan was not content merely to deplore the ills of Charles's rule in the 1680s, but went on to provide a vision of the godly sovereign. When Emanuel regained control of Mansoul, he imposed "new Laws, new Officers, new motives, and new ways" (85). The Diabolonians were committed to prison (Bunyan's touch of poetic justice), while Lord Understanding and Mr. Knowledge were given positions of responsibility. In addition to providing Mansoul with ample ministers of the Gospel, Emanuel bestowed a new and just charter (119–32, 137, 145).

During the brighter days of the 1670s, Bunyan depicted the life of the saints as a pilgrimage, but the Popish Plot, the exclusion crisis, Stephen College's execution, and the renewed repression of Nonconformists called for tougher imagery. Thus, *The Holy War* was conceived. Although Bunyan remained out of prison, he returned once more to the theme of persecution and suffering. It was because of sin, he said in *A Holy Life* (1683), that God had given the saints "over to the hand of the Enemy" and delivered them "to the tormentors."[44] Still, Bunyan resisted a call to arms. Instead he wrote at length about Christian suffering at the hands of the state in a poignant treatise entitled *Seasonable Counsel: or, Advice to Sufferers* (1684).

Setting aside the theme of conflict, Bunyan took up his pen to write once more of passive disobedience. Christians, he acknowledged, are all kings, but he was quick to qualify this democratic theme by insisting that each had dominion only over himself. The saint's duty is to mind his own business, attend to his calling, and let the magistrates fulfil their responsibilities. If the rulers are wicked, the Christian can do no more than cry to God for deliverance, for all other attempts to secure relief are impermissible. "Let not talk against governors, against powers, against men in authority be admitted. . . . Meddle not with those that are given to change." The believer is obligated to fear God, honor the monarch, and render appropriate duty to the magistrates, which entails obeying them and thanking God for their rule.[45]

The positive nature of Christian suffering is critical to the entire discourse. It is not enough simply to endure persecution, for the saint must *actively* suffer for righteousness by willingly accepting affliction instead of sinful action. Rather than rebel, Christians must "sit still and be quiet, and reverence the ordinance of God: I mean affliction" (708, 710–11). Suffering thus becomes an aspect of Christian worship. "Let us learn like Christians to kiss the rod, and love it." While persecution is providentially determined, it is also a just consequence of sin. "The rod is fore-determined, because the sin of God's people is foreseen. . . . Let us not look upon our troubles as if they came from, and were managed only by hell" (707, 725, 737). This point is crucial, for it prohibits active rebellion against agents of persecution, the tools of God in the providential administration of suffering for the cleansing and edification of the elect. Only in this context is it possible for Bunyan, after more than a dozen years in prison, to proclaim that he has

> ofttimes stood amazed both at the mercy of God, and the favour of the Prince towards us; and can give thanks to God for both: and do make it my prayer to God for the king, and that God will help me with meekness and patience to bear whatever shall befall me for my professed subjection to Christ, by men. (707)

The positive affirmation of suffering was reinforced by a deeper understanding of the role of sovereigns and magistrates in the divine scheme. According to Bunyan, God has not only ordained the powers that be, but now orders them as well. They serve as his rod or staff for the ultimate benefit of his people. As his ministers, one of their functions is to execute his wrath on those who commit evil, but they are also his agents even when they persecute the saints. Eventually—and ironical-ly—the elect will be avenged when the persecutors, though divine agents, are punished, but that task is reserved solely to God. In the mean-time, Bunyan was convinced that the rage of the persecutors was always kept within the bounds determined by God. Every magistrate could therefore be said to render some good to Christians, even if it was only to exercise a purging function (705–06, 724–25, 737, 739). Acceptance of the doctrine of providence was basic to Bunyan's entire argument: "Let us take heed of admitting the least thought in our minds of evil, against God, the king, or them that are under him in employ, because, the cup, the king, all men, and things are in the hand of God." Tyrannicide is flatly unacceptable. Bunyan pointed to the story of Abishai in 1 Samuel 26.7–8 as an illustration of a good man who, because of an erroneous conscience, contemplated killing a king. One who cannot obey a ruler because of scruples of conscience has no option but to suffer meekly and patiently.[46]

Rather early in this discourse on Christian suffering, Bunyan went out of his way to signal his quiescent intentions to the masters of the Stuart state.

> I speak not these things, as knowing any that are disaffected to the govern-ment; for I love to be alone, if not with godly men, in things that are conve-nient. But because I appear thus in public, and know not into whose hands these lines may come, therefore thus I write. I speak it also to show my loyalty to the king, and my love to my fellow-subjects; and my desire that all Christians should walk in ways of peace and truth. (709)

In 1684 Bunyan was still in contact with Cokayne, who had been fined for illegal preaching in 1682 and 1683, though Palmer had died in 1679 and Owen in 1683. Griffith was fined for illegal preaching in 1684, two years after a member of his congregation admitted knowing Richard Goodenough, a Rye House plotter in 1683. Another of Bunyan's London associates, the Independent minister Richard Wavel, was frequently ar-rested in 1683 and 1684, and one of Bunyan's regular printers, Francis

Smith, continued to experience legal difficulties in this period.[47] No wonder, then, that Bunyan felt he might be under observation and suspected of complicity in seditious plotting. There is, however, no evidence to connect Bunyan with active resistance to the Stuart regime.

The works Bunyan published in the period between 1685 and his death in 1688 contain only scattered references to the themes of magistracy, obedience, and suffering. In his *Discourse upon the Pharisee and the Publican,* which deals essentially with justification and prayer, Bunyan reiterated his theme that God would avenge the elect against unjust magistrates, judges, and tyrants.[48] The companion notion of suffering was again stated in the poetic lines of *A Discourse of the . . . House of God* (1688):

> A Christian for *Religion* must not fight,
> But put up *wrongs,* though he be in the *right.*[49]

In the same year Bunyan returned in *Solomon's Temple Spiritualized* to his essentially positive view of kingship. As in *The Holy City,* he thought monarchs would some day be highly impressed with the glory of the church.[50]

Some of Bunyan's most important statements on the state and the role of Christian obedience appear in his posthumous publications, particularly *Of Antichrist and His Ruin* and *An Exposition of the First Ten Chapters of Genesis.* The posthumously published works were probably written either in the period between 1666 and 1672 or between 1682 and 1688. The former is a period of apparently little literary activity, unless, as is probable, Bunyan used this period to compose *The Pilgrim's Progress.* The bitterness of prison life would help explain the explosively apocalyptic imagery in *Of Antichrist and His Ruin,* and the obvious political overtones of this work and the commentary on Genesis would account for his reluctance to see them through the press. The commentary, moreover, lay unfinished, perhaps because he was working on it at the time of his release. But there is nothing in the other posthumous works that would account for a lengthy delay in publication, and it therefore seems likely that all of these works date from the mid-1680s. But were the critical millenarian tract and the Genesis commentary written in the last years of Charles II's reign, against a background of remodeling and the imposition of Anglican domination? Or do they date from James II's reign, with its heightened fear of Popery under a Catholic monarch, but also with two Declarations of Indulgence and an overt attempt to woo the support of Dissenters and offer them positions of authority? Unquestionably, the first part of this period was one of intensified radical activity that included the abortive Rye House Plot and Monmouth's futile rising.

The prefatory epistle to *Of Antichrist,* written, as I have argued elsewhere, in mid- or late 1682, contains a profession of loyalty to the king as well as a warning to Christians not to blame temporal authorities, especially monarchs, for the affliction of the church. They "seldom trouble churches of their own inclinations. . . ."[51] The root cause of such vexation, Bunyan averred, was sin. As so often in his writings, he turned to Scripture to substantiate his case. Although the Persian kings hindered the Jews from building their temple, the Jews treated them tenderly and lovingly, submitting their bodies and goods, enduring affliction, serving them faithfully, and preserving their lives from the hands of assassins. If Persian decrees contravened divine law, the Jews remained loyal to God, "yet with that tenderness to the king, his crown and dignity, that they could at all times appeal to the righteous God about it" (73).

Bunyan gave monarchs a distinctive apocalyptic function. The Antichrist could be toppled only by the aid of kings, with the preachers slaying "her" soul and the sovereigns her body. This role, Bunyan explained, is divinely allotted to monarchs because of the gross abuse inflicted on them by the Antichrist. In undertaking this task, God will strip the rulers of all compassion in order to achieve total destruction. Certain kings (including Charles II?), however, are sufficiently bewitched by the Antichrist to stand by her, and thus by divine judgment must be "left in the dark." Providentially, other rulers will be enticed away from the Antichrist by God in order that "he might train them up by the light of the gospel, that they may be expert, like men of war, to scale her walls, when the king of kings shall give out the commandment to them to do so" (61, 74, 88). With this return to the imagery of *The Holy War,* Bunyan has provided a militancy that is lacking in the quiescent *Seasonable Counsel,* written later, in the aftermath of the Rye House Plot. The violent images in *Of Antichrist* extend to the destruction of the Antichrist by sword-wielding kings who serve as divine agents to punish evil. The justice of such scourging is appropriate because the Antichrist has "turned the sword of the magistrate against those that keep God's law" and has made that sword "the ruin of the good and virtuous, and a protection to the vile and base" (72, 77).

Deliverance from the Antichrist, Bunyan avowed, is certain but not yet at hand. Before she can be overthrown,

> there will be such ruins brought both upon the spirit of Christianity, and the true Christian church state, before this Antichrist is destroyed, that there will for a time scarce be found a Christian spirit, or a true visible living church of Christ in the world. . . . (66)

From the depths of desolation God will call upon monarchs and other temporal rulers to deliver the elect from the grasp of the Antichrist. Obviously reflecting the concerns of the Nonconformists with whom he came into contact in the mid-1680s, Bunyan repeatedly urged the saints patiently to await the time when the kings would commence their work of deliverance. The task will begin in God's time, and if this does not occur as rapidly as Christians hope, they must, Bunyan exhorted, seek the fault in themselves. "Know that thou also hast thy cold and chill frames of heart, and sittest still when thou shouldest be up and doing." Displaying sympathy for rulers, Bunyan reminded his readers that they were responsible for the government of entire kingdoms and additionally were hampered by the presence of flattering Sanballats and Tobiases (62, 73, 74).

Toward monarchs, then, the saints must be patient and understanding. "Let the king have verily a place in your hearts, and with heart and mouth give God thanks for him; he is a better saviour of us than we may be aware of, and may have delivered us from more deaths than we can tell how to think."[52] Perhaps Bunyan was contemplating here about how favorably Charles II compared to Mary I and Philip II, or perhaps even to Louis XIV. Bunyan insisted that every saint has a responsibility to pray for the king to have wisdom, a long life, an awareness of any conspiracies against him, and the ability to drive evil persons away.

Reflecting on the discourse *Of Antichrist*, Tindall concluded rather skeptically that Bunyan's "fulsome exculpation" of temporal rulers was due more to prevailing political conditions than to pity or love (135). After the striking condemnation of Charles II in *The Holy War*, it is indeed difficult to find Bunyan looking upon monarchs positively.

An Exposition of the First Ten Chapters of Genesis sets a different tone, so much so that Tindall has referred to it as an "exercise in veiled sedition" and, less provocatively, "a prophetical allegory of seventeenth-century politics." While there is some merit in this characterization, he is incorrect in arguing that Bunyan refers unequivocally to kings as tyrants, and does not try to conceal the notion of open warfare between saint and ruler.[53] The crucial passages deal with the accounts of Cain and Nimrod.

To Bunyan, Cain was a destroyer, a curse, a disciple of the devil, and "a figure of all such as make false and strange delusions. . . ." In contrast to Abel and his descendants, who were destined to be victims of persecution, Cain's posterity became rulers and lords who "tyranically afflict[ed] and persecute[d]. . . ."[54] When Cain murdered his brother, he was attempting to extirpate all true religion. With apocalyptic overtones, Bunyan even wrote of the great conflict between the armies of the Lamb and of Cain. Here, then, was the perfect occasion for Bunyan to espouse a theory of tyrannicide, but he went no further than to allow the godly to call for divine vengeance on their persecutors. Indeed, tyrants were virtually brushed aside as nuisances: "Tyrants matter nothing, . . . nor how much they destroy . . ." (445–47, 456). Rather than overthrowing them, the Christian must hope for their salvation, bless them while they curse, and pray for them while they persecute. Admittedly, said Bunyan, tyrants were used by Satan to threaten and molest the church, but in the face of laws contrary to Christian principles the saints had to "stand their ground, and not . . . shrink like Saul, till God shall send others to take part with them." Tyrannical persecution served a useful function by purging the church of carnal predilections (437, 445, 456, 473).

Like the Seeker William Erbery, Bunyan regarded Nimrod as the instigator of absolute monarchy. Perhaps in company with some of the Baptists, he even viewed Nimrod as a symbol of Charles II, though he may have been thinking of Louis XIV or James II.[55] The biblical image of Nimrod as a hunter dovetailed nicely with Bunyan's depiction of Nimrod and others of his ilk as persecutors, for "the life, the blood, the extirpation of the contrary party, is the end of their course of hunting" (497). Thus Bunyan reminded his audience that subsequent persecutors in Scripture were compared to Nimrod.[56] This interpretation was common enough, being found, for example, in the annotations to the Geneva Bible, which make Nimrod "a cruel oppressor & tyrant" (Genesis 10.8):

"His tyrannie came into a proverbe as hated bothe of God and man: for he passed not to commit crueltie even in Gods presence"(Genesis 10.9).

Bunyan was at pains to make Nimrod the creator of an iniquitous state religion, reminding Nonconformists of the established church in their own country. In the biblical account, Bunyan claimed rather freely, those who did not accede to Nimrod's religion faced persecution. "That sin therefore which the other world was drowned for was again revived by this cursed man, even to lord it over the sons of God, and to enforce idolatry and superstition upon them . . ."(497). First Nimrod and then his followers ostentatiously exalted themselves by utilizing the state church to reinforce their political supremacy. On this point the radical influence on Bunyan is unmistakable: his thesis evokes the old Leveller and Digger assertion that the established clergy are a crucial prop of the monarchy.[57] In sharp contrast to the Levellers and Diggers, however, Bunyan had no interest in pulling up monarchy root and branch.

Despite his basic indifference to constitutional polity, Bunyan was sharply critical of absolute monarchy. "First the tyranny began at Babel itself, where the usurper was seen to sit in his glory. . . ."[58] But Nimrod, the usurper, was, for Bunyan, the founder of absolute monarchy, leaving the inescapable conclusion that absolute kings are tyrants. Nimrod was particularly insidious, in Bunyan's estimation, because he provided an example for inferior rulers to impose their own "pretended" religion rather than the simplicity of the Gospel. "Hence note, that what cities, that is, churches soever have been builded by persons that have come from Romish Babel, those builders and cities are to be suspected for such as had their founder and foundation from Babel itself" (498). Bunyan's direct link between absolute monarchy and Catholicism suggests that the immediate object of his attack in this commentary was James II or Louis XIV, not Charles II, who professed the Roman faith only on his death-bed. If Nimrod in fact suggests James II, the composition of this work probably followed *Of Antichrist and His Ruin*. Bunyan probably began the commentary in the period from about 1686 to 1688, with his death accounting for its incompletion.

The commentary on Genesis is neither hostile to monarchy per se nor a call to violent action as a means of deposing tyrants. Instead the political thrust of the commentary is directed at absolute monarchs (tyrants) and state churches which persecute those who reject their tenets. With respect to the futility of forcing the ungodly and the godly alike into one ecclesiastical institution, Bunyan mused, "What laws have been made, what blood hath been shed, what cruelty hath been used, and what flatteries and lies invented, and all to make these two waters and people one?"[59] Bunyan does not hesitate to castigate persecutors, even those who carry on this work in the guise of a reason of state, but nowhere in the work does he call on the saints to rise and overthrow them (489).

Several of the other posthumous works return to themes that appeared in Bunyan's earlier publications. One of the most interesting reflects the dismay manifested in *The Holy War* when Diabolus trampled the statutes of Shaddai. On one level this was a sign of the reprobate's disrespect for divine maxims, but on another it was an attack on the Magna Carta. Bunyan was sarcastic in his criticism of those who had no respect for the common law, regardless of their social status: "The old laws, which are the Magna Charta, the sole basis of the government of a kingdom, may not be cast away for the pet that is taken by every little gentleman against them."[60] This contrasts sharply with the view of extreme radicals, such as the Leveller Richard Overton, who referred disdainfully to the Magna Carta as "a beggerly thing, containing many markes of intollerable bondage. . . ."[61]

Respect for the law—and ultimately the monarch—was also expressed in *Paul's Departure and Crown.* At the head of every statute, Bunyan observed, was the phrase, "Be it enacted by the King's most excellent Majesty," which was intended to make the law respected and glorious. Bunyan understood, too, the general popularity of the monarchy among the masses, for "we see . . . what power and place the precepts of kings do take in the hearts of their subjects, every one loving and reverencing the statute, because there is the name of the king." Because of such respect, rebellion was a word that made the world tremble.[62] These are odd statements indeed if Bunyan was the inciter to sedition that Tindall makes him out to be.

Bunyan nevertheless cautioned against placing excessive trust in princes, citing Psalm 118.8–9 and Psalm 146.3. The Stuarts, he hinted, had betrayed such trust in the recent past. In *Israel's Hope Encouraged,* he remarked ruefully that since the discovery of the infamous Popish Plot, "our days indeed have been days of trouble, . . . for then we began to fear cutting of throats, of being burned in our beds, and of seeing our children dashed in pieces before our eyes." The proper course of action, he asserted, would have been to trust in God, but instead the people put their faith in Charles II, Parliament, the city of London, good mayors and sheriffs, and anti-papal statutes. From the perspective of the reign of the Catholic James II, Bunyan regarded this trust as misplaced.[63] Yet he refused to call for a political revolution, reminding his readers in *The Saints' Knowledge of Christ's Love* that monarchs had their power from God and exercised it within his restraints. God retains "the bridle . . . in his own hand, and he giveth reins, or check, even as it pleaseth him." This was always done, Bunyan assured his readers, for the well-being of the elect.[64]

In one of his last works, *The House of the Forest of Lebanon* (1692), Bunyan took the opportunity to refute those who continued to cling to the old Fifth Monarchy idea about instituting the kingdom of God by force.[65] It was "extravagant," he insisted, to think of such a kingdom in temporal terms, or that it might be inaugurated by physical weapons.

> I confess myself alien to these notions, and believe and profess the quite contrary, and look for the coming of Christ to judgment personally, and betwixt this and that, for his coming in Spirit, and in the power of his word to destroy Antichrist, to inform kings, and so give quietness to his church on earth; which shall assuredly be accomplished, when the reign of the beast . . . is out.[66]

As for the church, its role in these chiliastic events was not one to alarm the state. A hint of *The Holy War*'s militancy remains, for the church is portrayed as "God's tower or battery by which he beateth down Antichrist," but the weapons are only spiritual—the word of God, whose destructive power is restricted to Satan, sin, and lovers of evil (534). Perhaps more significantly, Bunyan insisted that this spiritual war is not offensive but defensive. To temporal authorities, the church poses no threat, for the saints "know their places, and are of a peaceable deportment" (526, 534, 536). The church has no mission to destroy monarchs, subvert kingdoms, or cause desolation. Christ "designs the hurt of none; his kingdom is not of this world, nor doth he covet temporal matters; let but his wife, his church alone, to enjoy her purchased privileges [which are concerns of the soul], and all shall be well." If, however, the saints are afflicted by persecution, those responsible will ultimately be slain by the sword of the Spirit, a threat Bunyan reinforced by quoting

Revelation 11.5. Yet the church itself, Bunyan contended, engaged in no sedition.[67]

Throughout his career, excepting only his youthful period of military service (which predated his conversion), Bunyan stood constant in his advocacy of passive disobedience to state decrees that contravened divine precepts. In his own judgment he was no more guilty of sedition than were Jesus and Paul, Jeremiah and Daniel.[68] He came closest to treasonable assertions in *The Holy War,* with its striking parallels between Diabolus and Charles II, but nowhere in his writings does he call for Nonconformists to take up arms against a tyrannical Stuart sovereign. Neither is there any evidence to indicate that Bunyan plotted insurrection, despite the accusations of his enemies. Bunyan was no political revolutionary. Only if his recurring references to persecuting rulers and their ultimate judgment at the hands of God were misinterpreted as a call to rebellion could his views be seditious in their effect. There was indeed a militancy in works such as *The Holy War* and *Of Antichrist and His Ruin,* but this was a militancy of the spirit, not the sword. Compared to *Seasonable Counsel,* such works reflect the inherent tension embodied in the very concept of passive resistance. While the exhortations to suffer patiently in *Seasonable Counsel* exemplify passivity, so the more militant works encourage the saints to resist the forces of evil, albeit always in the context of a spiritual struggle.

Two things stopped Bunyan from advocating violent action. One was his conviction that temporal authorities always acted as divine agents, no matter how cruelly they persecuted the saints. Tyrannicide was therefore impossible because it was tantamount to an act against God himself. The other restraining factor was the positive way in which Bunyan conceived of suffering. It was not merely something to be endured but virtually an act of worship, calling for the active participation of the believer through willing acceptance. As Bunyan indicated in *Seasonable Counsel,* in the confrontation with the Stuart state, victory was only possible for those who could find "joy under the cross," the spiritual experience of suffering for the right cause in the right way (739). "Wherefore, my brethren, my friends, my enemies, and all men," Bunyan concluded, "what religion, profession, or opinion soever you hold, fear God, honour the king, and do that duty to both which is required of you by the Word and law of Christ, and then . . . you shall not suffer by the power for evil-doing" (741). In the end, the sword would bow to the Spirit.

DAVID HERRESHOFF

Marxist Perspectives on Bunyan

Expressions of affinity and respect for Bunyan have been coming from
Marxist historians and critics at least since the 1930s.[1] Robert G.
Collmer's "Bunyan and the Marxists" takes note of two examples—
Jack Lindsay's *John Bunyan: Maker of Myths* (1937) and Christopher Hill's
Milton and the English Revolution (1977). In the forty years between the
appearance of these two studies and beyond, there have been others, and
in 1978 Marxist scholars celebrated the 350th anniversary of Bunyan's
birth with a conference at Humboldt University in the German Democratic Republic. "If the world should be turned upside down by Marxists," Collmer wonders, "would Bunyan once again rise as a prominent
writer?"[2] Perhaps the Bunyan Conference at Humboldt is an omen that
in a post-capitalist world Bunyan would not cease to be read and studied. But this essay's purpose is not prophecy but description and apprais-
al of Marxist contributions to Bunyan studies from Jack Lindsay onwards.

Aside from the admiration and pleasure a great writer provokes in
sensitive readers, sometimes against their wills, what, it may be asked,
draws Marxists to Bunyan? Readers of Marxist Bunyan scholarship will
be able to find several possible answers to this question in literature.
Among them is that Marxists with a knowledge of the history of their
own movement are open to feelings of identification with participants
in past struggles between orthodoxy and heterodoxy, between establishment and dissent, and among rival currents of dissent which agitated
the intellectual and spiritual milieu of Bunyan's life. Sometimes these
feelings of identification take the form of contention over cultural leg-

acy; is Bunyan "ours" or "theirs" or perhaps both? would be a way of formulating the issue, with "ours" referring to a presumed secular and proletarian interest and "theirs" to a Christian and bourgeois one. Marxists concerned with this issue do not, as will be seen, respond in unison. There is good reason for the lack of unanimity.

Though anticlerical from its inception and representing itself as an explicable phase in the development of thought rather than a revelation, Marxism in fact wrestles with concerns which Christians confronted for centuries before its birth. This is perhaps easier to see at present than it was in the nineteenth century, when the first generation of Marxists was closer to the anti-clericalism of the Enlightenment and the French Revolution than are their present-day successors, for they then confronted an organized Christianity more distant in outlook from the revolutionary dissenters of Bunyan's young manhood than are many Christians of the late twentieth century (particularly, though not exclusively, some in the Third World). And Marxism, in some present versions, is not so implacable toward philosophical idealism as it was in the heyday of Kautsky and Lenin. Although Marxist historical materialism can never accept the primacy of the word, yet the Marxist project is a revolution which will succeed only if fought for by human beings who are conscious of their aims. The idea whose time has come enters history with the power of a material force through the minds embracing it; the revolution is the work of a conscious class incarnating an idea, the proletariat as collective messiah. Such thoughts have struck some but not all Marxists writing about Bunyan in the past decade.

Another reason for Marxists' being attracted to Bunyan is that he is seen by them as a guide who can show them to a wicket gate beyond which they can get a clear view into the political landscape of the English Revolution and its aftermath. And since revolutionary landscapes are of the greatest interest to Marxists, the attraction is strong. The great drama of revolution and counterrevolution played out in mid-seventeenth-century England was for Marx and Engels one of the decisive moments in the rise of capitalism, the English link between the German Reformation and the rise of the Dutch Republic in the sixteenth century and the French Revolution in the eighteenth. But for them the language in which the issues of the English Civil War, the Commonwealth, and the Restoration were fought through does not accurately describe what was at stake; the language, rather, tends to use a diction

which clothes the interest and aspirations of social classes in the authority of Scripture.

   Readers of recent Marxist Bunyan scholarship will discover that the
ideological clothing metaphor is alive and well in the prose of some but
not all of the writers to be considered here. Whatever its surviving
merit, in its original use it expressed a sense of historical irony but also a
historical optimism. The idea was that the actors enter upon the stage of
history and do and say things there which have other meanings than
what they think they do. The perceived situation is the reverse of that
which Isaiah describes when he calls the Assyrian army the rod of God's
anger. Not understanding that they are the punishing weapon of an
angry God, the Assyrians think of themselves merely as successful
plunderers. In seventeenth-century England, by contrast, contending
factions which feel themselves to be acting in obedience to God's will
are in fact advancing the material interests of different classes. The implied historical optimism in the clothing metaphor is in the faith that
future struggles are to be waged in a language revelatory of naked truth.
If the Puritan revolutionaries could see their world only through a glass,
darkly, the proletarian revolutionaries will see historical reality face to
face.

   How, it may now be asked, have the Marxists under discussion here
fitted Bunyan into this scheme? Jack Lindsay in his *John Bunyan: Maker of
Myths* (1937) provides one answer. Lindsay characterizes Bunyan as the
product of family and social crises not understood by Bunyan, and he
eventually develops explanations of how such a man came to write *The
Pilgrim's Progress*:

> [O]ur business here is to get beneath the form in which the search [for under-
> standing and reconciliation] presented itself to Bunyan, and to find the per-
> sonal and social bedrock on which he raised his superstructure of anxiety,
> terror and hope, despair and reconciliation. It was an inevitable accompani-
> ment of Bunyan's torment that he should not be able to realize the personal
> and social roots of his troubles. . . . The only meaning he could possibly
> have attached to them was that they were hindrances to attaining the goal of
> reconciliation with the Father. If he had been able to see their relation as the
> underlying causes of his states of mind, his whole problem would have ceased
> to exist.[3]

In his digging toward the "bedrock," the "roots," the "underlying

causes" shaping Bunyan's consciousness, Lindsay proceeds under the
sign of Freud as well as of Marx. The "Father" is alternately divine and
diabolical and ambiguously present in Bunyan's biological father, whose
prompt remarriage after the death of Bunyan's mother is presumed to
have been traumatic for Bunyan. Because Bunyan could only "tran-
scribe his states of mind in terms of the contemporary religious idiom,"
he formulates his problems in language "in which the social strife and
the family discord are confused and blended" (8). Marxist analysis, in
Lindsay's view, requires that the social be seen as more important than
the personal.

> Both the devil and god are father-figures, derived immediately from family
> experience but finding their deeper meaning rooted in social reality. . . .
> The battle between devil and god thus represents a profound inner conflict,
> the individual refraction of social issues. . . . It was the fierceness of resis-
> tance which he had to overcome within himself . . . [which gave] clarity
> and urgency to *Grace Abounding* and *The Pilgrim's Progress.* . . . (10–11)

For Lindsay, Bunyan's quarrels with others yield rhetoric; his quarrels
with himself yield poetry.

But what is this supremely important social reality? For Lindsay,
Bunyan's work was involved with larger historical processes, including
the contemporaneous class-war; one battlefield of that war, according
to Lindsay's account, was in the people's churches:

> Thwarted of socially-constructive self-expression, they devised their
> churches as compensations. The bourgeois, who still wanted strict form and
> control, built up the Presbyterian form, an excellent system of committees
> knitted together; the lower classes turned more toward Independency, the
> local free church feeling itself in communion with its brother-churches ev-
> erywhere, but not linked up. These two forms together comprised the whole
> skeletal machinery for a complete democracy. . . . They were, so to speak,
> constructions *outside society* of what the people felt that society lacked and
> must continue to lack while organized on a class-basis. (105)

So the whole Puritan movement in its gamut of organized tendencies is
really a means of ushering in an alternative society to the one defended
by the temporarily disestablished Anglicans.

Lindsay's responses to and claims for *The Pilgrim's Progress* are per-

vaded by democratic, anti-elite sentiment. The book's power for Bunyan's generation, he says, lay in its concentration of "the ideas and images of a whole vast body of popular literature—the body which had for
centuries alone been close to the living needs of men and women" (167–
68). And the attractiveness of the book is enhanced for Lindsay by the
plebeian status of its author: "The 'Christian Life' is the theme. Which in
fact means the life of John Bunyan, tinker, who soldiered through the
Civil War, represented in terms of Christian imagery" (168).

In concert with Bunyan's use of popular themes and sources, Lindsay
values the author's reliance on vernacular speech. Lindsay's analysis
weaves together secularism and popularism, acknowledging Bunyan's
power to capture—and even amplify—popular idiom and rhythm without falling back upon a biblically based style. Given the circumstance,
acknowledged by Lindsay, that the language of class struggle in the
seventeenth century was scriptural, how strange that "the common
speech" remained undefiled by biblical rhythms and diction! Scientism
appears in the conclusion of Lindsay's discussion of style: "It is an example of the way diverse social forces intertwine, that while Bunyan was
creating this style of direct narrative, the Royal Society was requiring
that prose become plain, unlaboured, simple." Appropriately Lindsay
notes Bishop Sprat's preference for "the language of artisans, country-
men, and merchants before those [sic] of wits and scholars" in concluding that "socially divided as they were, deeply separated in ideology,
[Bunyan] and the scientist were making up a whole" (176). In the Marxist view of 1937, science and the people are good and religion, at best,
irrelevant.

Considering *The Pilgrim's Progress* as an allegory, Lindsay ranges easily
through the mythology and literature of several nations for comparisons. Grouping it "with the other basic fantasies of world literature:
Don Quixote, The Odyssey, The Golden Ass, Gulliver, Gargantua" (177),
Lindsay points to mythological analogues at the same time he sees the
overall narrative in Marxist (and Freudian terms):

> The battle with the monster in the earth-cleft is the common folk-image of
> the birth-struggle. A monster such as Apollyon has the same meaning as, say,
> the Minotaur whom Theseus slays after tracking down the lair through the
> wandering maze, or Cacus whom Hercules tracks down to his den. These
> monsters are male, the destroying Father in his ugliest shape. The Pilgrim's

imprisonment by a giant, and his escape from the dark cell, are paralleled by
countless tales in folklore and myth, of which that of Ulysses in the Cyclops'
cave, or that of Jack the Giant-killer, will serve as examples. The crossing
of the Slough or of the River belongs to the commonest type of birth-
symbolism. The ceaseless sound of 'many waters' pervading the bridge-jail
would help in arousing birth-memories in Bunyan. . . . (183–84)

Nonetheless, Lindsay points out, this is a fantasy based as much on reality as mythology. The sound of "many waters" is clearly from Bunyan's
experience, and Lindsay later likens Christian's burden to Bunyan's
tinker's wallet, "which marked him out as a despised toiler as he trudged
the roads" (186).

Next Lindsay offers a reading of *The Pilgrim's Progress* as dream. The
story, which on the surface involves "personal salvation," is actually
founded on an "underlying social basis":

> The impression conveyed by the allegory is the exact opposite of what it
> literally professes. The phantasms of good and evil become the real world;
> and in encountering them the Pilgrim lives through the life that Bunyan had
> known in a definite place and time. . . . There are comrades and enemies,
> stout-hearts and cravens, men who care only for the goal of fellowship and
> men of greed and fear; and these are the men of contemporary England.
>
> The Celestial City is the dream of all England, all the world, united in
> Fellowship. Meanwhile there was, for Bunyan, the little congregation of
> Bedford who were doing their best in a world of distorting pressures. (194)

These interpretations are a consistent series of materialist seculariza-
tions of Bunyan's dream-vision. They imply a millenarian reading of it
as well.

In *The Holy War*, according to Lindsay, Bunyan "inverted the method
of *The Pilgrim's Progress*. In the latter work he had used the theme of the
lonely and isolated salvationist to depict the bustling world in which he
himself had come to grace. In *The Holy War* he used the image of a whole
society to express the psychology of the individual of his day" (212). But
Lindsay also reads the book as a disguised account of struggles between
Bedford and the Stuart monarchy, "a picture of the social convulsions of
his age" (213). The town of Mansoul, besieged by the Diabolonians,
Lindsay sees as representative of Bedford, "the society of the godly
united against the feudalist foe" (217). From the pages of *The Holy War*

Lindsay infers an "uprush of revolutionary emotion" in Bunyan. He takes the book to be a forecast of the 1688 Revolution: "And also, in the dim future, the day of full social unity" (219). Here again we meet Lindsay's version of Bunyan as secular revolutionary eager for action, a version possibly descriptive of the young Parliamentary trooper of the 1640s but surely an anachronism when applied to the Baptist preacher of the 1680s. "Underneath, he longs for the active revolutionary struggle. He depicts with the heartiest of joyful accord the ruthless suppression of the Diabolonians" (221).

Alick West, like Jack Lindsay a pioneer of British Marxist literary criticism, published a study of Bunyan in his essay collection *The Mountain and the Sunlight: Studies in Conflict and Unity*, in 1958. He was one of a group of writers associated with the Communist Party of Great Britain of whose shared characteristics Arnold Kettle writes:

> Firstly, their work is imbued with a sense of closeness to the millions of working-class people who have participated in the labour movement, and reveals a corresponding attempt to write in simple, direct language to which working-class people can respond. Secondly, there is in their writing a strong consciousness of the progressive aspects of the English literary heritage, especially the work of Shakespeare, Milton, Bunyan, the Romantic poets and the 19th-century novelists. But perhaps most significant of all is a certain suspicion of the kind of 'ideological' criticism found in the work of continental Marxists trained in the Hegelian tradition.[4]

West's Marxist criticism may be distinguished from Lindsay's by his inclination to allow a longer tether than Lindsay and to pull less insistently on the author he has collared. West acknowledges what Zhdanovite socialist realism does not, that

> A work may talk revolution; but if it does not show revolution through society's creative movement, it is not fulfilling its function as literature. . . . Or a work may talk reaction; but if it conveys the sense of the social movement it condemns, the manifestly reactionary work is more valuable than the manifestly revolutionary. (7)

This approach to the relation between literature and ideology permits West to take the trouble to try to understand and expound those tenets of Bunyan's faith which seem to him significant for the student of

Bunyan's mind and art. To him the central issue is the relation between law and grace. In analyzing it he remained of course a historical materialist:

> The Baptists of Bedford, as elsewhere, were artisans, mechanics, small shop-keepers. Their livelihood depended on trade, and trade could not prosper in social disorder. It required freedom, but not anarchy. This need of organisation and social order underlies the conflict between grace and law, between the Christ within and the Christ without. The extreme conceptions current among the Ranters and the early Quakers that since there was identity between the individual soul and Christ the law had no power, could no more be accepted in practice by artisans and shopkeepers than by the bourgeoisie. They also needed the power of the law, for they also had lives and property to be protected; and if the law's power was to be recognised, that demanded belief in a Christ without, separate from and above the individual soul. (144–45)

Another distinguishing feature of West's Bunyan criticism is his appreciation of the author's individualism. Lindsay appears to incline toward that tendency in Marxism which celebrates the collective by devaluing the individual, forgetting that Marx and Engels desired a society in which "the free development of each is the condition of the free development of all." West's view comes out in his discussion of *Grace Abounding,* a work which he believes accomplishes something other than its author intended as it becomes the story of a unique consciousness rather than of a representative one: "Before *Grace Abounding* there had been few books in English literature where a man thinks with such energy that he is I; there had been none spoken by a mechanic to his fellow artisans" (147).

The new value of the self articulated by Bunyan is a product of the Reformation, requiring "the unity of common devotion to the cause of Christ against Antichrist. In the growing strength of that unity Protestantism saw the meaning of history; and the achievement of conscious participation in that unity is the new meaning which Bunyan gives to 'I' " (151). West invites us to

> Contrast with the unconsciously social existence of the peasantry in a medieval village the self-awareness with which Bunyan the tinker devotes himself to the aim which he and his fellows have consciously set before themselves. (151)

And West sees himself and the version of Marxism for which he speaks as continuators of the Bunyanesque revolutionary individualism of the Reformation:

> In a number of *Encounter* current at the time these lines are being written, Mr. Koestler is sorrowing that man ever cut the navel string that bound him to God. In Dr. Leavis's backward gaze at the popular tradition of the middle ages there is a similar regret: the wisdom of the past is lost. Did Bunyan thus revere what was in his day similar wisdom—Catholicism? Wisdom for Bunyan was the spirit of the men and women who had lived and died for Protestantism. His voluntary devotion of his conscious self to the same cause was an act of that humanism in which Catholicism saw, and sees, its greatest enemy. (152)

The Catholicism which West had in mind in 1958 was the church of Monsignor Fulton J. Sheen's homilies against humanism and Cardinal Spellman's call to arms in behalf of God and the Free World, not the church of Central American peasants, Polish proletarians, and antinuclear American bishops of the 1980s.

West's reading of *The Pilgrim's Progress* is consistent with his reading of *Grace Abounding*. In both he discerns "tension between humanism and religion" (158); the stronger the humanism, the weaker the allegory. Breaking out of the form of allegory for West is a matter of creating representations of human character of such persuasive power as will convince readers that as "the courage and the combats have been real, so is the victory" (160).

The focus of realism in *The Pilgrim's Progress,* for West, is Vanity Fair, which symbolizes the growing tension between the marketplace, the basic economic movement of Bunyan's time, and the kind of idealism represented by the pilgrims. The fact that Faithful is put on trial and burned at the stake in Vanity Fair while Christian escapes both trial and punishment by the people of Vanity signifies for West an ambiguous resolution of this conflict. This plot in turn shows an ambivalent reaction to the rise of capitalism among the Dissenters, particularly the Baptists, who were helping to bring into being a system which in important ways was not in harmony with their values and aspirations. Indeed their "conception both of personal relationships and of democracy implicit in their religious organisation, with no priestly authority and equal obligation on all members to help each other in winning salvation, was radi-

cally different from what the bourgeois revolution brought into being"
(162). The moral of the plot, as drawn by West, is that

> pilgrims must stand firm against the unjust and inhuman power of the
> market, which takes no account of the value of the human soul; they must
> stand firm even unto death. But the Christian must not make this antagonism
> between money and the soul into the great issue of life and death, as it would
> appear to be if Faithful were the hero and the book had ended with his being
> burned. (162)

Marxism as practiced by West allows Bunyan to be what he is, a man
concerned with the way to the next world. It is close to the Marxism of
Arnold Kettle, who thinks

> Mr. Lindsay is wrong to identify in too facile a way Bunyan's Celestial City
> with modern man's goal of fellowship. Bunyan believed in a life after death
> and there is no point in insinuating that, had he known better, he would have
> believed in something else. What is important is that the positive quality of
> Bunyan's belief in a life after death and the actual tensions of mortal struggle
> which (as Mr. Lindsay excellently brings out) give the prose its muscular,
> colloquial vitality go far to negate the antihumanist, defeatist character of
> the myth itself.[5]

It is the participation of Bunyan, "the jailed dissenting tinker," in the
life of a seventeenth-century England wracked with problems which,
for West, makes possible Bunyan's vivid imitation of that life. The soli-
tary pilgrim setting out for the next world, for instance, is a flesh-and-
blood being in that life as well as an artist's dream:

> [W]e find a figure like Bunyan's pilgrim, stopping his ears lest the cries of his
> wife and children should hold him back from going where he knows he must.
> The wife of one of the Anabaptists of Münster related at the trial after the
> rising had been put down, how in the night her husband, the peasant Hans
> Ber, got up from his bed and made ready to go on a journey. 'Where are you
> going?' she asked him. He answered: 'I do not know. God knows.' She im-
> plored him to remain and help bring up the children, but he replied, 'I must
> go to find out the will of the Lord.' And he went to join the Anabaptists, and
> met his death. (154)

West sees this German peasant as a brother of Christ and of Bunyan himself when, contemplating the consequences of defying the temporal authorities in the cause of faith, he recalls in *Grace Abounding:* "Oh, I saw in this condition I was as a man who was pulling down his house upon the head of his wife and children; yet thought I, I must do it, I must do it" (154–55). This sort of foregrounding of the connections between art and life is characteristic of British Marxist criticism while it remained independent of Continental theorists.

Christopher Hill's lifelong immersion in seventeenth-century studies was largely, as he says, a consorting with Muggletonians, Levellers, Diggers, Quakers, Anabaptists, Antinomians, and Fifth Monarchy men,[6] and his practice in telling one from the other has equipped him to see and declare what Bunyan shares with, and by what Bunyan is to be distinguished from, the exuberant political and religious left wing of the English Revolution. The seventeenth-century hero of the British Marxists is Gerrard Winstanley, and Hill is alert to spot links between Winstanley and Bunyan, calling them "the great seventeenth-century literary figures to whom we should turn as representatives of our common humanity" (266). Winstanley and Bunyan, according to Hill, share the radical commitment to the life of action. " 'Action is the life of all,' cried Winstanley, 'and if thou dost not act, thou dost nothing.' Clarkson and Bunyan echoed him" (333).

But compared to Milton, Hill finds Bunyan to be a rather unsatisfactory ally from the past. Bunyan lacks the "this-worldly emphasis" which Milton shares with the radicals. Nevertheless he sees Bunyan relating to Seekers, Ranters, and early Quakers "in the same way" as do Milton, George Fox, and Lodowick Muggleton (457). Hill prefers Milton's individualism to Bunyan's because

> the this-worldliness of his thought makes him far less concerned with his own soul or with the after life than many of his contemporaries. . . . There is in him none of that fevered search for personal salvation that we find in Vaughan on the one hand, in Bunyan on the other. Milton is concerned with Christ's kingdom, the good society, rather than with personal consolations or rewards. (460)

In the tercentenary year of the publication of *The Pilgrim's Progress,* Hill delivered one of *The John Bunyan Lectures* at Bedford. In it he balances his thesis of the withdrawal of the dissenting sects from political

involvement after the Restoration against the conception that during
the whole period between the outbreak of the Civil War and 1688 a
divorce of religion from politics is an impossibility. It is an impossibility
in the midst of the flood tide of radicalism because millenarian hopes
impelled Christian radicals into revolutionary activity designed to
cooperate in establishing the reign of Christ. It is an impossibility during
the ebb because growing repression of dissent then made the very per-
petuation of nonconforming congregations an act of political defiance.

Filling in this pattern of analysis, Hill shows the political concerns of
Bunyan's congregation in the 1650s. The congregation put forward the
names of candidates to represent Bedford in the Barebones Parliament.
It held a meeting of thanksgiving after the proposal to crown Cromwell
king was abandoned. After the Restoration it fell silent on political issues.[7]

In Hill's scheme of the course of English events between 1642 and
1688, there were two revolutions, one long, one short, one within the
other. The longer of the two secured the defeat of absolutism in state
and church and the supremacy of Parliament as the executive committee
of the gentry and merchants. The shorter, and rapidly frustrated revolution, takes up the years between the end of the civil war in 1646 and the
suppression of the radicals in the early 1650s. In 1660, in reaction to that
second revolution, "the alarmed men of property—former royalists and
former Parliamentarians—sank their differences in order to recall
Charles II. . . . But now he was junior partner to the gentry that Parliament represented" (9). The Revolution of 1688 Hill sees as a confirmation of the political settlement of 1660 made necessary by James II's
abortive attempt to revert to prerevolutionary absolutism.

Bunyan was fourteen years old at the beginning of the long revolution
and he died just before its completion. His outlook as a mature man,
according to Hill, was indelibly marked by his experience of the revolutionary excitement which infused the army and the meetings of Dissenters in the period of the revolution within the revolution: "Few of us
think again after we are thirty, and Bunyan was no exception" (23–24).
Bunyan's outlook was the product of a period

> when what we feebly call religious toleration had established itself. Any
> group of men and/or women who so wished could get together, elect a
> chairman—often a so-called "mechanic preacher," a man who worked six

days a week. Under him they conducted religious discussions, which often strayed very far from what we would regard as "religious," in the narrow sense of the word, into economics, morals and politics, as we saw Bunyan's meeting discussing kingship in 1657. They had escaped from the control of their betters. (11)

As he distinguishes Bunyan's among the many voices of dissent, it becomes clear that Hill's sympathies lie more with the radical extremists of the time, the Quakers, Diggers, Ranters, and Milton, than with Bunyan (12). It is almost as if he chides Bunyan when he dates his "conversion and his rejection of the Ranters" from "the years in which the radicals were being suppressed, and the men of property were reestablishing a state church and a censorship" (20). This makes Bunyan's Calvinism a response to loss of hope in the imminence of the millennium. Hill associates "some of the less attractive features of Bunyan's thought" with the author's Calvinism. These include the idea that the torments of the damned in hell will be a delight to God, and the rugged individualism which impels Christian to put his fingers in his ears so as not to hear the cries of his wife and children as he departs from the City of Destruction, a performance "Bunyan defended . . . in a later treatise: 'Thy soul is thy own soul . . . ; thou shalt not lose *my* soul by *thy* laziness' " (21).

For Hill, Calvinism is a continuation of medieval belief in utter human helplessness in the face of uncontrollable natural and supernatural powers, a belief which science was threatening to subvert.

Only a visionary like Bacon could suggest the possibility of human beings controlling their own destiny. . . . For a brief period during the Interregnum the millenarian ideas of those who hoped to bring about Christ's kingdom on earth fused with the optimism of the scientists who thought that within a generation or two nature could be brought under human control.

Hill's favored champion of this fusion is Winstanley, for whom the resurrection "was a metaphor for the rising of Reason and the spirit of cooperation in all men and women, after which oppression would cease and churches would no longer be needed" (21). When Bunyan was reaching maturity that dream was fading, and Hill sees his rejection of Ranter and Quaker ideology as related to that disillusion:

the particular poignancy of *The Pilgrim's Progress* (as of *Paradise Lost*) springs from the tension between the vision and the reality, the dream and the all-too-real world. Starting from fallen man, Milton and Bunyan both show the divine in man as slowly winning its way back, in Milton's case to "a Paradise within thee, happier far," to be won on earth as the radicals had hoped; in Bunyan's to a tough confidence that could triumph over the torments and early death which were the normal fate of the propertyless itinerant. (26)

From Lindsay through Hill, British Marxist criticism of Bunyan shows both continuity and change. Lindsay's Freudianism is not continued by subsequent writers. West inclines to afford freer play to the relation between the aesthetic and the ideological and greater weight to the claims of the individual in relation to the collective; so does Kettle. Hill revives the milieu in which Bunyan lived and wrote. A widening of the Marxist perspectives seems to be in progress.

E. P. Thompson's *The Making of the English Working Class* considers briefly how *The Pilgrim's Progress* was read in its own century and, further, between the subsidence of the English Revolution and the eruption of the French; in fact, Thompson assigns it a primary place alongside Thomas Paine's *Rights of Man* as "one of the two foundation texts of the English working-class movement." Thompson credits Bunyan as the vehicle which preserves "slumbering Radicalism" throughout the eighteenth century, calling him, along with Paine, Cobbett, and Owen, the writers who "contributed most to the stock of ideas and attitudes which make up the raw material of the movement from 1790–1850."[8] During the generations separating the English revolution of the seventeenth century and the working-class insurgency of the nineteenth which culminated in Chartism, the English Dissenters, by means of political quietism, kept aglow "in the imagery of sermons and tracts and in democratic forms of organisation" habits of radical thought and action "which might, in any more hopeful context, break into fire once more" (30).

In Christian's "What shall I do?" Thompson hears the voice "of those who lost at Putney, and who had no share in the settlement of 1688" (32). The answer they found to Christian's cry, he suggests, was to search for the interior kingdom of personal salvation. He sees in Christian's journey

the inner spiritual landscape of the poor man's Dissent—of the 'tailors, leather-sellers, soap-boilers, brewers, weavers and tinkers' who were among Baptist preachers—a landscape seeming all the more lurid, suffused with passionate energy and conflict, from the frustration of these passions in the outer world. . . . (32)

The inner journey of the quietist seeker, of course, is far from tranquil. Thompson sees the spiritual world as constantly threatened by the outer world—primarily by the State, which Bunyan symbolizes in Apollyon, the seemingly fantastic monster that accosts Christian much as the county magistrates who tried to stop Bunyan's field-preaching. Such attacks can over time weaken resistance, and Thompson sees in the characters of Messrs. By-ends, Hide-the-World, Save-All, and Money-Love an anticipation by Bunyan of the degeneration of Dissent in the eighteenth century: "What they have lost is their moral integrity and their compassion; the incorruptible inheritance of the spirit, it seems, could not be preserved if the inheritance of struggle was forgotten" (34).

Like Arnold Kettle, Thompson eschews the total secularization of *The Pilgrim's Progress* attempted by Lindsay. He agrees with Max Weber that the focus of interest in the book is on the world to come. Yet this focus yields "some emotional compensation for present sufferings and grievances: it was possible not only to imagine the 'reward' of the humble but also to enjoy some revenge on their oppressors, by imagining their torments to come" (34). This side of other-worldliness, in Thompson's view, is all to the good. But

in stressing the positives in Bunyan's imagery we have said little of the obvious negatives—the unction, the temporal submissiveness, the egocentric pursuit of personal salvation—with which they are inseparably intermingled; and this ambivalence continues in the language of humble Nonconformity far into the 19th century. (34)

Thus does Thompson winnow out Bunyan's chaff from his wheat. There are two Bunyans: the revolutionary Puritan and the quietist Dissenter, and the harvest is equally accessible to Bunyan's contending heirs.

When the context is hopeful and mass agitations arise, the active energies of the tradition are most apparent: Christian does battle with Apollyon in the real world. In times of defeat and mass apathy, quietism is in the ascendant, reinforcing the fatalism of the poor: Christian suffers in the Valley of Humiliation, far from the rattling of coaches, turning his back on the City of Destruction and seeking a way to the spiritual City of Zion. (34)

Paraphrastic analysis of this passage discloses several elements in Thompson's approach to Bunyan's contribution to the political culture of the English working class. First is his association of moments or periods of rising militancy with heightened consciousness of "the real world." Corollary to this is his association of times of growing passivity among the oppressed with weakening connections with reality and an increase in fantasizing. Second is the suggestion that the mood of the historical moment prompts readers to find in Bunyan either the active, combative optimist or the passive, other-worldly fatalist, and that there is much in Bunyan to nourish either mood. Readers of Bunyan, however, may be perplexed by Thompson's interpretation of battling and suffering as antitheses. For if "Christian suffers in the Valley of Humiliation, far from the rattling of coaches" (in the real world), he also battles there; it is in that place that he encounters Apollyon, in the fantasy world of literature and dream and faith in things unseen. For Bunyan struggle and pain are not mutually exclusive opposites but a dialectical, interpenetrating unity. It is never safe to assume that a Marxist historian will always prove to be more Marxist in his way of thinking than will a Baptist preacher. Furthermore the inclination to counterpose a (good) reality to a (bad) fantasy world has not always been part of the Marxist method. For Promethean Marx one of the traits distinguishing human beings from other creatures is the capacity to rear structures in the imagination before embodying them in brick and timber.[9]

Ellen Cantarow's "A Wilderness of Opinions Confounded: Allegory and Ideology" studies *The Pilgrim's Progress* as an important example of a literary production showing the breakdown of allegory as a functioning literary mode and the rise of the bourgeois novel.[10] Hers is the only piece of Marxist criticism of Bunyan thus far considered to concern itself with questions of form and genre in any systematic way. She argues that allegory's "formal characteristics are peculiarly suited to convey conservative and authoritarian notions, and that it isn't a medium in which ideas of historical and social change prosper; [and] that during the period in which it was a dominant literary form, it justified ruling-class ideologies, which were conservative" (215). These claims she supports in analyses of *Piers Plowman* and *The Faerie Queene*. Of Langland's poem she concludes that it is, "if anything, reformist" (247), committed to bettering, not overturning, medieval English institutions: "Langland isn't telling us that the institutions of feudalism must be changed, but rather that each man and woman in the feudal hierarchy must conform to the laws divinely ordained for the just functioning of the system. In other words, Langland was no radical" (221).

As for Spenser, he is equally committed to a ruling-class ideology which represents the social order as ordained, natural, and permanent. *The Faerie Queene,* she points out, is not historical fact but instead "ideology, which rationalised ruling-class reactions to historical fact" (237). And what kind of literature is "historical fact"? That kind in which the oppressed speak for themselves (216). And to the extent that that voice is unalloyed it must find the form of allegory an impediment to clear speech. Why? Because with Langland and Spenser "allegory existed to idealize what in theory were held to be proper relationships between the feudal and renaissance ruling classes and the masses of the people governed, and it idealized the institutions that consolidated ruling-class power" (216).

Bunyan's allegory, according to a consensus which includes Cantarow, does not idealize the relationship between the rulers and the ruled in any place where Apollyon holds sway. The social context of the book, as she observes, is what she calls the Baptist "community of artisans and farmers." The book's attitude toward the social order is not reformist: "Within its evangelism, in its emphasis on individual soul-searching, in its concentration on the afterlife to be attained through self-examination, an expression of lower-class interest appears, which is quite unlike the conservative notion of 'just hierarchy' " (247). Unlike *Piers Plowman,*

> *The Pilgrim's Progress* . . . does not treat institutional abuses with the idea of proposing their correction. When Bunyan portrays corruption, as he does in the trial of Christian and Faithful at Vanity Fair, the implication is that the system in which such events occur is irredeemable. This implication is largely the result of the fact that the system is seen from below, rather than being described from above. (247)

Rounding out her portrait of Bunyan as plebeian, uncompromising other-worldly revolutionary, Cantarow calls his description of the Palace Beautiful "a fictional wish-fulfillment of ultimate social justice (indeed, of a kind of socialism) for the poor" (247).

But how, it might be asked, do these sentiments and aspirations manage to find embodiment in an allegory—a form, it will be remembered, "peculiarly suited to convey conservative and authoritarian notions"? Cantarow's answer is "that at the onset of bourgeois democracy, allegory as a dominant literary form declines" (218). It remains for Cantarow to show evidence of that decline in *The Pilgrim's Progress*. The demonstration proceeds from consideration of the social and political milieu of the text to a focus on its form and esthetic.

Cantarow acknowledges her debt to Thompson's placement of Bunyan's work within a social context and she accordingly views the years of Bunyan's maturity as a time when the revolutionary excitement of the 1640s shifted from the political to the religious arena. The Stuart Revolution's repression of sectarians forced class sentiment "to pulse through the heart of evangelism, and this was fatal for activism" (248). At the same time, in an analogous process, Bunyan was writing *The Pilgrim's Progress,* a book in which revolutionary energies are imprisoned in an innately inhospitable form and necessarily deformed by it.

> In the glorification of this sentiment allegory becomes no less categorical and ahistorical than it is in aristrocratic usage; its idealizing character is simply used to promote the escapism peculiar to evangelism. In this the quintessential characteristic of allegory seems to be its incompatibility with notions of social transformation, its ahistorical and counterrevolutionary nature.

No explanation is offered at this point as to why allegory is a more suitable vehicle for representing quests for the world to come than for struggles toward the secular millennium. Instead, as is customary among secularist critics of Bunyan, Cantarow summons Winstanley as exemplar of a better way of thinking than Bunyan's: "[W]hile men are gazing up to Heaven, imagining after a happiness, of fearing a Hell after they are dead, their eyes are put out, that they see not what is their birthrights, and what is to be done by them here on Earth while they are living. . . ."[11]

Winstanley's words are indeed a telling expression of the voice of the left wing of secular millenarianism of the 1640s, and it is by no means unlikely that when they were uttered Bunyan thought that way also, but it is beside the point in a discussion of the relation between ideology and allegory.

Approaching the center of her discussion, Cantarow finds that the difference between the allegory of *The Pilgrim's Progress* and the allegories of Langland and Spenser can be found in the authors' differing class sympathies.

> "Mistrust," "Timorous," "Pliable," "Obstinate," "Hopeful" all represent states of mind and feeling. When it comes to the figures of greater social stature in the work, more "conventional" allegorical categories are often (though not invariably) applied—thus "Hategood," "Worldly-Wiseman," "Money-Love," are members of the upper classes. (248)

But this reversal or transposition of class relationships—the assertion rests on Cantarow's observation that Bunyan's allegorical villains tend to be upper class while Langland's and Spenser's do not—is not "the essential difference" between *The Pilgrim's Progress* and the two earlier allegories. Rather, "It is in Bunyan's insistence on the effect his book was to have on his reader's life that one finds the seeds of an entirely different attitude towards fiction than any preceding the late seventeenth century. For it depends on a new relationship between the author and his audience" (248–49). This new relationship may be seen in Cantarow's interpretation of Bunyan's invitation to the reader (in his prefatory poem) to "lay my Book, thy Head and Heart together." She reads this line as

> a statement about the affective experience of literature, an experience that stands in marked contrast to the experience of literature as that was understood through the Renaissance: one experienced art according to pre-established rules existing in the art form itself, rules that dictated one's reactions. . . . Now, the notion that the reader's response to literature and art should be a criterion of its success, and that its major significance should inhere there, points to the development of a different esthetic. (249)

She perceives in *The Pilgrim's Progress* a transition from the didactic relationship of allegory to the affective relationship of the novel. Bunyan's is a book which retains "the impersonal, ahistorical and generalizing quality of allegory" and yet acquires "a strangely intimate tone." It abandons the normal verse form of allegory for prose, and within the confines of prose it renounces "the rhythms of scriptural prose" in favor of "plain, straightforward, relatively unadorned statements framed in colloquial and everyday speech" (251).[12] It presents the individualist hero as a feeling, reacting subject and does not merely objectify him as a character to whom things happen. These are narrative techniques Cantarow sees as novelistic rather than allegorical. *The Pilgrim's Progress* is a precursor of the novel as "a new, a bourgeois," literary form, which, "because of the particular point in history at which Bunyan was writing, and because of his place in a particular class and culture," presents us with "a new kind of expression straining at the bonds of the old" (252).

Papers read at the Bunyan-Kolloquium held at Humboldt University on the 350th anniversary of Bunyan's birth reiterate, develop, or modify points, observations, and findings of these earlier Marxist critical works. Joan Bellamy's "John Bunyan and the Democratic Tradition" finds close similarity in style between Bunyan and Winstanley.[13] Defining Puritan as inclusive of all "classes and strata who engaged in the struggle, at some stage or another, in the revolution" (219), she evaluates *The Pilgrim's Progress* as "a high point of Puritan culture which transformed into art important ideas and ways of writing which had been created during the 50 years of struggle for a new England against monarchy and episcopacy, for a just and democratic church and state" (218). Bellamy illustrates the matrix from which Bunyan's work emerges by quoting from William Prynne, John Bastwick, John Lillburne, and Winstanley, a gamut of militants and martyrs ranging from Presbyterians through a Leveller and a Digger. In Winstanley's *Fire in the Bush* she locates a passage of dialogue between the soul and fear which concerns "the psychological effects of oppression." It puts her in mind of *The Pilgrim's Progress* and "might have been written by Christian" (220).

Bellamy abandons Lindsay's and Cantarow's attempts, already discussed here (pp. 165 and 180), to see in Bunyan's writing a vernacular style uninfluenced by the Bible. Such language as used by Prynne, Bastick, Lillburne and Winstanley, she says, "addressed essentially to a popular readership, derived in part from the Bible, in part from the idioms of ordinary speech. They borrowed familiar rhetorical devices from sermons and prayers, and they also created dialogues and elements of dramatic characterisation" (221).

Bunyan's style, Bellamy claims, approximates this description (221).

Among Bunyan's forerunners, it is "in Winstanley that the Biblical echoes come through most lyrically" (222).

In arguing for continuity between Bunyan and his predecessors Bellamy is silent about the divergences in outlook which distinguish Bunyan from them, and above all from Winstanley and his secular communist millenarianism. The same cannot be said about Thomas Metscher in his "Subversive, Radical and Revolutionary Traditions in European Literature between 1300 and the Age of Bunyan." Metscher takes on E. P. Thompson, and by implication Bellamy as well, in stressing the "stark individualism" of Bunyan's allegory. Where Bellamy organizes a "democratic" supra-class continuum which includes both Winstanley and Bunyan, Metscher proposes a competition between contradictory tendencies in the English Revolution which counterpose Winstanley and Bunyan. He sees *The Pilgrim's Progress* as "a direct and authentic expression not of early socialist but of radical petit-bourgeois, in fact radical *protestant* ideology, as a literary embodiment of the search for 'kalvinistische Heilsgewissheit' . . . in the traditions of bourgeois rather than plebian radicalism,"[14] a distinction he sees as significant. Metscher notes that, in contrast to Bunyan, for Winstanley "it is not the 'I' but the 'we' that is the central matter of concern" as the subject of history: "It might be suggested, at least in the sense of a working hypothesis, that it is this *we*, the concept of the *common self* which is the decisive criterion to establish the identity of a genuine *proletarian* tradition and distinguish it from those of *petit-bourgeois radicalism*" (13). The two traditions personified in Winstanley and Bunyan "express different forms of social and cultural experience: that of collective labour . . . and that of the small commodity owner working for himself," each related in that both, in their period, are revolutionary traditions, but united only with respect to what they are against, not what they are for (12–13).

Having tentatively placed Bunyan, Metscher tests that placing by means of a rapid and brilliant survey of the tendencies in European literature since Dante, named in the title of his essay. With Metscher there appears to be a total break with the habit, observable in some Marxist critics, of automatically counterposing the secular and the religious. Commenting on St. Francis' "The Song of Brother Sun," he notes that as a prayer it is in "a form in which *individual experience* [is] able to articulate itself" (15). And in the faith of Meister Eckhart and other mystics in the individual soul's unmediated access to God he finds both an anticipation of Protestantism and "a clear indication of the mystic's hidden (often perhaps unconscious) rebellion against the institutions of the feudal system—against the very ideology of Church institution as such" (16).

Unwilling to "secularize" the beliefs, language, and struggles of earlier centuries, Metscher nonetheless remains a Marxist. He changes the emphasis, not the doctrine.

> Without underestimating the historic significance of the non-religious traditions—the "new realism" in the drama, in the novel, in lyric poetry—despite Cervantes and Shakespeare, as it were, it is evident that in the centuries between 1300 and 1700 *the major ideological battles were fought in religious form.* Even in Winstanley . . . the language is that of revolutionary Christianity, inspired by a radical reading of the Bible. The first authentic texts of what can with good reason be called genuine proletarian literature are certainly religious: a spontaneous dialectical materialism in radical Christian guise. (16)

Though the thought is not foreign to other Marxists, there is no hint in Metscher that Christianity (as text and source of ideas, not as institution) ever impeded the radical impulse; on the contrary, Metscher argues,

> the tradition of radical religious literature is perhaps the most contradictory, and for us certainly the most difficult to assess. The *Bible,* translated into the vernacular, and particularly in the use made of it by the sects and by radical Protestantism, certainly functioned as a subversive text. In Münzer, Winstanley—and even right up to Blake's "The Everlasting Gospel"—it becomes the revolutionary handbook of the times. (15)

With Thomas Metscher and, most notably among others, with Christopher Hill, Marxist criticism demonstrates a capacity to describe, evaluate, and enjoy Bunyan without feeling obliged to recruit him.

In his "Realistische Allegorie in John Bunyans *The Pilgrim's Progress,*" Georg Seehase calls the book "ein allegorischer epischer Prosaroman mit realistichen Strukturen." This would seem to take care of the problem of genre classification. However, Seehase is less interested in form than he is in ideological content and the book's reception and literary influence. He sees the book as the source of one of the constituting elements of the English novel of the eighteenth century. That element is Bunyan's "*ideologisch-moralistische Intonation.*" The novelists of the eighteenth century managed to appropriate this intonation from Bunyan minus its religious garb; it is the ideological content which they make use of.[15]

Aware that German editions of *The Pilgrim's Progress* which serve the cause of Christian propaganda continue to appear, Seehase believes it is feasible to prepare an edition at least of the First Part to serve the needs of socialist publishing policy. It would be provided with a suitable and appealing commentary. In order to produce such an edition, Marxist scholars must first elucidate for themselves why and how they are charmed by Bunyan's work (208). Referring to a secularist mediation of Gotthold Ephraim Lessing, according to whom Greek sculpture, though often superficially motivated by religion, is most powerful when the artist concentrates on delight, Seehase suggests that he and his co-thinkers have a relation to Bunyan like Lessing's to Greek art: "in modern reading pleasure from Bunyan's work, the debate succeeds" (208). If one concedes that Bunyan is ineradicably possessed of a religious false consciousness, however, *The Pilgrim's Progress* can only be understood as, at the most, a belles-lettristic tract illustrative of the Bible. Seehase wants more for the book than that; he wants to annex it to the domain of the socialist heritage (*Bereich sozialistischer Erberezeption*) (208-09). The way to do that is to emphasize Bunyan's contributions to the progress of art and therefore to the progress of society. Those contributions are to be chiefly found in his demonstration that allegory can be made to describe living reality and in his creation of an epic hero and a narrator who provide models for the novelists of the following century (212–15).

It is the thesis of Günter Walch in "John Bunyan—Dichter der Plebejischen Fraktion: Revolutionärer Puritanismus und Allegorie" that Bunyan finds in the centuries-old literary and folk traditions of allegory the appropriate medium for the shaping of his theme of the individual's search for wholeness. He shapes this theme from the plebeian standpoint, uniting in its shaping the historical and the spiritual (*von Historischem und Numinosem*). By means of this literary form, with its conditioning function, he derives the possibilities of allegorical style in contradictory tension in a creative manner and thereby transforms the genre. In advancing this thesis Walch arrays himself against a distinguished company from the past: Goethe, Schopenhauer, and Yeats, as well as Wolfgang Iser and Alick West. All these, he suspects, have betrayed a prejudice against allegory.[16]

Walch's essay is courteous and careful in its disagreements with some earlier Marxist scholarship. If he contradicts Lindsay and West in some matters, he also acknowledges his debt to them. The tone of the discussion is caught in his remark that "In general it must be said with appropriate modifications for English literature in the revolutionary seventeenth century what Spriewald says of the Marxist interpretation of the poetry of the dawn of the bourgeois revolution, we remain 'noch in den Anfangen.' "[17] Still in the beginning but intent on pursuing the quest, I would add.

Forty years is a rather long beginning for any school of criticism, unless the school is destined to endure for centuries. But it is enough to remind us of Bunyan's enduring charm. It may be that the productions of the school tell us more about the hopes, intentions, and methods of the critics than about the achievement of the artist criticized. No matter—it remains a body of criticism worth the attention of students of Bunyan's reception in this century. In a review of this criticism, several developments become visible. An inclination grows to allow the past a certain autonomy; resolute efforts to recruit Bunyan for the proletarian revolution give way to a willingness to let Bunyan be Bunyan. Marxist critics appear to be undergoing a distancing from the anticlerical matrix of their doctrine, encouraged perhaps by theological and practical developments among Christians in the present century. One sign of this distancing is that Lindsay's assertion that the vital and memorable in Bunyan's art owes nothing to the Bible has been reconsidered and dropped in the later criticism. Lindsay's psychoanalyzing of Bunyan also appears to have no continuators among subsequent Marxist critics.

British Marxists have naturally done most of the Marxist criticism of Bunyan. In some instances their criticism reveals national characteristics which distinguish it from the products of Zhdanovite socialist realist criticism. Thus West celebrates Bunyan's individualism and refuses to use the ideology of a writer as a criterion for the worth of a literary work.

For Hill and other British Marxists the seventeenth-century hero is Winstanley rather than Bunyan. The relation of religion and politics is one of Hill's major themes. He stresses the impossibility of divorcing politics from religion in a period of fervent millenarian hopes. Understanding the social meaning of *The Pilgrim's Progress* requires fitting its author into a period when those hopes were ebbing. He discovers a retreat from politics as usually conceived, but Establishment repression of Dissenters after the Restoration made simple persistence in organized nonconformity a political act.

E. P. Thompson judges *The Pilgrim's Progress* to have been one of the two chief literary inspirations of the English working-class movement (the other being *The Rights of Man*). Thompson regards Bunyan as a prophet of a this-worldly degeneration of the dissenting community in the eighteenth century. He believes the vicissitudes of English workers' hopes for bettering their condition prompted working-class readers of Bunyan to see in him either an active contender against the powers that be or a passive submitter to their yoke.

The papers read at Humboldt University to celebrate the 350th anniversary of Bunyan's birth reiterate or modify earlier Marxist criticism in several ways. There is continued unease about Bunyan's individualism, expressed in a quarrel over whether Bunyan should be classed as a pioneer of socialist collectivism or of petit-bourgeois individualism. There are no further attempts to identify a Puritan vernacular style uninfluenced by the Bible. A counterposing of the secular and the religious, to the detriment of the latter, is no longer automatic. Allegory, once regarded as a reactionary art weapon of the upper classes, is seen to have other possibilities.

U. MILO KAUFMANN

The Pilgrim's Progress *and* The Pilgrim's Regress: *John Bunyan and C. S. Lewis on the Shape of the Christian Quest*

John Bunyan and C. S. Lewis, in *The Pilgrim's Progress* and *The Pilgrim's Regress,* exploit two different and complementary metaphors for describing the Christian quest. Bunyan develops the metaphor of the one-way quest, while Lewis develops the metaphor of the two-way quest. To be fair with Lewis, one should add that he too finds good use for the metaphor of the one-way quest, but uses it in a way quite different from Bunyan. While in *The Pilgrim's Progress* the one-way quest of pilgrimage reflects how individual Christian calling can in fact call one beyond this world, in *The Pilgrim's Regress* the one-way component of the narrative expresses a more general, even universal vocation—the divine calling of all individuals beyond the finite to the infinite in a dialectic of desires and images. Set against this cosmic and universal vocation is that more specifically Christian vocation which Lewis develops under the metaphor of a two-way quest, with the first leg of the quest not understood for what it truly is until its completion. For Lewis, then, the essential nature of the Christian life is expressed not in the move beyond the world, even though the world and all within it is under judgment much as in Bunyan, but rather in a redemptive return into the world, in the vision earned at the world's extremities. The return involves the recovery of communal and traditional forms of thought and worship. Lewis is more sensitive than is Bunyan to the tension between world-denying and world-affirming modes, as well as that between the light which enlightens every person (John 1.9) and the lights which define

individual Christian pilgrimage as well as that of Christian com-
munities.

In the course of this discussion I shall want to define further the model
of the one-way quest as expressive of certain core-convictions of Christian tradition. Against that background I shall consider how progress
and stasis relate to the one-way quest in Bunyan's masterpiece, hoping
to qualify a position on the matter advanced by Stanley Fish in his
Self-Consuming Artifacts. Then, I shall consider one-way and two-way
quests in Lewis's *The Pilgrim's Regress,* indicating how Lewis assumes a
more inclusive perspective than does Bunyan in portraying the shape of
the Christian journey. Finally, and briefly, I shall acknowledge certain
evidence which softens the contrast between these two allegorists.

Bunyan and the One-Way Quest

Bunyan's *The Pilgrim's Progress* is a notable example of the one-way
quest, but in literature the two-way version is of course the more natural and common. Ordinarily the hero's expedition involves a departure
and a return. But in one-way questing, asymmetry is of the essence. The
seeker does not begin at home, but rather hopes to end there.

The one-way quest commonly stresses life and time as vectors, irreversible in nature. Change is real, growth is real, gain and loss are real.
It is the threat of irreversible loss, or irrevocable tragedy, as well as the
promise of enduring gains and irrevocable good, which imparts to the
one-way quest its peculiar power.

In Christian belief, of course, time is irreversible and finite. Those
two predications are in fact interrelated. For if time were limitless, any
event would be in theory if not in fact reversible, much as every statement to be found in Jorge Borges's infinite library of Babel must also
have its every permutation and falsification in that limitless store of the
possible combinations of twenty-two letters.

The one-way quest serves to express not only the ultimacy of history,
but also the ultimacy of moral careers lived out in history. Morality
involves all the asymmetries of good and ill, of inclusion and exclusion,
of affirmation and denial. On the cosmic scale, such an asymmetrical
moral plot is notably portrayed in the canon of Milton's poetry, wherein

the scope of evil is circumscribed in a directed sequence of crises, or
kairoi: the war in Heaven, the Nativity, the temptation and passion of
Christ, the apocalyptic close of history. Milton's is a seminally Christian
interpretation of cosmic history, and its moral plotting of that history
features resolutions that exclude, deny, and vanquish evil.

In something of the same vein, T. H. White's young Arthur says to
Merlyn, "If I were to be made a knight . . . I should pray to God to let
me encounter all the evil in the world in my own person, so that if I
conquered there should be none left, while if I were defeated, it would
be I who would suffer for it." Merlyn responds, "That would be extremely presumptuous of you . . . and you would be conquered, and
you would suffer for it."[1] True moral resolution means for young
Arthur the eradication of evil, or its tragic alternative, the death of the
hero.

In biblical religion the asymmetry of one-way quest is grounded in
God's righteousness, and in his validating of human history through his
call upon it. Alan Watts nicely sums up the claim for God's goodness:

> What belongs essentially and exclusively to God is inflexible righteousness,
> and historical Christianity simply has not tolerated any notion of God as an
> Absolute "beyond good and evil." Thus the Being of being, the Ultimate
> Reality, has—for the Christian mentality—a definite character, a specific
> and particular will, such that goodness does not exist merely in relation to
> evil but is, from everlasting, the very essence of God.[2]

While Watts condemns this position for being aberrant vis-à-vis the
perennial philosophy, it is certainly one held by both Bunyan and Lewis.
To take morality seriously is to take seriously the prospect of life as an
editing. One proceeds by exclusions. In moral terms, the end is both less
and more than what one begins with.

Beyond the absolutizing of morality, there is also in biblical religion
the attaching of enduring meaning to historical process. Biblical religion sees history as oriented toward an end beyond it, yet present in it.
No one better summarizes the boldness of the Christian conception than
does the German Oscar Cullman. Cullman, like Watts, recognizes the
presence of offense in the acceptance of asymmetry.

In primitive Christianity's constructing of an inclusive time-line,
Cullman says,

that which is so offensive for modern thought . . . becomes particularly clear, namely, the fact that *all Christian theology in its innermost essence is Biblical history;* on a straight line of an ordinary process in time God here reveals himself, and from that line he controls not only the whole of history, but also that which happens in nature![3]

A more recent formulating of this linear aspect of Christian belief is provided by Harvey Cox, who, referring to the battle between Hebrew prophetism and the nature-religion of the Canaanites, observes that the conflict was "between two views of man. Was man enmeshed in nature and akin to its vitalities and powers, or was man an historical creature, called by a God who acted in historical events and who required him to take responsibility for himself and his world on the way to an open future?" In Hebrew religion nature was not ignored, but brought into history. "The Canaanite fertility festivals became occasions to celebrate Yahweh's promises for the future."[4]

The phrase "called by a God who acted in historical events" is certainly applicable to the dynamics of Christian's career in *The Pilgrim's Progress,* as is the phrase "on the way to an open future." Still, the forward momentum of Bunyan's narrative is compromised in several ways, and we shall not well understand the work until we have grasped the relationship therein between quest and present attainment.

Plainly, in *The Pilgrim's Progress* Christian's forward movement is compromised by vacillation and retreat, but, more important, Bunyan hints that the Christian life is indeed at least as much a matter of rest as it is of movement. This latter truth is grounded first in the narrative circumstance of the dreaming narrator's exploring in his "Denn" the manifold implications of Christian conversion. The Christian life is synchronous in the sense that the entire structure of truths lived out is captured in the Puritan analogy of faith. But the reader's impression that movement is not the whole truth is grounded too in Bunyan's fidelity to Calvinist determinism. Calvinist theology stressed the reality of a finished work of grace, realized by the convert in the moment he grasps the fact of his election. This feature of Calvinist belief Bunyan expressed with disarming sincerity near the climax of his *Grace Abounding.* His laying hold of saving assurance is somehow contingent upon his achievement of a double vision that enabled him to take in at once his heavenly and earthly state. It happened, he says,

> as I was passing the field, and that too with some dashes on my conscience, fearing lest yet all was not right, suddenly this sentence fell upon my Soul, *Thy righteousness is in Heaven;* and methought withall, I saw with the eyes of my Soul Jesus Christ at God's right hand, there, I say, as my Righteousness; so that wherever I was, or whatever I was a doing, God could not say of me, *He wants my Righteousness,* for that was just before him.[5]

He goes on to notice that his varying frames of mind, so poignantly portrayed in early pages of his spiritual record, do not affect his righteousness for better or worse "for my Righteousness was Jesus Christ himself, *the same yesterday, and to-day, and for ever,* Heb. 13.8" (73).

He goes on to describe the new doubleness of vision, that power to hold the heavenly and finished fact in tension with the vicissitudes of the immediate and unfinished, even more succinctly: "Twas glorious to me to see his exaltation, and the worth and prevalencie of all his benefits, and that because of this; Now I could look from my self to him," and Bunyan gathers that indeed, in Christ he is at present in heaven. "Now could I see myself in Heaven and Earth at once; in heaven by my Christ, by my Head, by my Righteousness and Life, though on Earth by my body or person" (73). In this discovery Bunyan is at one with Calvinist tradition, which stressed the possibility of a heavenly life now, of crossing heaven's threshold while yet in the flesh. I have discussed this at some length elsewhere, and here will cite only the words of the Calvinist Bishop of Exeter and Norwich, Joseph Hall, who says of the Christian believer that "He walks on Earth, but converses in Heaven; having his Eyes fixed on the invisible, and enjoying a sweet Communion with his God, and Saviour; while all the rest of the World sits in Darkness, he lives in a perpetual Light; the Heaven of Heavens is open to none but him."[6]

This doubleness of vision described by both Hall and Bunyan can be related quite handily to the matter of pilgrimage. Insofar as the soul finds itself in Christ, it has already achieved its end, it has returned to God, its source. Sin and loss have been corrected in redemption and restoration. And yet—and how vital to a full appreciation of Bunyan's narration this fact is—the vision *is* double. One rests, but one also undertakes quests, learning, growing, choosing, enacting that pursuit of holiness which is the Christian response to calling.

It should not surprise us that when Stanley Fish turns his perceptive eye upon the "progress" of *The Pilgrim's Progress,* he can argue that it is scarcely a progress at all.

> [T]he prose itself consistently disappoints the expectations generated by the title. These include (1) the negotiation by one or more pilgrims of a fixed and graduated set of obstacles (2) a direct and progressive relationship between the number of obstacles negotiated and the piling up of spiritual "points" toward a definite goal (3) a growing sense of accomplishment and self-satisfaction (in the reader as well as in the characters) which accelerates as the pilgrims draw nearer to the Heavenly City. What we find, however, are (1) a route whose landmarks and dangers vary with the inner state of those who travel it (2) no direct relationship at all between the point (in space and time) one has reached and the attainment of the ultimate reward, and (3) a pattern of backslidings and providential rescues that works to subvert the self-confidence of pilgrim and reader alike.
>
> In short, *The Pilgrim's Progress* is antiprogressive. . . .[7]

I read Fish as making two valid and helpful claims about Bunyan's narrative. The first is that Christian's wayfaring is not to be seen, finally, as primarily a matter of his own doing. A self-made Christian pilgrimage is indeed a pseudo-artifact, consumed in the process of its disclosure to us. The second is that Christian's course contains a host of antiprogressive elements: doublings back, divagations, losses.

Lest, however, this argument seem to snatch from us all right to speak of one-way quest and progress, let me add first that Fish does not deny the general outlines of a progress, and second that he is more faithful to the descriptive than to the prescriptive side of Bunyan's vision. Christian vocation prescribes a progress, however faultily it is realized.

In broad outline, of course, Christian does move forward from the City of Destruction to the Celestial City. To this manifest achieved progress I would add the details of the several elements of irreversibility in the story. Christian enters the way through a wicket gate, never to retrace that initial choice. Upon seeing the Cross his burden falls away, never to return.

Then in time there is experienced the winsome reality of Beulah Land, the vestibule of Heaven, where God's marriage-covenant is re-

newed and the sun shines night and day. This land, we are carefully told,
lies beyond the Valley of the Shadow of Death, out of the reach of the
Giant Despair, and "neither could the pilgrims from this place so much
as see Doubting Castle. Here they were within sight of the City they
were going to."[8] The language makes despair and doubt appear impossible for these wayfarers. Here, the very seeing of the heavenly goal
moves them. Bunyan is at no loss in presenting the progressive as well as
the antiprogressive elements of pilgrimage.

The more important matter, though, is the distinction to be made
between the descriptive and the prescriptive side of Bunyan's vision.
What Fish has done is to point attention to the way pilgrims act as
contrasted with how they are called upon to act. There can be no doubt
that Bunyan's faith prescribes a genuine progress. It is this that Christian
bears witness to when he says,

> If I go back to mine own Countrey, *That* is prepared for Fire and Brimstone;
> and I shall certainly perish there. If I can get to the Coelestial City, I am sure
> to be in safety there. I must venture: To go back is nothing but death, to go
> forward is fear of death, and life everlasting beyond it. I will go forward. (43)

It is part of Bunyan's honesty in describing actual pilgrimage that he
should have Christian, immediately after this rousing declaration, discover that he had left his roll behind in the arbor where he had slept, so
he must in fact retrace his steps. But the prescriptive truth remains un-
compromised; life is ahead, step by step, and death is behind.

This one-way quest is, I suggest, a response to Christian vocation
which must have as its invarying expression a moral seriousness. Still,
morality is always ancillary, never primary, since it is vocation which
defines pilgrimage. The distinction is one which Bunyan makes carefully in his much-discussed and much-misunderstood episode of Hypocrisy and Formalist. The timing for the appearance of these false pilgrims
is crucial. They appear on the scene almost immediately after Christian's regeneration, when three shining ones provide him with new
clothing, a mark on his forehead, and a "Roll with a Seal upon it." These
of course are the evidence of his calling. He is to present the roll when he
arrives at the Celestial Gate, in a kind of key-in-lock consummation of
his quest. Formalist and Hypocrisy appear when they do to point up the
spurious. They represent the two eternal abuses of the moral life alien-

ated from calling, from direct response to the God who calls. Formalist is observing the rules for their own sake. Morality becomes an end in itself. Hypocrisy is observing the rules for appearance's sake. In neither case is morality an authentic response to the calling God.

A further damning truth about these inauthentic responses to the call is that they resist genuine change, progress, or self-transcendence in growth. Legalism is apt to conform to the good fully seen and understood. But calling is from without to the beyond, to what escapes immediate comprehension. Hypocrisy is apt to calculate conduct on the basis of ulterior and yet immediate ends. Again, transcendence of the immediate is forfeited. In due time Christian, with Formalist and Hypocrisy, comes to the hill Difficulty, where one false pilgrim takes the side road called Danger, and the other, Destruction, which leads him into a "wide field full of dark Mountains, where he stumbled and fell, and rose no more" (42). Such is the end of those who have no true calling from Christ, who have not repented and truly believed, and whose moral choosing—implied in the names Formalist and Hypocrisy—is not equal to the challenge of the one-way quest of holiness.

The most dramatic and summary version of this truth is to be seen in the case of one poor fool named Ignorance, who in fact takes the pilgrim's way to the very end, making who knows how many apt moral choices in the process. He crosses the River of Death at the same ford where Christian does, but the city's king will not come down to welcome him, and we learn in the last paragraph of the First Part that the angels descend, bind Ignorance hand and foot, and carry him to the door that opens in the side of Heaven's Mount. Bunyan's narrator observes, "Then I saw that there was a way to Hell, even from the Gates of heaven, as well as from the City of Destruction" (163).

The one-way quest of Bunyan's Christian is, then, a paradigm of the Christian affirmation of creation, time, growth, moral distinctions, and calling. As one-way, rather than two-way trip, Christian's journey is a flight from unambiguous and unmitigated peril, a moral career, an education in grace, an irreversible altering of landscape for all who follow him, but first and last it is a continuing response to divine calling, in a process of self-transcendence. Bunyan's one-way quest is the Way of Holiness as his pilgrim is careful to tell Apollyon in the Valley of Humiliation. One ends with a holiness he did not have at journey's beginning, and which he in no wise earned.

C. S. Lewis and the Two Quests

If in the case of *The Pilgrim's Progress* the central issue of narrative structure concerns stasis and movement, in the case of Lewis's sequel, *The Pilgrim's Regress,* the central issue concerns the integration of one- and two-way quest, for in fact there are two distinct journeys in the Lewis work.

The framing journey is one-way, the pilgrim John's response to a call from altogether beyond the world. This is a general vocation, one which the author makes plain comes to all men, in all times. It is a calling couched in the mystery of desire or longing, for which no earthly object proves to be an adequate end. Such calling is quite other than the specifi- cally Christian one to which Bunyan's pilgrim responds, though, like Christian's call, this call draws man beyond the world. The second quest in *The Pilgrim's Regress* is that which describes the convert's regress or return from the world's edge into the community of men for witness and redemptive work.

For Bunyan's pilgrim, conversion comes near the opening of his one- way quest and the River of Death defines the transition into the next world. For Lewis's pilgrim, conversion does not come until the traveler passes through the spiritual death and rebirth defined by death's river at the world's edge, and his specifically Christian pilgrimage begins, rather than ends, at this point. John's regress is, then, the analogue to Christian's progress. His two-way quest is constituted, we see, from the contrary movements of two distinct vocations. The first calls beyond the world, only to be revealed as the vehicle or concomitant—Lewis is not clear on the matter—of another, specifically Christian, calling which directs John back to all he had left behind.[9]

Throughout his writings Lewis is consistent in associating longing with a one-way quest which leads beyond this world to realities not hitherto experienced. In his sermon-essay "The Weight of Glory," for example, he describes moments of intense longing as "only the scent of a flower we have not found, the echo of a tune we have not heard, news from a country we have never yet visited."[10] Here, transparently, is the language of one-way quest. The journey is no recovery of home, but the discovery of the new yet wholly appropriate object. The quest is a re- sponse to calling, and the calling persists despite the sad truth that most education is directed to silencing it. Nearly all the modern philosophies, says Lewis, intend "to convince us that the good of man is to be found on this earth" (5).

John's experience of this call comes when he has just begun his flight from the impossible rules of his home.

> Then came the sound of a musical instrument, from behind it seemed, very sweet and very short, as if it were one plucking of a string or one note of a bell, and after it a full, clear voice—and it sounded so high and strange that he thought it was very very far away, further than a star. The voice said, Come.[11]

In his helpful exposition of longing, which appears as an introduction to the third edition of *The Pilgrim's Regress,* Lewis writes that "the human soul was made to enjoy some object that is never fully given—nay, cannot even be imagined as given—in our present mode of subjective and spatio-temporal experience" (10).

As with Christian's journey, this one-way quest or vocation transcends even while it incorporates morality. John is guided for much of his journey by Vertue, though the moment comes when he must lead his guide, now blind. The message is much like Bunyan's. Vertue attends, but does not constitute the calling which shapes the one-way quest. And this accommodation of morality is a recognition of the ultimate and eternal, in the Christian purview. God, says Lewis in *The Problem of Pain,*

> may be more than moral goodness: he is not less. The road to the promised land runs past Sinai. The moral law may exist to be transcended: but there is no transcending it for those who have not first admitted its claim upon them, and then tried with all their strength to meet that claim, and fairly and squarely faced the fact of their failure.[12]

Lewis, in his *Letters to Malcolm,* finds another way to lodge claims for the eternal consequences of the moral life. Somehow for man in Heaven, as with God, morality will have been transcended, but in a way which yet preserves the asymmetry of good and evil: "In the perfect and eternal world the Law will vanish. But the results of having lived faithfully under it will not."[13] What, then, of the evil which has been part of the individual pilgrim's past? Is it all merely leached from memory? Lewis

196 U. Milo Kaufmann

seems to believe otherwise. A transfiguration will occur. In his preface to *The Great Divorce,* he declares that earthly life

> will not be found by anyone to be in the end a very distinct place. I think, earth, if chosen instead of Heaven, will turn out to have been, all along, only a region in Hell: and earth, if put second to Heaven, to have been from the beginning a part of Heaven itself.[14]

In this retroactive transfiguration of the personal past we have, I suppose, a definitive comment upon journey as one-way quest. Journeying is not the return to home or source so much as the linear pursuit of a transfiguring end. The traveler ends as far more than he began, with far more than he had at the opening of his quest.

It is remarkable that Lewis was able early and late to honor this model of the one-way quest even though, as *Surprised by Joy* and *The Pilgrim's Regress* make clear, it could not be readily reconciled with the facts of his own conversion and subsequent Christian career. His conversion was in several important ways a recovery—of his childhood faith, of the traditional formulations which were a matrix for that faith, and of the community of men which the child is participant in unawares and which the intimately personal aspect of the quest spurred by longing could serve to conceal. Specifically *Christian* pilgrimage must, for Lewis, employ the language of the two-way quest.

All this is well described in John's contemplative vision just prior to his conversion, as he looks across a landscape of light. Many other travelers are present, and "as John looked round upon the people he saw that they were approaching some high walls and great gates. And, at the shape of the towers clustered above him, a memory, very deeply buried, stirred in his mind, first sweet, then uneasy, then spreading through the pool of his mind in widening circles of dismay . . . (164–65). He realizes that he is gazing upon those same towers which as a child he had seen on the summit of the Eastern mountains. These are the towers associated with the Landlord and his black hole. To consider Christian commitment is to involve oneself in community, in tradition, in the recovery of much one may have imagined he had forever outgrown. After his conversion, John is permitted a vision of his Island, beyond the western end of the world:

And the morning wind, blowing off-shore from it brought the sweet smell of the orchards to them, but rarefied and made faint with the thinness and purity of early air, and mixed with a little sharpness of the sea. But for John, because so many thousands looked at it with him, the pain and the longing were changed and all unlike what they had been of old: for humility was mixed with their wildness, and the sweetness came not with pride. . . . There was fear in it also, and hope: and it began to seem well to him that the Island should be different from his desires, and so different that, if he had known it, he would not have sought it. (171–72)

The gloss which Lewis provides sums up the mystery here. "The goal is, and is not, what he had always Desired" (172). The difficulty, of course, is that the traveler's two quests do not have identical objects. For a time the two quests are coincident, but a moment comes when they diverge. The one-way quest must ever lead beyond the world. The specifically Christian journey, for Lewis, returns man to the world. The paradox is set forth well in *Surprised by Joy.* "I had hoped that the heart of reality might be of such a kind that we can best symbolize it as a place; instead, I found it to be a Person."[15]

Vocation in and for the world, as distinguished from the more general calling beyond all boundaries, finds its end in the person of God incarnate, and so in the present joining of temporal and eternal. There is a this-worldly end, object of the Christian's two-way quest. John the pilgrim concedes this: "And at the very best it now seemed that the last of things was at least more like a person than a place, so that the deepest thirst within him was not adapted to the deepest nature of the world" (148). The deepest nature of the world is personal. This is "the last of *things*" (emphasis mine). But all things are finite, and desire reaches finally beyond all things. When Lewis returns to this difficult issue in *Surprised by Joy,* he assures us that his conversion meant that the subject of joy, or otherworldly longing, "has lost nearly all interest" for him (238). Yet the works he wrote after his autobiography, especially *Till We Have Faces,* do not wholly support that claim.

I think we may fairly sum up the complex matter in this fashion: longing or *Sehnsucht* in Lewis's works marks a one-way quest which leads dialectically and ineluctably beyond all finite things. The process of his conversion and subsequent repossession of this world is marked by primarily immediate ends. These ends, encompassed in the person of

Christ and in the Christian community functioning within the world, validate the world. They summon the pilgrim to his necessary regress.

On two points, I think, Lewis remains obscure to the last. First, he leaves his reader uncertain as to how *Sehnsucht* masked or served the more immediate ends of Christian vocation, which it apparently did in summoning John to the point at which his conversion could occur. Second, Lewis both affirms and denies the possibility of describing what lies beyond images and things. All images must be broken, and yet the imagery of goodness still attaches to the Transcendent Caller. Lewis, it may be, must retreat behind the same defense that Milton used. A mind finite as ours, but unfallen, would know good without knowing evil—would, that is, know being as good without making a differentiation that marks the merely finite.

A Coda

A brief qualification of the contrast I have been developing between Bunyan and Lewis is in order here. The discussion of one-way as distinguished from two-way quest points up how Lewis features the redemptive return to the world while Bunyan features the flight from the world. The danger of such a distinction is that it can imply Bunyan's neglect of the Christian's involvement in this world, and it is certainly true that the pilgrimage of the First Part of *The Pilgrim's Progress* is uncompromising in its rejection of worldly entanglements. We recall Christian and Faithful's response to the offerings of Vanity Fair, which include wives and children as well as honors and lands. Of course, in their very setting forth on pilgrimage they had already made the sort of decision which their resolute behavior in Vanity Fair reaffirms. To be a pilgrim is to acknowledge that the entire present world stands under the divine judgment.

The situation in the Second Part is more complex, however. All readers of the two parts have undoubtedly noted their markedly differing mood and tempo. Though both present flight and pilgrimage, the later journey does not abandon the present world with the same intransigence that we find in the earlier. Christiana and the others, like Feeble-mind and Ready-to-halt, who constitute the entourage of Great-heart are, in their diverse weaknesses, a clear figuration of the church as redemptive community, healing and strengthening the less advantaged of the world. Moreover, after Christiana is called across the River of Death we learn that her children and their families remain "for the Increase of the Church in that Place where they were for a time" (311). This closing scene, framed as it is by the sweet assurances of Eden and the unyielding certainty of death, is a resonant evocation of the church firmly planted in this world, mediating the hope in which both Christian and Christiana pursued their quests.

Admittedly, we do not see in either part of *The Pilgrim's Progress* the sort of counter-movement which the regress of Lewis's pilgrim constitutes. Yet the close of the Second Part makes it clear that Bunyan understands the Christian life to include a continuing redemptive role for the church in the world. Though Bunyan vexes the logic of his allegory a bit by this locating of Christian's family as an outpost on the very threshold of death and heaven (have *they* no pilgrimage to make, after all?), he chooses to avoid all those images of return which might compromise the meanings apparent in the spiritual progress as one-way quest.

Notes

Bunyan's Proverbial Language

1. See, for example, John Kelman, *The Road: A Study of John Bunyan's "Pilgrim's Progress"* (1912; rpt. Port Washington: Kennikat, 1970) 2: 17–18; Henri Talon, *John Bunyan: The Man and His Works,* trans. Barbara Wall (London: Rockliff, 1951) 126–27, 208–09, 221; Lynn Veach Sadler, *John Bunyan* (New York: Twayne, 1979) 42, 61, 70, 88. See also the notes in *The Miscellaneous Works of John Bunyan,* gen. ed. Roger Sharrock (Oxford: Clarendon, 1976–   ), hereafter cited parenthetically as "Oxford Bunyan"; as well as in John Bunyan, *The Pilgrim's Progress from This World to That Which Is to Come,* ed. James Blanton Wharey, 2nd ed. rev. Roger Sharrock (Oxford: Clarendon, 1960), hereafter cited parenthetically as *PP;* John Bunyan, *Grace Abounding to the Chief of Sinners,* ed. Roger Sharrock (Oxford: Clarendon, 1962), hereafter cited parenthetically as *GA;* and John Bunyan, *The Holy War,* ed. Roger Sharrock and James F. Forrest (Oxford: Clarendon, 1980).

2. *The Works of John Bunyan,* ed. George Offor, 3 vols. (Glasgow: Blackie and Son, 1856) 3: 30; hereafter cited parenthetically as "Offor."

3. Hussey, "The Humanism of John Bunyan," in *The Pelican Guide to English Literature: From Donne to Marvell,* ed. Boris Ford (Baltimore: Penguin, 1968) 3: 220–21.

4. Taylor, *The Proverb and Index* (1931; rpt. Hatboro, Pa.: Folklore Associates, 1962) 3. Subsequent references are to this text.

5. Whiting, "The Nature of the Proverb," *Harvard Studies and Notes in Philology,* 14 (1932), 302.

6. *The Rhetoric of Aristotle,* trans. R. C. Jebb, ed. J. E. Sandys (Cambridge: Cambridge Univ. Press, 1909) 176; quoted in Whiting, 277.

7. Whiting, 279–83.

8. Janet E. Heseltine, "Introduction," *The Oxford Dictionary of English Proverbs,* 2nd ed., ed. W. G. Smith, rev. Paul Harvey (Oxford: Clarendon, 1948) x. Subsequent references are to this text.

9. Owst, *Literature and Pulpit in Medieval England,* 2d rev. ed. (1961; rpt. New York: Barnes & Noble, 1966) 40–46.

10. Wilson, "English Proverbs and Dictionaries of Proverbs," *The Library* 4th ser. 26 (1945): 64–67.

11. *The Arte of English Poesie by George Puttenham,* ed. Gladys D. Willcock and Alice Walker (Cambridge, Mass.: Harvard Univ. Press, 1936) 154. However, Rosemund Tuve, *Elizabethan and Metaphysical Imagery* (Chicago: Univ. of Chicago Press, 1947) 284–99, has shown that figurative language went far beyond mere ornamentation for the Elizabethans and Jacobeans. An image was an argument. Richard Weaver, *The Ethics of Rhetoric* (Chicago: Henry Regnery, 1953) 57, amplifies by reminding us that those who argue from similitude also have "a belief in a oneness of the world, which causes all correspondence to have probative value. Proponents of this view tend to look toward some final, transcendental unity, and as we might expect, this type of argument is used widely by poets and religionists. John Bunyan used it constantly; so did Emerson."

12. Peacham, *The Garden of Eloquence* (1593; facs. rpt. Gainesville: Scholars' Facsimiles & Reprints, 1954) 86. Subsequent references are to this text.

13. Howell, *Lexicon Tetraglotton* (1660) 2.

14. Gascoigne, "Dulce bellum inexpertis," in the *Posies* (1572); quoted in George Boas, *Vox Populi: Essays in the History of an Idea* (Baltimore: Johns Hopkins Univ. Press, 1969) 27.

15. Joan Marie Lechner, *Renaissance Concepts of the Commonplace* (New York: Pageant, 1962) 211.

16. See Mario Praz, *Studies in Seventeenth Century Imagery,* 2 vols. (London: Warburg Institute Studies, 1939–47).

17. For example, M. P. Tilley, *Elizabethan Proverb Lore in Lyly's "Euphues" and in Pettie's "Petite Palace," with Parallels from Shakespeare* (New York: Macmillan, 1926); F. P. Wilson, "Shakespeare and the Diction of Common Life," *Proceedings of the British Academy* 27 (1941): 167–97; M. P. Tilley, *A Dictionary of the Proverbs in England in the Sixteenth and Seventeenth Centuries* (Ann Arbor: Univ. of Michigan Press, 1950); Archer Taylor, "Proverbs in the Plays of Beaumont and Fletcher," *Southern Folklore Quarterly* 24.2 (1960): 77–100; Archer Taylor, "Proverbs and Proverbial Phrases in the Plays of John Marston," *Southern Folklore Quarterly* 24.3 (1960): 193–216; Archer Taylor, "Proverbs and Proverbial Phrases in Roger L'Estrange, *The Fables of Aesop,*" *Southern Folklore Quarterly* 26.3 (1962): 232–45; Richard Levin, "Proverbial Phrases in the Titles of Thomas Middleton's Plays," *Southern Folklore Quarterly* 28.2 (1964): 142–45; Charles G. Smith, *Spenser's Proverb Lore, with Special Reference to His Use of the Sententiae of Leonard Culman and Publius Syrus* (Cambridge, Mass.: Harvard Univ. Press, 1970); and R. W. Dent, *Shakespeare's Proverbial Language* (Berkeley: Univ. of California Press, 1981).

18. William Haller, *The Rise of Puritanism* (New York: Columbia Univ. Press, 1938) 23.

19. Dent, *The Plaine Mans Path-way to Heauen* (London, 1607; 1st published 1601) 151–53, hereafter cited parenthetically as "Dent." The italics, which are mine, underscore proverbs catalogued as follows in M. P. Tilley, *A Dictionary of Proverbs in England in the Sixteenth and Seventeenth Centuries:* T391, B768; O25, H532, A112, S78, H474, C915,

W123, B50, and P45. All subsequent catalogue numbers given in the text conform to Tilley.

20. Sharrock, *John Bunyan* (London: Hutchinsons, 1954) 112. Subsequent references are to this text.

21. Ricks, "Short Is Sweet," *London Review of Books* 3–16 February 1983: 13.

22. See Ralph Lever, *The Arte of Reason, Rightly Termed Witcraft; Teaching a Perfect Way to Argue and Dispute* (London, 1573) 197; quoted in Sister Miriam Joseph, *Shakespeare's Use of the Arts of Language* (New York: Columbia Univ. Press, 1947) 309.

23. Richardson, *English Preachers and Preaching, 1640–1670* (New York: Macmillan, 1928) 74; and Mitchell, *English Pulpit Oratory from Andrewes to Tillotson* (1932; rpt. New York: Russell & Russell, 1962) 101.

24. Weaver: 25, 7, 17, 18.

25. Tindall, *John Bunyan: Mechanick Preacher* (New York: Columbia Univ. Press, 1934) 50.

26. Sharrock, *John Bunyan*, 47.

27. For an illuminating comparison of the elected Christian and the gifted folktale hero whose abilities to solve riddles indicates his affinity with the "underlying order of things," see Nick Davis, "The Problem of Misfortune in *The Pilgrim's Progress*" in *The Pilgrim's Progress: Critical and Historical Views,* ed. Vincent Newey (Totowa: Barnes & Noble, 1980) 182–204. This essay and the one by David Seed in the same collection, "Dialogue and Debate in *The Pilgrim's Progress*," 69–90, properly insist upon the primacy of one's verbal skills as the indicator of spiritual stature or election in Bunyan's allegory.

28. Although Faithful calls the last sentence in this passage a "proverb," neither Tilley nor any of the other dictionaries confirm it.

Bunyan's Satire and Its Biblical Sources

1. Brean S. Hammond, "*The Pilgrim's Progress:* Satire and Social Comment," in *The Pilgrim's Progress: Critical and Historical Views,* ed. Vincent Newey (Totowa, N.J.: Barnes & Noble, 1980) 124.

2. A. Richard Dutton, " 'Interesting but tough': Reading *The Pilgrim's Progress,*" *Studies in English Literature* 18 (1978): 447; Elizabeth Adeney, "Bunyan: A Unified Vision?" *Critical Review* 17 (1974): 103. Adeney focuses on comic rather than satiric aspects of *The Pilgrim's Progress.* Henri Talon's *John Bunyan: The Man and his Works,* trans. Barbara Wall (London: Rockliff, 1951) is sensitive to Bunyan's humor but does not discuss it in detail; see 205, 207–08, 219, 319. Except in connection with the essays of Hammond and Adeney, satire and comedy are seldom mentioned in the recent annotated bibliography by James F. Forrest and Richard Lee Greaves, *John Bunyan: A Reference Guide* (Boston: G. K. Hall, 1982), and Greaves does not allude to this side of Bunyan in his retrospective article, "Bunyan Through the Centuries: Some Reflections," *English Studies* 64 (1983): 113–21.

3. For a discussion of how Bunyan's mind worked with biblical texts, see my article,

"Bunyan's Special Talent: Biblical Texts as 'Events' in *Grace Abounding* and *The Pilgrim's Progress,*" *English Literary Renaissance* 11 (1981): 329–43.

4. John Bunyan, *The Pilgrim's Progress,* ed. James Blanton Wharey, 2nd ed. rev. Roger Sharrock (Oxford: Clarendon, 1960) 10. Subsequent references are to this text.

5. Obstinate's words recall Proverbs 26.16: "The sluggard is wiser in his own conceit than seven men that can render a reason." However, the real sluggard is Obstinate himself, who—rather than going on pilgrimage—is choosing to remain in the City of Destruction.

6. Bunyan's margin on p. 13 cites Titus 1.2 as an ultimate guarantee that the biblical citations in his story possess a truth older than that of any worldly authorities. In that verse Paul greets Titus "In hope of eternal life, which God, that cannot lie, promised before the world began."

7. All statements in this paper about biblical sources and the frequency with which certain words occur in the Bible are based on Robert Young's *Analytical Concordance to the Bible,* 22nd Am. ed. (New York: Funk & Wagnalls, 1955). This is a concordance to the King James or Authorized Version, which Bunyan almost always prefers. A modern work like Young's shows how often Bunyan reproduces the precise language of particular biblical passages.

8. The pilgrim's wary attitude toward Atheist reflects Bunyan's own experience with the problems of unbelief. See *Grace Abounding,* ed. Roger Sharrock (Oxford: Clarendon, 1962) 31, 102.

9. The importance of the eleventh and twelfth chapters of Hebrews in the creation of *The Pilgrim's Progress* is discussed in my article, "Bunyan and the Epistle to the Hebrews: His Source for the Idea of Pilgrimage in *The Pilgrim's Progress,*" *Studies in Philology* 79 (1982): 279–96.

10. Since Bunyan was so reticent about his extra-biblical reading, it is difficult to judge just how much his treatment of the world's three lusts owes to Christian tradition. From the early Fathers on, commentators attempted to interpret and harmonize the 1 John passage with Adam and Eve's temptations—which were often seen as threefold (Genesis 3)—and with the three temptations of Jesus (Matthew 4 and Luke 4; see Donald R. Howard, *The Three Temptations: Medieval Man in Search of the World* [Princeton: Princeton Univ. Press, 1966] 42–75). Bunyan may well have been in touch with pre-Reformation Christianity orally, through the conservative preaching that he heard in Bedfordshire (G. R. Owst, *Literature and Pulpit in Medieval England* [Cambridge: Cambridge Univ. Press, 1933] 97–109). By having Adam the first offer Faithful his three daughters ("*The lust of the flesh, the lust of the eyes, and the pride of life*"), Bunyan associates the world's three lusts with the heritage of sin from Adam's fall (69). However, he does not make a point-by-point comparison to the Genesis 3 account or to the three temptations of Jesus—although, as noted below, in the Vanity Fair episode he does dramatize the devil's offer of the kingdoms of the world (89). In the scene leading up to Christian's entrance at the Wicket Gate, Bunyan comes close to invoking another traditional tripartite formula—the world, the flesh, and the devil; Christian reflects that the arguments of Mr. Worldly-Wiseman flow "only from the flesh," and Good-Will pulls him in through the gate to escape the arrows of Beelzebub (24–25). But devils appear only

briefly in *The Pilgrim's Progress,* while the flesh is usually presented among the other attractions of the world.

11. The pun on Faithful's name is used by Evangelist in anticipation of the event (87).

12. The names of By-ends' kindred suggest at least two pertinent biblical references. The phrase "smooth man" occurs in the King James Version only in the description of Jacob, who is cheating Esau out of his birthright (Genesis 27.11). By-ends' parson, Mr. Two-tongues, recalls Paul's warning about the conduct of clergy in the early church: "Likewise must the deacons be grave, not doubletongued, not given to much wine, not greedy of filthy lucre" (1 Timothy 3.8).

13. Mr. Hold-the-World's words contain a heavy irony of which he is presumably unconscious. His opening phrase is taken from the instructions of Jesus to his disciples:

> Behold, I send you forth as sheep in the midst of wolves: be ye therefore wise as serpents, and harmless as doves. But beware of men: for they will deliver you up to the councils, and they will scourge you in their synagogues; and ye shall be brought before governors and kings for my sake, for a testimony against them and the Gentiles. (Matthew 10.16–18)

Mr. Hold-the-World is not likely to meet this sort of fate, but the description perfectly sums up the recent martyrdom of Faithful.

14. Ignorance has received particular praise from readers who have not appreciated Bunyan's book as a whole. Roger Sharrock mentions that "James Foster, an enlightened eighteenth-century Dissenting Preacher, used to say that none of the characters in *The Pilgrim's Progress* spoke sense except Ignorance." Sharrock, *John Bunyan* (London: Hutchinsons, 1954) 92–93. When Alfred Noyes wrote an attack on *The Pilgrim's Progress* at the time of the tricentennial anniversary of Bunyan's birth, he also defended this character: "Study the fate of poor Mr. Ignorance who, both in his conversation with these vain and boastful pilgrims, Christian and Hopeful, and in his unassuming approach (without trumpets) to the Celestial City, strikes one as a far better Christian and a far more honest man." Noyes, "Bunyan—a Revaluation," *The Bookman* (London) 75 (October 1928): 14. As Roland Mushat Frye has suggested, Ignorance may indeed be intended as a portrait of the Christian moralist who "refuses to acknowledge that he is himself not good, but a sinner." Frye, *God, Man, and Satan: Patterns of Christian Thought and Life in Paradise Lost, Pilgrim's Progress, and the Great Theologians* (Princeton, N.J.: Princeton Univ. Press, 1960) 117. If so, Bunyan has failed to marshal his biblical texts in ways that have convincingly chastised many other would-be pilgrims. For some observers, the lash of his satire has recoiled upon him.

15. The names of these four characters—Bats-eyes, Inconsiderate, Light-mind, and Know-nothing—seem to be an ironic recollection of a verse in Isaiah. The prophet is looking forward to a time when all of Israel will understand God's actions: "That they may see, and know, and consider, and understand together, that the hand of the Lord hath done this, and the Holy One of Israel hath created it" (41.20). Bunyan's scene plainly implies that the time has not yet arrived.

16. "Bubble" is not a biblical word, but Roger Sharrock notes that in Quarles's *Emblemes* it is a frequent image for the world's vanity (351).

17. For a definitive study of Bunyan's later views about the separatist church, as they are incorporated in the Second Part of *The Pilgrim's Progress,* see John R. Knott, Jr., "Bunyan and the Holy Community," *Studies in Philology* 80 (1983): 200–25.

Bunyan's Scriptural Acts

Excerpts from this paper were read, in preliminary forms, at conventions of the Modern Language Association, 27–30 December 1982, in Los Angeles, and 27–30 December 1984, in Washington, D.C.

1. *A Sermon Preached before the Honourable House of Commons, at Westminster, March 31, 1647* (Cambridge, 1647) 56–57. In quotations from early printed sources, I have regularized *i, j, u, v,* and *w,* and have expanded abbreviations to conform to modern usage.

2. This is the form of the title in the list of books licensed for publication on 18 February 1678; see Geoffrey F. Nuttall, "The Heart of *The Pilgrim's Progress,*" in *Reformation Principle and Practice: Essays in Honour of Arthur Geoffrey Dickens,* ed. Peter Newman Brooks (London: Scolar Press, 1980) 229. Hereafter quotations from *The Pilgrim's Progress* are from the edition of J. B. Wharey, 2nd ed. rev. Roger Sharrock (Oxford: Clarendon, 1960). References given in the text are usually preceded by the abbreviation *PP.*

3. *The Literary Culture of Nonconformity in Later Seventeenth-Century England* (Leicester: Leicester Univ. Press; Athens: Univ. of Georgia Press, 1987).

4. See Dayton Haskin, "*The Pilgrim's Progress* in the Context of Bunyan's Dialogue with the Radicals," *Harvard Theological Review* 77 (1984): 73–94.

5. See Christopher Hill, *The World Turned Upside Down: Radical Ideas during the English Revolution* (New York: Viking, 1972) 328–31; and Hill, "John Bunyan and the English Revolution," *Marxist Perspectives* 7.2 (1979): 8–26.

6. Some especially significant recent studies treating *The Pilgrim's Progress* as fiction are the following: Barry Qualls, *The Secular Pilgrims of Victorian Fiction: The Novel as Book of Life* (Cambridge: Cambridge Univ. Press, 1982); Carolyn Van Dyke, *The Fiction of Truth: Structures of Meaning in Narrative and Dramatic Allegory* (Ithaca: Cornell Univ. Press, 1985), chap. 4; Leopold Damrosch, Jr., *God's Plot and Man's Stories: Studies in the Fictional Imagination from Milton to Fielding* (Chicago: Univ. of Chicago Press, 1985); and Michael McKeon, *The Origins of the English Novel 1600–1740* (Baltimore: Johns Hopkins Univ. Press, 1987) chap. 8.

7. Of course, *The Pilgrim's Progress* is filled with promises and threats. This is in fact one of the principal features of Bunyan's assimilation of the Bible to the romance tradition, a "source" for English fiction recently reexamined by McKeon; see especially chaps. 1, 7, and 8. But my point is that Bunyan gave up seeing the Bible almost exclusively in terms of promises and threats (see *Grace Abounding*) and came to see it primarily as recording something more like *res gestae.*

8. See Hill, *World Turned Upside Down,* 320–26.

9. See, for example, Robert Greville, Lord Brooke, *A Discourse Opening the Nature of*

that Episcopacie, Which Is Exercised in England (1642) 2. 7. 116; quoted from the fascimile in *Tracts on Liberty in the Puritan Revolution, 1638–1647*, ed. William Haller, 3 vols. (New York: Columbia Univ. Press, 1933) 2: 160.

10. *Scripture a Perfect Rule for Church-Government: Delivered in a Sermon at Margarets Westminster, before sundry of the House of Commons* (1643) 34.

11. "Truth Lifting Up Its Head," in *Works*, ed. George H. Sabine (1941; rpt. New York: Russell & Russell, 1965) 123.

12. Unless otherwise noted, biblical quotations are from the Authorized Version.

13. *A Paraphrase and Annotations Upon all the Books of the New Testament*, 2nd ed. (1659) 1–12.

14. *The Journal of George Fox*, rev. ed. John L. Nickalls (London: Religious Society of Friends, 1975) 8, 33, 115.

15. *The Seventeenth Century Background* (1934; rpt. Garden City: Doubleday, 1953) 72.

16. *Grace Abounding to the Chief of Sinners*, ed. Roger Sharrock (Oxford: Clarendon, 1962) 66; emphasis in original. Subsequent references are to this text.

17. The phrase "methodically humble" derives from Geoffrey Hartman, "The Interpreter: A Self-Analysis," in *The Fate of Reading* (Chicago: Univ. of Chicago Press, 1975) 3–19.

18. Working along different lines, attempting to trace the development of the novel out of Puritan fictions, Damrosch (especially in chap. 2) depicts Bunyan as a writer not yet able to break free of myth, though in the experience of writing *The Pilgrim's Progress* he began to glimpse the autonomy of fictional representations.

19. *John Bunyan*, Courtenay Studies in Reformation Theology, 2 (Abingdon, Eng.: Sutton Courtenay, 1969) 23. On Bunyan's interpretive procedures in relation to those of Calvin, see Thomas H. Luxon, "Calvin and Bunyan on Word and Image: Is There a Text in Interpreter's House?" *English Literary Renaissance*, 18 (1988): 438–59.

20. On "openings," see Georgia B. Christopher, "The Verbal Gate to Paradise: Adam's 'Literary Experience' in Book X of *Paradise Lost*," *PMLA* 90 (1975): 73–74, 77. Cf. also her book, *Milton and the Science of the Saints* (Princeton: Princeton Univ. Press, 1982) 4, 136ff., et passim.

21. See *The Commentaries of M. John Calvin upon the Actes of the Apostles, Faithfully translated out of Latine into English for the great profite of our countrie-men, By Christopher Fetherstone* (London, 1585), n.p. Subsequent page references are to this text.

22. On Calvin's understanding of the Incarnation, see Kilian McDonnell, *John Calvin, the Church and the Eucharist* (Princeton: Princeton Univ. Press, 1967).

23. On the doctrine of accommodation in the Renaissance, see C. A. Patrides, "*Paradise Lost* and the Theory of Accommodation," in *Bright Essence: Studies in Milton's Theology*, ed. William B. Hunter (Salt Lake City: Univ. of Utah Press, 1971) 159–63.

24. Mislabeled 70, the page number should read 54.

25. Page 205. Cf. Bunyan's remarks in The Conclusion (#4) to *Grace Abounding*, 102.

26. See *Confessions*, 8.12. Cf. Christopher, *Milton and the Science of the Saints*, 50–51.

27. Cudworth, 3. The text for the sermon was 1 John 2.3–4.

28. See *Complete Prose Works of John Milton*, gen. ed. Don M. Wolfe, 8 vols. (New

Haven: Yale Univ. Press, 1953–82) 2: 550. Milton's interest in the prophecy of Joel 2.28 is discussed by William Kerrigan, *The Prophetic Milton* (Charlottesville: Univ. Press of Virginia, 1974) 171–74.

29. *A Survey of the Spirituall Antichrist, Opening the Secrets of Familisme and Antinomianisme in the Antichristian Doctrine of John Saltmarsh, and Will. Del,* 1: 198–99, 218–19, 228, 242–43, et passim.

30. See Geoffrey F. Nuttall, " 'Unity with the Creation': George Fox and the Hermetic Philosophy," in *The Puritan Spirit: Essays and Addresses* (London: Epworth, 1967) 194–203.

31. See Dayton Haskin, "The Burden of Interpretation in *The Pilgrim's Progress,*" *Studies in Philology* 79 (1982): 256–78.

32. But see U. Milo Kaufmann, *The Pilgrim's Progress and Traditions in Puritan Meditation* (New Haven: Yale Univ. Press, 1966) and Dean Freiday, *The Bible—Its Criticism, Interpretation and Use—in 16th and 17th Century England,* Catholic and Quaker Studies No. 4 (Pittsburgh: s.n., 1979) 69–75. See also the recent Univ. of Chicago dissertation by Thomas H. Luxon, "Puritan Allegory and Bunyan's *Pilgrim's Progress*" (1984), especially 165ff.; John R. Knott, Jr., " 'Thou must live upon my Word': Bunyan and the Bible," in *John Bunyan: Conventicle and Parnassus: Tercentenary Essays,* ed. N. H. Keeble (Oxford: Clarendon, 1988), 153–70.

33. Though he does not treat Bunyan, Hans Frei discusses this model for thinking about scriptural texts in *The Eclipse of Biblical Narrative: A Study in Eighteenth and Nineteenth Century Hermeneutics* (New Haven: Yale Univ. Press, 1974) 2.

34. See Frei, chaps. 1–2.

35. See "The Authors Apology for his Book," *PP,* 7.

36. Cf. C. P. M. Jones, "The Epistle to the Hebrews and the Lucan Writings," in *Studies of the Gospels: Essays in Memory of R. H. Lightfoot,* ed. D. E. Nineham (Oxford: Basil Blackwell, 1955) 113–43. Jones observes that in his *Ecclesiastical History* (part 6, 14), Eusebius says that Clement of Alexandria had noted that Hebrews and Acts have the same complexion or style, and he averred that Luke must have translated into Greek a letter that Paul had originally written in Hebrew. Bunyan seems to have understood implicitly what Clement had argued for explicitly.

37. See "Notes on *The Pilgrim's Progress,*" in *The Complete Works of Samuel Taylor Coleridge,* ed. W. G. T. Shedd, 7 vols. (New York: Harper, 1853–84) 5: 257.

38. " 'With Great Delight': The Song of Solomon in *The Pilgrim's Progress,*" *English Studies* 68 (1987): 220–27.

39. "The Way and the Ways of Puritan Story: Biblical Patterns in Bunyan and His Contemporaries," *English* 33 (1984): 209–32; incorporated, in revised form, into *The Literary Culture of Nonconformity* as chap. 9.

40. *The Geneva Bible: A facsimile of the 1560 edition,* ed. Lloyd E. Berry (Madison: Univ. of Wisconsin Press, 1969) 54^r.

41. *The Miscellaneous Works of John Bunyan,* gen. ed. Roger Sharrock (Oxford: Clarendon, 1976) 1: 19. Subsequent page references are to this text.

42. See "The Authors Apology," 1. Cf. John R. Knott, Jr., "Bunyan's Gospel Day: A

Reading of *The Pilgrim's Progress,*" *English Literary Renaissance* 3 (1973): 443–61; incorporated in *The Sword of the Spirit* (Chicago: Univ. of Chicago Press, 1980) 131–63.

43. Cf. Rebecca Beal, "*Grace Abounding to the Chief of Sinners:* John Bunyan's Pauline Epistle," *Studies in English Literature* 21 (1981): 147–60.

44. Stranahan has counted nine citations; see "Bunyan and the Epistle to the Hebrews: His Source for the Idea of Pilgrimage in *The Pilgrim's Progress,*" *Studies in Philology* 79 (1982): 280n.

45. *Miscellaneous Works* 1: 79.

46. *A Paraphrase on the New Testament, with Notes, Doctrinal and Practical,* 3d ed. (London: T. Parkhurst, 1701), headnote to "The Acts of the Holy Apostles."

47. See Brainerd P. Stranahan, "Bunyan and the Epistle to the Hebrews," 279–96, and "Bunyan's Special Talent: Biblical Texts as 'Events' in *Grace Abounding* and *The Pilgrim's Progress,*" *English Literary Renaissance* 11 (1981): 329–43.

48. See Stranahan's count, "Bunyan and the Epistle to the Hebrews," 280n.

49. For a detailed treatment, see Dayton Haskin, "Bunyan, Luther, and the Struggle with Belatedness in *Grace Abounding,*" *University of Toronto Quarterly* 50 (1980–81): 300–13.

50. Cf. Felicity A. Nussbaum, " 'By These Words I Was Sustained': Bunyan's *Grace Abounding,*" *ELH* 49 (1982): 18–34; especially 26–27. On Bunyan's obsession with Esau, see 24–25.

51. See A. F. Scott Pearson, *Thomas Cartwright and Elizabethan Puritanism 1535–1603* (Cambridge: Cambridge Univ. Press, 1925) 25ff.

52. On the concept of "inaugurated eschatology," see Joachim Jeremias, in *The Parables of Jesus,* 2nd rev. ed. (New York: Scribner's, 1972), especially 115ff. While the seventeenth-century Quakers emphasized a "realized eschatology" that left little to be accomplished in the future, Bunyan generally thought in terms of this "inaugurated eschatology," which allows more scope to what has "not yet" happened. On Bunyan's marginal glosses, see Valentine Cunningham, "Glossing and Glozing: Bunyan and Allegory," in *John Bunyan: Conventicle and Parnassus,* ed. Keeble, 217–40.

53. See C. K. Barrett, "Stephen and the Son of Man," in *Apophoreta: Festschrift für Ernst Haenchen,* ed. W. Schneemelcher, Beihefte zur Zeitschrift für die neutestamentliche Wissenschaft, 30 (Berlin: Töplemann, 1964) 35ff.

54. *The Geneva Bible: a facsimile of the 1560 edition,* 2^r.

55. *The Oxford English Dictionary* includes among the senses of *gate* a "way, road, or path" and a "going, journey [or] course." For the latter definition it cites an example from 1677.

56. *Self-Consuming Artifacts: The Experience of Seventeenth-Century Literature* (Berkeley: Univ. of California Press, 1972), 229.

57. See Roland Mushat Frye, *God, Man, and Satan: Patterns of Christian Thought and Life in Paradise Lost, Pilgrim's Progress, and the Great Theologians* (Princeton: Princeton Univ. Press, 1960) 147; Henri Talon, *John Bunyan: The Man and His Works,* trans. Barbara Wall (Cambridge: Harvard Univ. Press, 1951) 149. Cf. John R. Knott, Jr., "Bunyan and the Holy Community," *Studies in Philology* 80 (1983): 220.

58. See I. Howard Marshall, *Luke: Historian and Theologian* (Grand Rapids: Zondervan, 1970) 153, 214.

59. Cf. Acts 19.23. See S. V. McCasland, " 'The Way,' " *Journal of Biblical Literature* 77 (1958): 222–30.

60. See David Gill, "Observations on the Lukan Travel Narrative and Some Related Passages," *Harvard Theological Review* 63 (1970): 199–221.

61. The distinctive nature of the Lukan writings is helpfully discussed by Charles H. Giblin, "Discerning Gospel Genre," *Thought* 47 (1972): 225–52.

62. *The Geneva Bible,* 54^r.

63. See Roger Thomas, "Comprehension and Indulgence," in *From Uniformity to Unity, 1662–1962,* ed. Geoffrey F. Nuttall and Owen Chadwick (London: SPCK, 1962) 189–253. Cf. Knott, "Bunyan and the Holy Community," 207, 223–24.

64. See Krister Stendahl, "The Apostle Paul and the Introspective Conscience of the West," *Harvard Theological Review* 56 (1963); rpt. in *Paul Among Jews and Gentiles* (Philadelphia: Fortress, 1976) 85–86; see also "Sources and Critiques" in the same volume, 125–33.

65. See C. F. Evans, " 'Speeches' in Acts," *Mélanges bibliques en hommage au R. P. Béda Rigaux,* ed. Albert Descamps and André de Halleux (Gembloux: Duculot, 1970) 287–302; and Jacques Dupont, "Les Discours Missionnaires des Acts des Apôtres," *Revue Biblique* 69 (1962): 37–60.

66. Cf. N. H. Keeble, "Christiana's Key: The Unity of *The Pilgrim's Progress,*" in *The Pilgrim's Progress: Critical and Historical Views,* ed. Vincent Newey (Totowa: Barnes & Noble, 1980) 1–20.

67. See Luther's *Lectures on Genesis, Chapters 6–14,* in *Luther's Works,* gen. ed. Jaroslav Pelikan and Helmut T. Lehmann, 55 vols. (St. Louis: Concordia; Philadelphia: Fortress, 1955–   ) 2: 179.

68. This incident has recently been studied by George Butler, "The Iron Cage of Despair and 'The Unpardonable Sin' in *The Pilgrim's Progress,*" *English Language Notes* 25 (1987): 34–38.

69. John's Gospel makes it explicit that memory plays this important a role when it recounts an incident from Jesus' life and then intrudes a post-resurrection reinterpretation into the narrative: "his disciples remembered that he had said this unto them; and they believed the Scripture, and the word which Jesus had said" (2.22). Cf. John Ashton, *Why Were the Gospels Written?* (Notre Dame: Fides, 1973) 82–84.

70. *Self-Consuming Artifacts,* 246, 250ff.

71. Cf. William York Tindall, *John Bunyan: Mechanick Preacher* (New York: Columbia Univ. Press, 1934) 190.

72. *Grace Abounding,* 84. Bunyan's tendency to see Foxe's *Book of Martyrs* as a supplement to the Scriptures was hardly unique; see, for instance, Stephen Marshall's sermon before both houses of Parliament after the victory at Naseby, 19 June 1645: *A Sacred Record to be Made of Gods Mercies to Zion* (London, 1645) 35–36. (Page 36 is mislabeled "63.")

73. Cf. McKeon's argument that "Christian's progress recapitulates the rise of the new gentility of early modern England" (311).

Allegory as Sacred Sport: Manipulation
of the Reader in Spenser and Bunyan

1. Richard Baxter, *A Christian Directory* (London, 1673) 97. Cf. John Milton, *Paradise Lost,* 5: 95–128.

2. Thomas Goodwin, *The Vanitie of Thoughts Discovered* (London, 1650) 14.

3. Thomas Hobbes, *Leviathan,* ed. Michael Oakeshott (Oxford: Basil Blackwell, 1955) 15.

4. Rymer, preface to the translation of Rapin's *Reflections on Aristotle's Treatise of Poesie* (1674); Dryden, preface to "Annus Mirabilis" (1666); Pope, "Essay on Criticism," line 82. These are cited in James Sutherland, *A Preface to Eighteenth Century Poetry* (Oxford: Clarendon, 1948) 7–9.

5. Sir Philip Sidney, *An Apology for Poetry, or The Defence of Poesy,* ed. Geoffrey Shepherd (London: T. Nelson, 1965) 104.

6. "Of Education," in John Milton, *Complete Poems and Major Prose,* ed. Merritt Y. Hughes (New York: Odyssey, 1957) 631. Subsequent references are to this text.

7. William Langland, *The Book Concerning Piers the Plowman,* ed. Rachel Attwater (London: Dent, 1957) 72.

8. V. A. Kolve, *The Play Called Corpus Christi* (Stanford: Stanford Univ. Press, 1965) 32.

9. Paul A. Olson, "*A Midsummer Night's Dream* and the Meaning of Court Marriage," *ELH* 24 (1957): 114.

10. *Comus,* 785f., in Hughes, 108. Note that line 784 echoes 1 Corinthians 2.9.

11. William Wordsworth, *The Prelude or Growth of a Poet's Mind,* ed. Ernest de Selincourt, 2nd ed. rev. Helen Darbishire (Oxford: Clarendon, 1965) 87.

12. C. S. Lewis, *The Allegory of Love, a Study in Medieval Tradition* (Oxford: Clarendon, 1936) chap. 7.

13. Charles Lamb, "Sanity of True Genius," *The Last Essays of Elia,* ed. Edmund Blunden (London: Oxford Univ. Press, 1935) 46–49.

14. See, for instance, W. L. Renwick's remarks on the need for an intensive study of Spenser's language in *Edmund Spenser,* R. A. Neil Lecture (Cambridge: Cambridge Univ. Press, 1952), passim.

15. All quotations from *The Faerie Queene* are taken from the text ed. A. C. Hamilton (London: Longman, 1980).

16. On the reader's involvement in the Cave of Mammon episode, see Harry Berger, Jr., *The Allegorical Temper: Vision and Reality in Book II of Spenser's Faerie Queene* (New Haven: Yale Univ. Press, 1957) 3–38. Mr. Berger holds that the allegory here "sets up a kind of tension between what the hero knows and what the reader knows" (37), the point of the same being a contrast between the reader's reaction to Mammon's temptations and Guyon's lack of reaction.

17. Milton, *Areopagitica,* in Hughes, 729.

18. Lewis, 325–33.

19. *The Pilgrim's Progress,* ed. James Blanton Wharey, 2nd ed. rev. Roger Sharrock (Oxford: Clarendon, 1960) 3–4. Subsequent references are to this text.

20. Johan Huizinga, *Homo Ludens: A Study of the Play Element in Culture* (London: Maurice Temple Smith, 1970), 22–24, 32.

21. *The Holy War*, ed. Roger Sharrock and James F. Forrest (Oxford: Clarendon, 1980) 116.

22. On the significance of Bunyan's choice of form, see James F. Forrest, "Vision, Form, and the Imagination in the Second Part of *The Pilgrim's Progress* (1684)," *The Journal of Narrative Technique* 13.2 (1983): 109–16.

23. *The Works of John Bunyan*, ed. George Offor, 3 vols. (Glasgow: Blackie and Son, 1856) 3: 398.

24. G. B. Shaw, *Dramatic Opinions and Essays*, 2 vols. (London: Archibald Constable, 1907) 2: 144.

25. Wolfgang Iser, *The Implied Reader: Patterns of Communication in Prose Fiction from Bunyan to Beckett* (Baltimore: Johns Hopkins Univ. Press, 1974) 4.

26. Stanley E. Fish, *Self-Consuming Artifacts: The Experience of Seventeenth-Century Literature* (Berkeley: Univ. of California Press, 1972) 226.

27. Milton, *Areopagitica*, in Hughes, 728.

Falling into Allegory: The "Apology" to *The Pilgrim's Progress* and Bunyan's Scriptural Methodology

1. See *The Pilgrim's Progress As Originally Published by John Bunyan, Being a Fac-simile Reproduction of the First Edition* (1875; rpt. Old Woking, Surrey: Gresham, 1978). For the title pages of subsequent editions see James B. Wharey's edition, rev. Roger Sharrock (Oxford: Clarendon, 1960).

2. In the seventeenth century, titles that exploited the pilgrimage metaphor became the marker for discursive religious tracts. To cite just a few examples: Christopher Lever, *The Holy Pilgrime, Leading the Way to Heaven. Or A Divine Direction in the Way of Life* (London, 1618); David Lindsay, *The Godly Mans Journey: Containing Ten Several Treatises* (London, 1625); and M. R., *The Pilgrim's Pass to the New Jerusalem: Or a Serious CHRISTIAN his Enquiries after Heaven* (London, 1659).

3. John Bunyan, *The Pilgrim's Progress from This World to That Which Is to Come*, ed. James B. Wharey, 2nd ed. rev. Roger Sharrock (Oxford: Clarendon, 1960) 1, line 9. All quotations, except where noted, follow this edition and will subsequently be cited by page or line number in the body of the text.

4. Henri Talon, *John Bunyan: The Man and His Works*, trans. Barbara Wall (London: Rockliff, 1951) 217; Roger Sharrock, "Personal Vision and the Puritan Tradition in Bunyan," *Hibbert Journal* 56 (1957–58): 47.

5. William York Tindall, *John Bunyan: Mechanick Preacher* (New York: Columbia Univ. Press, 1934) 43.

6. U. Milo Kaufmann, *The Pilgrim's Progress and Traditions in Puritan Meditation* (New Haven: Yale Univ. Press, 1966) 8.

7. See also John R. Knott, Jr. *The Sword of the Spirit: Puritan Responses to the Bible* (Chicago: Univ. of Chicago Press, 1980) 139–40.

8. Lawrence A. Sasek, *The Literary Temper of the English Puritans* (Baton Rouge: Louisiana State Univ. Press, 1961) 64.

9. George Puttenham, *The Arte of English Poesie by George Puttenham,* ed. Gladys D. Willock and Alice Walker (Cambridge: Harvard Univ. Press, 1936) 186.

10. See "An Advertisement to the Reader" appended to *The Holy War,* in *The Works of John Bunyan,* ed. George Offor (Glasgow: Blackie and Son, 1856) 3: 374. There Bunyan responds to readers who felt that the caliber of *The Pilgrim's Progress* far exceeded what a mechanick preacher was capable of and who had apparently accused him of actual plagiarism, by proclaiming that "Manner and matter too was all mine own" (line 15). Bunyan's status dictated his adoption of a naive persona:

> It came from mine own heart, so to my head,
> And thence into my fingers trickled;
> Then to my pen, from whence immediately
> On paper I did dribble it daintily. (lines 11–14)

As this passage makes clear, Bunyan himself is largely responsible for the belief that he "unconsciously" produced a literary masterpiece.

11. Kenneth B. Murdock, *Literature and Theology in Colonial New England* (Cambridge: Harvard Univ. Press, 1956) 49.

12. John Steadman, *The Lamb and the Elephant: Ideal Imitation and the Context of Renaissance Allegory* (San Marino: Huntington Library, 1974) 72.

13. For the changes in typeface which emphasize the change of speaker, I follow the third edition (1679), where it first occurred. Wharey and Sharrock both print "satisfied" rather than "*satisfy'd,*" for reasons that are unclear.

14. Edmund Spenser, "A Letter of the Authors," appended to *The Faerie Queene,* in his *Poetical Works,* ed. J. C. Smith and E. de Selincourt (Oxford: Oxford Univ. Press, 1912, rpt. 1977) 407.

15. One of the best brief accounts of how this landscape is created is in John R. Knott, Jr., "Bunyan's Gospel Day: A Reading of *The Pilgrim's Progress,*" *ELR* 3 (1973): 443–61.

16. Dante explains that *The Divine Comedy* is designed to be read and interpreted in the way scriptural texts are, and illustrates the point with a fourfold allegorical interpretation of Psalm 114.1–2. See Robert S. Haller, ed. and trans., *Literary Criticism of Dante Alighieri* (Lincoln: Univ. of Nebraska Press, 1973) 95–111, especially 99, and Haller's comments, xiii–xvi and 95. For the Latin text, see Letter X, in *Dantis Alagherii Epistolae,* ed. Paget Toynbee, 2nd ed. (Oxford: Clarendon, 1966).

17. Biblical quotations follow the King James Version unless otherwise noted.

18. It should be noted that Bunyan conspicuously avoids any reference to passages like Mark 4.11–12 in which parables are said to conceal truth from the unworthy lest they be saved.

19. See "From *Piers Plowman* to *Pilgrim's Progress:* The Generic and Exegetical Contexts of Bunyan's 'Similitude of a Dream,' " unpub. diss. (Brown University, 1983).

20. See *Grace Abounding to the Chief of Sinners,* ed. Roger Sharrock (Oxford: Clarendon,

1962) 8; Bunyan's wife brought him this book and Lewis Bayly's *The Practise of Pietie* (1612?).

21. John Bunyan, *The Life and Death of Mr. Badman,* in Offor, 3: 590. Subsequent references are to this text.

22. Knott, *Sword,* 153. Jacques Blondel makes a similar point: "l'allégorie, loin d'estomper le réel, cherche à le traduire, donc à le recréer, parcequ'il est apparu trop riche, trop insaisissable, pour être épuisé soit par l'observation directe, soit par un inlassable recours aux 'similitudes' " (Allegory, far from toning down the real, attempts to translate and thus to recreate it, because it has seemed too rich, too hard to capture, to be exhausted either by direct observation or by an untiring recourse to "similitudes"). Jacques Blondel, "Allégorie et Réalisme dans *The Pilgrim's Progress* de Bunyan," Etudes de Critique et d'Histoire Littéraire, no. 28 [61-63], *Archives des Lettres Modernes* 3 (1959): 5. This sheds light on Bunyan's peculiar position in literary history, between the death of one dominant form and the birth of another, the novel: "Bunyan nous paraît donc avoir recouru à l'allégorie d'abord par souci de réalisme, si l'on veut bien momentanément laisser au terme son ancienne signification scolastique. . . . Mais l'allégorie, d'autre part, a suscité un autre réalisme, celui-la même par lequel on designera ce que fera bientôt De Foe" (Bunyan thus seems to us to have had recourse to allegory first as a source of realism, if one wishes for the time being to allow the term its former scholastic signification. . . . But allegory, on the other hand, gave rise to another realism, the very one by which one defines what Defoe would soon do) (9).

23. Barbara K. Lewalski, *Protestant Poetics and the Seventeenth-Century Religious Lyric* (Princeton: Princeton Univ. Press, 1979) 6–7. For a much fuller discussion of the wealth of rhetoric books and manuals that extolled the poetic nature of Scripture, see Lewalski, 72–86.

24. John Smith, *The Mysterie of Rhetorique Unvailed* (London, 1657), sigs. A5–5ᵛ. Subsequent references are to this text.

25. John Prideaux, *Sacred Eloquence: Or, the Art of Rhetorick, As it is layd down in Scripture* (London, 1659) sig. A2.

26. Robert Ferguson, *The Interest of Reason in Religion; With the Import and Use of Scripture-Metaphors; and the Nature of the Union Betwixt Christ & Believers* (London, 1675) 367. Subsequent references are to this text. The *DNB* notes Ferguson's influence on dissenters and his role in the Popish Plot and the Monmouth Rebellion.

27. John Smith, "Of Prophecy," in *Select Discourses* (London, 1660) 172. Subsequent references are to this text. This John Smith, who died in 1652, cannot be the same as the author of the 1656 *Mysterie;* the Smith who wrote "Of Prophecy" was a Puritan divine, Cambridge Platonist, and orientalist associated with Emanuel and Queen's College.

The Spirit and the Sword: Bunyan and the Stuart State

1. John Bunyan, *Grace Abounding to the Chief of Sinners,* ed. Roger Sharrock (Oxford: Clarendon, 1962) 335; cf. 333. I am indebted to Robert Zaller for his critique of a draft of

this essay. All references to *Grace Abounding* in this essay are to paragraph, rather than page, number.

2. Richard L. Greaves, "John Bunyan and the Fifth Monarchists," *Albion* 13 (Summer 1981): 84–86.

3. *The Minutes of the First Independent Church (now Bunyan Meeting) at Bedford 1656–1766,* ed. H. G. Tibbutt (Publications of the Bedfordshire Historical Record Society, vol. 55, 1976) 36.

4. "A Relation of the Imprisonment of Mr. John Bunyan," *ad cal. Grace Abounding,* ed. Sharrock, 105. Subsequent references are to this text and abbreviate the title as RI.

5. RI, 106. The Welsh Independent Vavasor Powell similarly rejected advice to flee (after being summoned before the Privy Council). *The Life and Death of Mr. Vavasor Powell* (London, 1671) 131.

6. *The Works of John Bunyan,* ed. George Offor, 3 vols. (Glasgow: Blackie and Son, 1856) 1: 732n.

7. William York Tindall, *John Bunyan: Mechanick Preacher* (New York: Columbia Univ. Press, 1934) 137. Subsequent references are to this text.

8. Tindall, 136. For Powell, Knollys, Jessey, and Danvers, see *Biographical Dictionary of British Radicals in the Seventeenth Century,* ed. Richard L. Greaves and Robert Zaller, 3 vols. (Brighton: Harvester, 1982–84) s.vv.

9. John Brown, *John Bunyan (1628–1688): His Life, Times, and Work,* rev. Frank Mott Harrison (London: Hulbert, 1928) 146.

10. Cf. the similar silence of Monica Furlong, *Puritan's Progress: A Study of John Bunyan* (London: Hodder and Stoughton, 1975).

11. Sharrock, in *Grace Abounding,* 161.

12. There is a letter from Cobb to Roger Kenyon, dated 10 December 1670, that apparently has not been noticed by Bunyan scholars:

One Benyon was indicted upon the Statute of 35 Elizabeth, for being at a Conventicle. He was in prison, and was brought into Court and the indictment read to him; and because he refused to plead to it, the Court ordered me to record his confession, and he hath lain in prison upon that conviction, ever since Christmas Sessions, 12 Chas. II. And my Lord Chief Justice Keelinge was then upon the Bench, and gave the rule, and had the like, a year ago, against others. Benyon hath petitioned all the Judges of Assize, as they came [on] the Circuit, but could never be released. And truly, I think it but reasonable that if any one do appear, and afterwards will not plead, but that you should take judgment by *nihil dicit,* or confession.

Historical Manuscripts Commission 35, *Fourteenth Report,* Appendix, part 4: 86. This is definitive proof that Bunyan was not released and rearrested in 1666.

13. Bunyan did not accept the view of active resistance previously espoused by such British Protestants as John Knox and John Milton. See Richard L. Greaves, *Theology and Revolution in the Scottish Reformation: Studies in the Thought of John Knox* (Grand Rapids: Eerdmans, for Christian Univ. Press, 1980), chap. 7.

14. See *The Statutes of the Realm* (London: Dawsons of Pall Mall, 1819; rpt. 1963), 4.2: 841–43. The actual words of the statute are "under colour or pretence of any exercise of

Religion. . . ." The statute was clearly intended "for the preventinge and avoydinge of suche great inconvenyence and perills as might happen and growe by the wicked and daungerous practises of seditious sectaries and disloyall persons." Bunyan's understanding of the statute was correct.

15. Christopher Hill, *The World Turned Upside Down: Radical Ideas during the English Revolution* (New York: Viking, 1972) 328. Despite my occasional disagreements with Hill, his work is very valuable and always provocative.

16. Richard Baxter, *Reliquiae Baxterianae*, ed. Matthew Sylvester (London, 1696), bk. 1, pt. 1, sect. 77 (p. 53).

17. Robert Baillie, "Epistle" to *Anabaptism, the True Fountaine of Independency, Antinomy, Brownisme, Familisme* (London, 1646).

18. Cf., e.g., anon., *Light Shining in Buckingham-shire* (n.p., 1648), reprinted in Gerrard Winstanley, *Works*, ed. George H. Sabine (1941; rpt. New York: Russell & Russell, 1965) 615. In a far more radical vein than Bunyan would accept, another anonymous radical asserted that "God gave the office of a King in his wrath, and . . . Kings and Priests are Jewish ceremonies. . . ." *Tyranipocrit, Discovered with His Wiles, Wherewith He Vanquisheth* (Rotterdam, 1649) 3.

19. John Tillinghast, *Mr. John Tillinghasts Eight Last Sermons* (London, 1655) 68. For a summary of Fifth Monarchist political views, see B. S. Capp, *The Fifth Monarchy Men: A Study in Seventeenth-Century Millenarianism* (London: Faber and Faber, 1972) 50–55, 151–52.

20. Richard Baxter, *A Holy Commonwealth, or Political Aphorisms, Opening the True Principles of Government* (London, 1659) 121, 127. Subsequent references are to this text. In 1667, Bunyan's friend John Owen pleaded that "we have no form of government, *civil or ecclesiastical*, to impose on the nation. . . ." *The Works of John Owen*, ed. William H. Goold, 16 vols. (London: Johnstone and Hunter, 1850–53) 13: 549.

21. John Goodwin, *Anti-Cavalierisme, or, Truth Pleading as Well the Necessity, as the Lawfulness of This Present War* (London, [1642]) 7.

22. George Fox, *A Collection of the Several Books and Writings*, 2nd ed. (London, 1665) 118.

23. *I Will Pray with the Spirit*, ed. Richard L. Greaves, in *The Miscellaneous Works of John Bunyan*, gen. ed. Roger Sharrock (Oxford: Clarendon, 1976) 2: 283.

24. *Prison Meditations*, ed. Graham Midgley, in *The Miscellaneous Works of John Bunyan*, (Oxford: Clarendon, 1980) 6: 45. Subsequent references are to this text.

25. *One Thing Is Needful*, in *Miscellaneous Works*, 6: 72. Subsequent references are to this text.

26. *The Holy City*, in *The Works of Bunyan*, ed. Offor, 3: 410. Subsequent references are to this text. For Bunyan's millenarianism, see the introduction to *The Holy City*, ed. J. Sears McGee, in *The Miscellaneous Works of John Bunyan*, vol. 3 (Oxford: Clarendon, 1987).

27. Cf. *Light Shining in Buckingham-shire*, 613.

28. *Biographical Dictionary of British Radicals*, s.vv. Cokayne, Holmes, Palmer, and Tong.

29. For the persecution of Bedfordshire Nonconformists in this period, see W. M. Wigfield, *Recusancy and Nonconformity in Bedfordshire: Illustrated by Select Documents Between 1622 and 1842* (Publications of the Bedfordshire Historical Record Society, vol. 20, 1938) 167–72.

30. On the meetings of Dissenters see Public Record Office, State Papers 29/266/30; on the growth of conventicles, Public Record Office, State Papers 29/267/89.

31. Public Record Office, State Papers 29/260/23.

32. *Minutes of the First Independent Church,* 41–42.

33. Wigfield, *Recusancy and Nonconformity,* 179. Suspicion that the congregation was engaged in treasonable activity may have been a factor in its persecution in May 1670. See the account in *A True and Impartial Narrative of Some Illegal and Arbitrary Proceedings . . . in and near the Town of Bedford* (n.p., 1670).

34. Richard L. Greaves, "The Organizational Response of Nonconformity to Repression and Indulgence: The Case of Bedfordshire," *Church History* 44 (December 1975): 472–84.

35. *A Confession of My Faith,* in *The Works of Bunyan,* ed. Offor, 2: 593–94.

36. Printed in *Baptist Confessions of Faith,* ed. William L. Lumpkin (Chicago: Judson, 1959) 215. Cf. the comparable statements in other confessions, 169, 194, 283–84, 331. John Owen's view was similar: "*Magistracy* we *own as the ordinance of God,* and his majesty as the person set over us by his providence in the chief and royal administration thereof. In submission unto him, we profess it our duty to regulate our obedience by the laws and customs over which he presides in the government of these nations. . . ." *Works of Owen,* 13: 548; cf. 13: 578.

37. *A Confession of My Faith,* 601. Cf. Fox, *A Collection,* 120. In contrast, John Goodwin asserted that violent action against the civil authorities may be justified when their commands run counter to the maxims of God. *Anti-Cavalierisme,* 9–10.

38. *A Defence of the Doctrine of Justification by Faith,* in *The Works of Bunyan,* ed. Offor, 2: 322.

39. Richard L. Greaves, "The Last Imprisonment of John Bunyan," *Northamptonshire and Bedfordshire Life,* 5 (June 1975): 17.

40. *Calendar of State Papers, Domestic, 1680–81,* 416–17.

41. *The Holy War,* ed. Roger Sharrock and James F. Forrest (Oxford: Clarendon, 1980) 17, 25–26. Subsequent references are to this text.

42. Hill, *The World Turned Upside Down,* 329.

43. Winstanley, *Works,* 386; *The Holy War,* 67. The lack of a radical social perspective in *The Holy War* is also underscored by the absence of women in the narrative.

44. *The Holy Life,* ed. Richard L. Greaves, in *The Miscellaneous Works of John Bunyan,* (Oxford: Clarendon, 1981) 9: 265.

45. *Seasonable Counsel,* in *The Works of Bunyan,* ed. Offor, 2: 706, 708–09 (quoted), 738. Subsequent references are to this text.

46. *Seasonable Counsel,* 705, 707 (quoted), 709. In the Geneva Bible, the note to 1 Samuel 26.9 is careful to explain that the restriction against killing a monarch applies only to a "private cause: for Jehu slew two Kings at Gods appointment." Bunyan chose to ignore this.

47. *Biographical Dictionary of British Radicals,* s.vv. Cokayne, Goodenough, Wavel, and Smith.

48. *Discourse upon the Pharisee and the Publican,* in *The Works of Bunyan,* ed. Offor, 2: 217.

49. *A Discourse of the . . . House of God,* in *Miscellaneous Works,* 6: 302.

50. *Solomon's Temple Spiritualized*, in *The Works of Bunyan*, ed. Offor, 3: 474.

51. *Of Antichrist and His Ruin*, in *The Works of Bunyan*, ed. Offor, 2: 45. Subsequent references are to this text.

52. *Of Antichrist and His Ruin*, 74; cf. 62.

53. Tindall, *John Bunyan*, 134, 141.

54. *An Exposition of the First Ten Chapters of Genesis*, in *The Works of Bunyan*, ed. Offor, 2: 442, 445. Subsequent references are to this text. The Quakers too saw Cain as the symbol of a persecutor. Tindall, *John Bunyan*, 266.

55. Tindall, *John Bunyan*, 266; *An Exposition of Genesis*, 497.

56. Cf. Edmund Ludlow, *A Voyce from the Watch Tower, Part Five: 1660–1662*, ed. A. B. Worden, Camden Society, 4th series, (London: Royal Historical Society, 1978) 21: 11.

57. *An Exposition of Genesis*, 498; Winstanley, *Works*, 372; *Light Shining in Buckinghamshire*, 615.

58. *An Exposition of Genesis*, 498. Bunyan appears reluctant to admit openly, as did the Presbyterian Thomas Hall, that tyrants are ordained by God. "If Tyrants," said Hall, "were not ordained by God, we must exclude his providence from the greatest part of the world." According to Hall, tyrants are used by God to punish ungrateful and rebellious people, much as Bunyan said. Implicitly, Bunyan would have to accept God's role in ordaining tyrants. Like Bunyan, Hall repudiates antityrannical risings and calls for obedience as far as a Christian can, in good conscience, go. Hall, *The Beauty of Magistracy* (London, 1660) 43–44, 46.

59. *An Exposition of Genesis*, 420. Advocates of a stringently imposed religious uniformity argued in precisely the opposite manner that religious diversity would lead to armed conflict: "Different Opinions and Practices in matters of Religion . . . do naturally improve into contentious *Disputes;* and those Disputes, if not restrain'd, break out into Civil Wars." Anon., *A Seasonable Discourse Against Comprehension* (London, 1676) 10. To this argument, an anonymous Nonconformist, possibly John Humphrys, retorted in 1675 that the Dissenters were obedient to civil authority, though their ultimate loyalty was to God. As Bunyan himself argued, this position entailed no "disloyal or Rebellious Principles." *The Peaceable Design* ([London], 1675) sig. A4^r.

60. *Israel's Hope Encouraged*, in *The Works of Bunyan*, ed. Offor, 1: 600.

61. [Richard Overton], *A Remonstrance of Many Thousand Citizens* ([London?], 1646) 15.

62. *Paul's Departure and Crown*, in *The Works of Bunyan*, ed. Offor, 1: 732.

63. *Israel's Hope Encouraged*, 585.

64. *The Saints' Knowledge of Christ's Love*, in *The Works of Bunyan*, ed. Offor, 2: 21.

65. Bunyan's opposition to the more revolutionary Fifth Monarchists was based fundamentally on their use of violent means, not on their threat to magistracy and monarchical polity. In contrast, Thomas Hall condemned the Fifth Monarchists for seeking "a parity and equality amongst all Christians . . . [with] no Superiours, nor Inferiours, but all fellow-creatures well met. . . ." *The Beauty of Magistracy*, 18.

66. *The House of the Forest of Lebanon*, in *The Works of Bunyan*, ed. Offor, 3: 536–37. Subsequent references are to this text.

67. *The House of the Forest of Lebanon*, 516, 527 (quoted). The note to Revelation 11.5 in the Geneva Bible likewise explains that the killing is "by Gods worde. . . ."

68. *The Saints' Knowledge of Christ's Love*, 19; *An Exposition of Genesis*, 455; *The Water of Life*, in *The Works of Bunyan*, ed. Offor, 3: 556.

Marxist Perspectives on Bunyan

1. If the term "Marxism" is to retain a descriptive function, what it describes, it seems to me, must continue to maintain the standpoint of historical materialism. In my understanding of the outlook, historical materialism contends that the most important condition of human history is the way people make their livings. The way people do that and their technical means for doing it bring them into struggle with a more or less uncongenial natural environment and with other human groups and individuals with whom they relate as competitors, victims, or victimizers in the effort to get and keep worldly goods. These struggles, for better and worse, are changing the conditions in which human beings live and simultaneously transforming human nature. They began at the dawn of history with the emergence of the patriarchal family, of private property, and of the armed guarantor of these two institutions, the state. These institutions can be transcended in an economy of plenty made possible by the technical dynamism of capitalism. A fit goal for human beings struggling in history is a free association of producers which exalts the welfare of the species without demeaning the dignity of the individual; it is the society forecast in the *Communist Manifesto* in which "the free development of each is the condition of the free development of all." Its achievement would be a victory for the freedom of the human will over inherited economic and social limitations. It would usher in a situation in which historical materialism, as here described, would be outmoded as a representation of what is happening in history, for it would be a society in which ideals and desires rule, in which humanity lives a planned, deliberate life.

2. Robert G. Collmer, "Bunyan and the Marxists," *Christianity and Literature* 28. 1 (1978): 16.

3. Jack Lindsay, *John Bunyan: Maker of Myths* (London: Methuen, 1937) 8. Subsequent references are to this text.

4. Kettle, in Alick West, *Crisis and Criticism and Selected Essays*, Foreword by Arnold Kettle, Introduction by Elizabeth West (London: Lawrence and Wishart, 1975) 2. Subsequent references to Alick West's Bunyan essay are to this edition.

5. Kettle, *An Introduction to the English Novel* (London: Hutchinsons, 1951) 1: 42–43.

6. Christopher Hill, *Milton and the English Revolution* (New York: Viking, 1977) 457. Subsequent references are to this text.

7. Christopher Hill, "John Bunyan and the English Revolution," *Marxist Perspectives* 7.2 (1979): 8–9. Subsequent references are to this text.

8. E. P. Thompson, *The Making of the English Working Class* (New York: Vintage, 1966) 31. Subsequent references are to this text.

9. Karl Marx, *Capital*, trans. Samuel Moore and Edward Aveling (London: Lawrence and Wishart, 1974) 1: 174.

10. Ellen Cantarow, "A Wilderness of Opinions Confounded: Allegory and Ideol-

ogy," *College English,* 34. 2 (November 1972): 215–55. Subsequent references are to this text.

11. Quoted by Cantarow from Gerrard Winstanley, *Works,* ed. George H. Sabine (Ithaca, N.Y.: Cornell Univ. Press, 1941) 569; quoted on 248.

12. Notice that on the topic of the influence of biblical style we are back to Jack Lindsay, who thought there wasn't any.

13. Joan Bellamy, "John Bunyan and the Democratic Tradition," *Zeitschrift für Anglistik und Amerikanistik* 27.3 (1979): 219. Subsequent references are to this text.

14. Thomas Metscher, "Subversive, Radical and Revolutionary Traditions in European Literature between 1300 and the Age of Bunyan," *Zeitschrift für Anglistik und Amerikanistik* 29.1 (1981): 12. Subsequent references are to this text.

15. Georg Seehase, "Realistische Allegorie in John Bunyans *The Pilgrim's Progress,*" *Zeitschrift für Anglistik und Amerikanistik* 27.1 (1979): 216. Subsequent references are to this text.

16. Günter Walch, "John Bunyan—Dichter der Plebejischen Fraktion: Revolutionärer Puritanismus und Allegorie," *Zeitschrift für Anglistik und Amerikanistik* 27.3 (1979): 202.

17. "Allgemein muss aber für die englische Literatur des revolutionären 17. Jahrhunderts mit entsprechender Modifikation gelten, was Spriewald für 'die marxistische Interpretation der Dichtung aus der Zeit der frühbürgerlichen Revolution' konstatiert, dass sie nämlich 'noch in den Anfängen' stecke." Walch, 198.

The Pilgrim's Progress and The Pilgrim's Regress: John Bunyan and C. S. Lewis on the Shape of the Christian Quest

1. T. H. White, *The Sword in the Stone* (New York: Dell, 1963) 254–55.

2. Alan Watts, *Myth and Ritual in Christianity* (Boston: Beacon, 1968) 45.

3. Oscar Cullman, *Christ and Time,* trans. Floyd V. Filson (Philadelphia: Westminster, 1950) 23.

4. ·Harvey Cox, "Evolutionary Progress and Christian Promise," in *The Evolving World and Theology,* ed. Johannes B. Metz (New York: Paulist, 1967) 45.

5. John Bunyan, *Grace Abounding to the Chief of Sinners,* ed. Roger Sharrock (Oxford: Clarendon, 1962) 72. Subsequent references are to this text.

6. Joseph Hall, *The Christian* in *The Works of the Right Reverend Father in God Joseph Hall Lord Bishop of Norwich* (London, 1714) 338.

7. Stanley E. Fish, *Self-Consuming Artifacts: The Experience of Seventeenth-Century Literature* (Berkeley: Univ. of California Press, 1972) 229.

8. John Bunyan, *The Pilgrim's Progress from This World to That Which Is to Come,* ed. James Blanton Wharey, 2nd ed. rev. Roger Sharrock (Oxford: Clarendon, 1960) 154. Subsequent references are to this text.

9. The directionality of these several quests is significant. Christian's trip is south, in

a direction which Dante too had associated with the attainment of paradise. John's trip is west, to death, and then east again for the recovery of his world with Christian eyes. In Lewis's favorite work of science fiction, David Lindsay's *A Voyage to Arcturus,* Maskull's foot journey on Tormance, the planet of Arcturus, is ever to the north, in what admiring critic Harold Bloom calls "nothing but a remorseless drive to death." ("Clinamen: Towards a Theory of Fantasy," in *Bridges to Fantasy,* ed. George E. Slusser, Erick S. Rabkin, and Robert Scholes [Carbondale: Southern Illinois Univ. Press, 1982]. This reference is to p. 1 of an essay which runs pp. 1–21.) What Bloom sees as a gnostic fable, combining narcissism and prometheanism in its nightmarish condemnation of the created world, offers at least one notable likeness to *The Pilgrim's Regress,* in that for both books the framing quest is of an unworldly end—Maskull's Muspel-fire in one case, and John's Island in the other. But Lewis refuses to sanction any final negative judgment upon the present world. The extreme west proves to be both end and beginning, as it is in Donne's great hymn upon his illness which also affirms the entire map of the creation.

10. Lewis, "The Weight of Glory," in *The Weight of Glory and Other Addresses* (Grand Rapids: Eerdmans, 1965) 5. Subsequent references are to this text.

11. Lewis, *The Pilgrim's Regress: An Allegorical Apology for Christianity, Reason, and Romanticism* (Grand Rapids: Eerdmans, 1958) 24.

12. Lewis, *The Problem of Pain* (New York: Macmillan, 1962) 65.

13. Lewis, *Letters to Malcolm: Chiefly on Prayer* (New York: Harcourt Brace, 1964) 116. In his *A Preface to Paradise Lost* Lewis had drawn out the implications from Augustine's *De Civitate Dei* that "good can exist without evil, as in Milton's Heaven and Paradise, but not evil without good" (Oxford: Oxford Univ. Press, 1960) 67.

14. Lewis, *The Great Divorce* (New York: Macmillan, 1946) 7.

15. Lewis, *Surprised by Joy* (New York: Harcourt Brace, 1955) 230. Subsequent references are to this text.

Bibliography

Adeney, Elizabeth. "Bunyan: A Unified Vision?" *Critical Review* 17 (1974): 97–109.

Ashton, John. *Why Were the Gospels Written?* Notre Dame: Fides, 1973.

Augustine, Aurelius. *De Civitate Dei.* Oxford: Oxford Univ. Press, 1960.

Baillie, Robert. *Anabaptism, the True Fountaine of Independency, Antinomy, Brownisme, Familisme.* London, 1646.

Barrett, C. K. "Stephen and the Son of Man." *Apophoreta: Festschrift für Ernst Haenchen.* Ed. W. Schneemelcher. Berlin: Töplemann, 1964.

Baxter, Richard. *A Christian Directory.* London, 1673.

————. *A Holy Commonwealth, or Political Aphorisms, Opening the True Principles of Government.* London, 1659.

————. *A Paraphrase on the New Testament, with Notes, Doctrinal and Practical.* 3d ed. London, 1701.

————. *Reliquiae Baxterianae.* Ed. Matthew Sylvester. London, 1696.

Beal, Rebecca. "*Grace Abounding to the Chief of Sinners:* John Bunyan's Pauline Epistle." *Studies in English Literature* 21 (1981): 147–60.

Bellamy, Joan. "John Bunyan and the Democratic Tradition." *Zeitschrift für Anglistik und Amerikanistik* 27.3 (1979): 218–24.

Berger, Harry, Jr. *The Allegorical Temper: Vision and Reality in Book II of Spenser's Faerie Queene.* New Haven: Yale Univ. Press, 1957.

Blondel, Jacques. "Allégorie et Réalisme dans *The Pilgrim's Progress* de Bunyan." *Archives des Lettres Modernes* 3, no. 28 (1959).

Boas, George. *Vox Populi: Essays in the History of an Idea.* Baltimore: Johns Hopkins Univ. Press, 1969.

Brown, John. *John Bunyan (1628–1688): His Life, Times, and Work.* Rev. Frank Mott Harrison. London: Hulbert, 1928.

Bunyan, John. *Grace Abounding to the Chief of Sinners*. Ed. Roger Sharrock. Oxford: Clarendon, 1962.

———. *The Holy War*. Ed. Roger Sharrock and James F. Forrest. Oxford: Clarendon, 1980.

———. *The Miscellaneous Works of John Bunyan*. Gen. ed. Roger Sharrock. Oxford: Clarendon, 1976–

———. *The Pilgrim's Progress from This World to That Which Is to Come*. Ed. James Blanton Wharey. 2nd ed. rev. Roger Sharrock. Oxford: Clarendon, 1960.

———. *The Pilgrim's Progress As Originally Published by John Bunyan, Being a Facsimile Reproduction of the First Edition*. 1875. Old Woking, Surrey: Gresham, 1978.

———. *The Works of John Bunyan*. Ed. George Offor. 3 vols. 1854. Glasgow: Blackie and Son, 1856.

Butler, George. "The Iron Cage of Despair and 'The Unpardonable Sin' in *The Pilgrim's Progress*." *English Language Notes* 25 (1987): 34–38.

Calendar of State Papers, Domestic, 1680–81.

Calvin, John. *The Commentaries of M. John Calvin upon the Actes of the Apostles. . . .* Trans. Christopher Fetherstone. London, 1585.

Cantarow, Ellen. "A Wilderness of Opinions Confounded: Allegory and Ideology." *College English* 34.2 (November 1972): 215–55.

Capp, B. S. *The Fifth Monarchy Men: A Study in Seventeenth-Century Millenarianism*. London: Faber and Faber, 1972.

Christopher, Georgia B. *Milton and the Science of the Saints*. Princeton: Princeton Univ. Press, 1982.

———. "The Verbal Gate to Paradise: Adam's 'Literary Experience' in Book X of *Paradise Lost*." *PMLA* 90 (1975): 69–77.

Coleridge, Samuel Taylor. *The Complete Works of Samuel Taylor Coleridge*. Ed. W. G. T. Shedd. 7 vols. New York: Harper, 1853–84.

Collmer, Robert G. "Bunyan and the Marxists." *Christianity and Literature* 28.1 (1978): 14–16.

Cox, Harvey. "Evolutionary Progress and Christian Promise." *The Evolving World and Theology*. Ed. Johannes B. Metz. New York: Paulist, 1967.

Cudworth, Ralph. *A Sermon Preached before the Honourable House of Commons, at Westminster, March 31, 1647*. Cambridge, 1647.

Cullman, Oscar. *Christ and Time*. Trans. Floyd V. Filson. Philadelphia: Westminster, 1950.

Cunningham, Valentine. "Glossing and Glozing: Bunyan and Allegory." *John Bunyan: Conventicle and Parnassus: Tercentenary Essays*. Ed. N. H. Keeble. Oxford: Clarendon, 1988.

Damrosch, Leopold, Jr. *God's Plot and Man's Stories: Studies in the Fictional Imagination from Milton to Fielding.* Chicago: Univ. of Chicago Press, 1985.

Dante, Alighieri. *Dantis Alagherii Epistolae.* Ed. Paget Toynbee. 2nd ed. Oxford: Clarendon, 1966.

Davis, Nick. "The Problem of Misfortune in *The Pilgrim's Progress.*" *The Pilgrim's Progress: Critical and Historical Views.* Ed. Vincent Newey. Liverpool: Liverpool Univ. Press, 1980; Totowa: Barnes & Noble, 1980, 182–204.

Dent, Arthur. *The Plaine Mans Path-way to Heauen.* 1601. London, 1607.

Dent, R. W. *Shakespeare's Proverbial Language.* Berkeley: Univ. of California Press, 1981.

Dupont, Jacques. "Les Discours Missionnaires des Acts des Apôtres." *Revue Biblique* 69 (1962): 37–60.

Dutton, A. Richard. " 'Interesting but tough': Reading *The Pilgrim's Progress.*" *Studies in English Literature* 18 (1978): 439–56.

Evans, C. F. " 'Speeches' in Acts." *Melanges bibliques en hommage au R. P. Béda Rigaux.* Ed. Albert Descamps and André de Halleux. Gembloux: Duculot, 1970.

Ferguson, Robert. *The Interest of Reason in Religion; With the Import and Use of Scripture-Metaphors; and the Nature of the Union Betwixt Christ & Believers.* London, 1675.

Fish, Stanley E. *Self-Consuming Artifacts: The Experience of Seventeenth-Century Literature.* Berkeley: Univ. of California Press, 1972.

Forrest, James F., and Richard Lee Greaves. *John Bunyan: A Reference Guide.* Boston: G. K. Hall, 1982.

Forrest, James F. "Vision, Form, and the Imagination in the Second Part of *The Pilgrim's Progress (1684).*" *The Journal of Narrative Technique* 13.2 (1983): 109–16.

Fox, George. *A Collection of the Several Books and Writings.* 2nd ed. London, 1665.
———. *The Journal of George Fox.* Rev. ed. John L. Nickalls. London: Religious Society of Friends, 1975.

Frei, Hans. *The Eclipse of Biblical Narrative: A Study in Eighteenth and Nineteenth Century Hermeneutics.* New Haven: Yale Univ. Press, 1974.

Freiday, Dean. *The Bible—Its Criticism, Interpretation and Use—in 16th and 17th Century England.* Pittsburgh: s.n., 1979.

Frye, Roland Mushat. *God, Man, and Satan: Patterns of Christian Thought and Life in Paradise Lost, Pilgrim's Progress, and the Great Theologians.* Princeton: Princeton Univ. Press, 1960.

Furlong, Monica. *Puritan's Progress: A Study of John Bunyan.* London: Hodder and Stoughton, 1975.

The Geneva Bible: A facsimile of the 1560 edition. Ed. Lloyd E. Berry. Madison: Univ. of Wisconsin Press, 1969.

Giblin, Charles H. "Discerning Gospel Genre." *Thought* 47 (1972): 225–52.

Gill, David. "Observations on the Lukan Travel Narrative and Some Related Passages." *Harvard Theological Review* 63 (1970): 199–221.

Goodwin, John. *Anti-Cavalierisme, or, Truth Pleading as Well the Necessity, as the Lawfulness of This Present War.* London, [1642].

Goodwin, Thomas. *The Vanitie of Thoughts Discovered.* London, 1650.

Greaves, Richard L., and Robert Zaller, eds. *Biographical Dictionary of British Radicals in the Seventeenth Century.* 3 vols. Brighton: Harvester, 1982–84.

Greaves, Richard L. "Bunyan Through the Centuries: Some Reflections." *English Studies* 64 (1983): 113–21.

———. *John Bunyan.* Courtenay Studies in Reformation Theology, 2. Abingdon, Eng.: Sutton Courtenay, 1969.

———. "John Bunyan and the Fifth Monarchists." *Albion* 13 (Summer 1981): 83–95.

———, ed. *John Bunyan: The Doctrine of the Law and Grace Unfolded . . . The Miscellaneous Works of John Bunyan.* Vol. 2. Gen. ed. Roger Sharrock. Oxford: Clarendon, 1976.

———. *John Bunyan: Good News for the Vilest of Men . . . The Miscellaneous Works of John Bunyan.* Vol. II. Gen. ed. Roger Sharrock. Oxford: Clarendon, 1985.

———. *John Bunyan: Instruction for the Ignorant . . . The Miscellaneous Works of John Bunyan.* Vol. 8. Gen. ed. Roger Sharrock. Oxford: Clarendon, 1981.

———. "The Last Imprisonment of John Bunyan." *Northamptonshire and Bedfordshire Life* 5 (June 1975): 17.

———. "The Organizational Response of Nonconformity to Repression and Indulgence: The Case of Bedfordshire." *Church History* 44 (December 1975): 472–84.

———. *Theology and Revolution: Studies in the Thought of John Knox.* Grand Rapids: Eerdmans, for Christian Univ. Press, 1980.

Greaves, Richard L., and James F. Forrest. *John Bunyan: A Reference Guide.* Boston: G.K. Hall, 1982.

Hall, Joseph. *The Works of the Right Reverend Father in God Joseph Hall Lord Bishop of Norwich.* London, 1714.

Hall, Thomas. *The Beauty of Magistracy.* London, 1660.

Haller, Robert S., ed. and trans. *Literary Criticism of Dante Alighieri.* Lincoln: Univ. of Nebraska Press, 1973.

Haller, William. *The Rise of Puritanism.* New York: Columbia Univ. Press, 1938.

———, ed. *Tracts on Liberty in the Puritan Revolution, 1638–1647.* 3 vols. New York: Columbia Univ. Press, 1933.

Hammond, Brean S. "*The Pilgrim's Progress:* Satire and Social Comment." *The*

Pilgrim's Progress: Critical and Historical Views. Ed. Vincent Newey. Liverpool: Liverpool Univ. Press, 1980; Totowa: Barnes & Noble, 1980.

Hammond, Henry. *A Paraphrase and Annotations Upon all the Books of the New Testament.* London, 1659.

Hartman, Geoffrey. *The Fate of Reading.* Chicago: Univ. of Chicago Press, 1975.

Haskin, Dayton. "Bunyan, Luther, and the Struggle with Belatedness in *Grace Abounding.*" *University of Toronto Quarterly* 50 (1980–81): 300–13.

———. "The Burden of Interpretation in *The Pilgrim's Progress.*" *Studies in Philology* 79 (1982): 256–78.

———. "*The Pilgrim's Progress* in the Context of Bunyan's Dialogue with the Radicals." *Harvard Theological Review* 77 (1984): 73–94.

Hill, Christopher. "John Bunyan and the English Revolution." *Marxist Perspectives* 7.2 (1979): 8–26.

———. *Milton and the English Revolution.* New York: Viking, 1977.

———. *The World Turned Upside Down: Radical Ideas during the English Revolution.* New York: Viking, 1972.

Historical Manuscripts Commission 35, *Fourteenth Report,* Appendix, part 4.

Heseltine, Janet T. Introduction. *The Oxford Dictionary of English Proverbs.* Ed. W. G. Smith. 2nd ed. rev. Paul Harvey. Oxford: Clarendon, 1948.

Hobbes, Thomas. *Leviathan.* Ed. Michael Oakeshott. Oxford: Basil Blackwell, 1953.

Howard, Donald R. *The Three Temptations: Medieval Man in Search of the World.* Princeton: Princeton Univ. Press, 1966.

Huizinga, Johan. *Homo Ludens: A Study of the Play Element in Culture.* London: Maurice Temple Smith, 1970.

Hunter, William B., ed. *Bright Essence: Studies in Milton's Theology.* Salt Lake City: Univ. of Utah Press, 1971.

Hussey, Maurice. "The Humanism of John Bunyan." *The Pelican Guide to English Literature: From Donne to Marvell.* Ed. Boris Ford. Baltimore: Penguin, 1968.

Iser, Wolfgang. *The Implied Reader: Patterns of Communication in Prose Fiction from Bunyan to Beckett.* Baltimore: Johns Hopkins Univ. Press, 1974.

Jeremias, Joachim. *The Parables of Jesus.* 2nd rev. ed. New York: Scribner's, 1972.

Johnson, Barbara A. "From *Piers Plowman* to *Pilgrim's Progress:* The Generic and Exegetical Contexts of Bunyan's 'Similitude of a Dream.' " Diss., Brown Univ., 1983.

Jones, C. P. M. "The Epistle to the Hebrews and the Lucan Writings." *Studies of the Gospels: Essays in Memory of R. H. Lightfoot.* Ed. D. E. Nineham. Oxford: Basil Blackwell, 1955.

Joseph, Sister Miriam. *Shakespeare's Use of the Arts of Language.* New York: Columbia Univ. Press, 1947.

Kaufmann, U. Milo. *The Pilgrim's Progress and Traditions in Puritan Meditation.* New Haven: Yale Univ. Press, 1960.

Keeble, N. H. "Christiana's Key: The Unity of *The Pilgrim's Progress.*" *The Pilgrim's Progress: Critical and Historical Views.* Ed. Vincent Newey. Liverpool: Liverpool Univ. Press, 1980; Totowa: Barnes & Noble, 1980.

————, ed. *John Bunyan: Conventicle and Parnassus: Tercentenary Essays.* Oxford: Clarendon, 1988.

————. *The Literary Culture of Nonconformity in Later Seventeenth-Century England.* Leicester: Leicester Univ. Press; Athens: Univ. of Georgia Press, 1987.

————. "The Way and the Ways of Puritan Story: Biblical Patterns in Bunyan and His Contemporaries." *English* 33 (1984): 209–32.

Kelman, John. *The Road: A Study of John Bunyan's "Pilgrim's Progress."* 1912. Port Washington: Kennikat, 1970.

Kerrigan, William. *The Prophetic Milton.* Charlottesville: Univ. Press of Virginia, 1974.

Kettle, Arnold. *An Introduction to the English Novel.* London: Hutchinsons, 1951.

Knott, John R., Jr. "Bunyan and the Holy Community." *Studies in Philology* 80 (1983): 200–25.

————. "Bunyan's Gospel Day: A Reading of *The Pilgrim's Progress.*" *English Literary Renaissance* 3 (1973): 443–61.

————. *The Sword of the Spirit: Puritan Responses to the Bible.* Chicago: Univ. of Chicago Press, 1980.

————. " 'Thou must live upon my Word': John Bunyan and the Bible." *John Bunyan: Conventicle and Parnassus: Tercentenary Essays.* Ed. N. H. Keeble. Oxford: Clarendon, 1988.

Kolve, V. A. *The Play Called Corpus Christi.* Stanford: Stanford Univ. Press, 1965.

Lamb, Charles. *The Last Essays of Elia.* Ed. Edmund Blunden. London: Oxford Univ. Press, 1932.

Langland, William. *The Book Concerning Piers the Plowman.* Ed. Rachel Attwater. London: Dent, 1957.

Lechner, Joan Marie. *Renaissance Concepts of the Commonplace.* New York: Pageant, 1962.

Lewalski, Barbara K. *Protestant Poetics and the Seventeenth-Century Religious Lyric.* Princeton: Princeton Univ. Press, 1979.

Lever, Christopher. *The Holy Pilgrime, Leading the Way to Heaven. Or a Divine Direction in the Way of Life.* London, 1618.

Levin, Richard. "Proverbial Phrases in the Titles of Thomas Middleton's Plays." *Southern Folklore Quarterly* 28.2 (1964): 142–45.

Lewis, C. S. *The Allegory of Love, a Study in Medieval Tradition.* Oxford: Clarendon, 1936.

————. *The Great Divorce.* New York: Macmillan, 1946.

_____. *The Letters to Malcolm: Chiefly on Prayer*. New York: Harcourt Brace, 1964.

_____. *The Pilgrim's Regress: An Allegorical Apology for Christianity, Reason, and Romanticism*. Grand Rapids: Eerdmans, 1958.

_____. *The Problem of Pain*. New York: Macmillan, 1962.

_____. *Surprised by Joy*. New York: Harcourt Brace, 1955.

_____. *The Weight of Glory and Other Addresses*. Grand Rapids: Eerdmans, 1965.

The Life and Death of Mr. Vavasor Powell. London, 1671.

Lindsay, David. *The Godly Mans Journey: Containing Ten Several Treatises*. London, 1625.

Lindsay, Jack. *John Bunyan: Maker of Myths*. London: Methuen, 1937.

Ludlow, Edmund. *A Voyce from the Watch Tower, Part Five: 1660–1662*. Ed. A. B. Worden. Camden Society, 4th series. London: Royal Historical Society, 1978.

Lumpkin, William L., ed. *Baptist Confessions of Faith*. Chicago: Judson, 1959.

Luther, Martin. *Luther's Works*. Gen. ed. Jaroslav Pelikan and Helmut T. Lehmann. 55 vols. St. Louis: Concordia; Philadelphia: Fortress, 1955– .

Luxon, Thomas H. "Calvin and Bunyan on Word and Image: Is There a Text in Interpreter's House?" *English Literary Renaissance* 18 (1988): 438–59.

_____. "Puritan Allegory and Bunyan's *Pilgrim's Progress*." Diss. Univ. of Chicago, 1984.

Marshall, I. Howard. *Luke: Historian and Theologian*. Grand Rapids: Zondervan, 1970.

Marshall, Stephen. *A Sacred Record to be Made of Gods Mercies to Zion*. London, 1645.

Marx, Karl. *Capital*. Trans. Samuel Moore and Edward Aveling. 2 vols. London: Lawrence and Wishart, 1974.

McCasland, S. V. " 'The Way'." *Journal of Biblical Literature* 77 (1958): 222–30.

McDonnell, Kilian. *John Calvin, the Church and the Eucharist*. Princeton: Princeton Univ. Press, 1967.

McGee, J. Sears, ed. *John Bunyan: Christian Behaviour . . . The Miscellaneous Works of John Bunyan*. Vol. 3. Gen. ed. Roger Sharrock. Oxford: Clarendon, 1987.

McKeon, Michael. *The Origins of the English Novel 1600–1740*. Baltimore: Johns Hopkins Univ. Press, 1987.

Metscher, Thomas. "Subversive, Radical and Revolutionary Traditions in European Literature between 1300 and the Age of Bunyan." *Zeitschrift für Anglistik und Amerikanistik* 29.1 (1981): 12–20.

Midgley, Graham, ed. *John Bunyan: The Poems. The Miscellaneous Works of John Bunyan*. Vol. 6. Gen. ed. Roger Sharrock. Oxford: Clarendon, 1980.

Milton, John. *Complete Poems and Major Prose*. Ed. Merritt Y. Hughes. New York: Odyssey, 1957.

————. *Complete Prose Works of John Milton.* Gen. ed. Don M. Wolfe. 8 vols. New Haven: Yale Univ. Press, 1953–82.

The Minutes of the First Independent Church (now Bunyan Meeting) at Bedford 1656–1766. Ed. H. G. Tibbutt. Publications of the Bedfordshire Historical Record Society, vol. 55, 1976.

Mitchell, W. Fraser. *English Pulpit Oratory from Andrewes to Tillotson.* 1932. New York: Russell & Russell, 1962.

Murdock, Kenneth B. *Literature and Theology in Colonial New England.* Cambridge: Harvard Univ. Press, 1956.

Newey, Vincent, ed. *The Pilgrim's Progress: Critical and Historical Views.* Liverpool: Liverpool Univ. Press, 1980; Totowa: Barnes & Noble, 1980.

Nussbaum, Felicity A. " 'By These Words I Was Sustained': Bunyan's *Grace Abounding.*" *ELH* 49 (1982): 18–34.

Nuttall, Geoffrey F. "The Heart of *The Pilgrim's Progress.*" *Reformation Principle and Practice: Essays in Honour of Arthur Geoffrey Dickens.* Ed. Peter Newman Brooks. London: Scolar Press, 1980.

————. " 'Unity with the Creation': George Fox and the Hermetic Philosophy." *The Puritan Spirit: Essays and Addresses.* London: Epworth, 1967.

Olson, Paul A. "*A Midsummer Night's Dream* and the Meaning of Court Marriage." *ELH* 24 (1957): 95–119.

[Overton, Richard]. *A Remonstrance of Many Thousand Citizens.* [London?], 1646.

Owen, John. *The Works of John Owen.* Ed. William H. Goold. 16 vols. London: Johnstone and Hunter, 1850–53.

Owst, G. R. *Literature and Pulpit in Medieval England.* Cambridge: Cambridge Univ. Press, 1933; 2nd ed. 1961. New York: Barnes & Noble, 1966.

Patrides, C. A. "*Paradise Lost* and the Theory of Accommodation." *Bright Essence: Studies in Milton's Theology.* Ed. William B. Hunter. Salt Lake City: Univ. of Utah Press, 1971.

The Peaceable Design. [London], 1675.

Peacham, Henry. *The Garden of Eloquence.* 1593. Gainesville: Scholars' Facsimiles & Reprints, 1954.

Pearson, A. F. Scott. *Thomas Cartwright and Elizabethan Puritanism 1535–1603.* Cambridge: Cambridge Univ. Press, 1925.

Praz, Mario. *Studies in Seventeenth Century Imagery.* 2 vols. London: Warburg Institute Studies, 1939–47.

Prideaux, John. *Sacred Eloquence: Or, the Art of Rhetorick, As it is layd down in Scripture.* London, 1659.

Public Record Office, State Papers 29/260/23; 29/266/30; 29/267/89.

Puttenham, George. *The Arte of English Poesie by George Puttenham.* Ed. Gladys D. Willcock and Alice Walker. Cambridge: Harvard Univ. Press, 1936.

Qualls, Barry. *The Secular Pilgrims of Victorian Fiction: The Novel as Book of Life.* Cambridge: Cambridge Univ. Press, 1982.

R., M. *The Pilgrim's Pass to the New Jerusalem: Or a Serious CHRISTIAN his Enquiries after Heaven.* London, 1659.

Renwick, W. L. *Edmund Spenser.* Cambridge: Cambridge Univ. Press. 1952.

Richardson, Caroline. *English Preachers and Preaching, 1640–1670.* New York: Macmillan, 1928.

Ricks, Christopher. "Short Is Sweet." *London Review of Books* 3–16 February 1983: 13.

Rutherford, Samuel. *A Survey of the Spirituall Antichrist.* . . . N.p., 1648.

Sadler, Lynn Veach. *John Bunyan.* New York: Twayne, 1979.

Sasek, Lawrence A. *The Literary Temper of the English Puritans.* Baton Rouge: Louisiana State Univ. Press, 1961.

A Seasonable Discourse Against Comprehension. London, 1676.

Seed, David. "Dialogue and Debate in *The Pilgrim's Progress.*" *The Pilgrim's Progress: Critical and Historical Views.* Ed. Vincent Newey. Totowa: Barnes & Noble, 1980, 69–90.

Seehase, Georg. "Realistische Allegorie in John Bunyans *The Pilgrim's Progress.*" *Zeitschrift für Anglistik und Amerikanistik* 27.1 (1979): 208–17.

Sharrock, Roger. *John Bunyan.* London: Hutchinsons, 1954.

———. "Personal Vision and the Puritan Tradition in Bunyan." *Hibbert Journal* 56 (1957): 47–60.

Shaw, G. B. *Dramatic Opinions and Essays.* 2 vols. London: Archibald Constable. 1907.

Sidney, Sir Philip. *An Apology for Poetry, or The Defense of Poesy.* Ed. Geoffrey Shepherd. London: T. Nelson, 1965.

Slusser, George E., Erick S. Rabkin, and Robert Scholes, eds. *Bridges to Fantasy.* Carbondale: Southern Illinois Univ. Press, 1982.

Smith, Charles G. *Spenser's Proverb Lore, with Special Reference to His Use of the Sententiae of Leonard Culman and Publius Syrus.* Cambridge: Harvard Univ. Press, 1970.

Smith, John. *The Mysterie of Rhetorique Unvailed.* London, 1657.

Smith, John. *Select Discourses.* London, 1660.

Spenser, Edmund. *The Faerie Queene.* Ed. A. C. Hamilton. London: Longman, 1980.

———. *Poetical Works.* Ed. J. C. Smith and E. de Selincourt. 1912. Oxford: Oxford Univ. Press, 1977.

The Statutes of the Realm. London: Dawsons of Pall Mall, 1819; rpt. 1963.

Steadman, John. *The Lamb and the Elephant: Ideal Imitation and the Context of Renaissance Allegory.* San Marino: Huntington Library, 1974.

Stendahl, Krister. "The Apostle Paul and the Introspective Conscience of the West." *Harvard Theological Review* 56 (1963): 199–215.

Stranahan, Brainerd P. "Bunyan and the Epistle to the Hebrews: His Source for the Idea of Pilgrimage in *The Pilgrim's Progress.*" *Studies in Philology* 79 (1982): 279–96.

———. "Bunyan's Special Talent: Biblical Texts as 'Events' in *Grace Abounding* and *The Pilgrim's Progress.*" *English Literary Renaissance* 11 (1981): 329–43.

———. " 'With Great Delight': The Song of Solomon in *The Pilgrim's Progress.*" *English Studies* 68 (1984): 220–27.

Sutherland, James. *A Preface to Eighteenth Century Poetry.* Oxford: Clarendon, 1948.

Talon, Henri. *John Bunyan: The Man and His Works.* Trans. Barbara Wall. London: Rockliff, 1951.

Taylor, Archer. *The Proverb and Index.* 1931. Hatboro: Folklore Associates, 1962.

———. "Proverbs and Proverbial Phrases in the Plays of John Marston." *Southern Folklore Quarterly* 24.3 (1960): 193–216.

———. "Proverbs and Proverbial Phrases in Roger L'Estrange, *The Fables of Aesop.*" *Southern Folklore Quarterly* 26.3 (1962): 232–45.

———. "Proverbs in the Plays of Beaumont and Fletcher." *Southern Folklore Quarterly* 24.2 (1960): 77–100.

Thomas, Roger. "Comprehension and Indulgence." *From Uniformity to Unity, 1662–1962.* Ed. Geoffrey F. Nuttall and Owen Chadwick. London: SPCK, 1962.

Thompson, E. P. *The Making of the English Working Class.* New York: Vintage, 1966.

Tilley, M. P. *A Dictionary of the Proverbs in England in the Sixteenth and Seventeenth Centuries.* Ann Arbor: Univ. of Michigan Press, 1950.

———. *Eliabethan Proverb Lore in Lyly's "Euphues" and in Pettie's "Petite Palace,"* with Parallels from Shakespeare. New York: Macmillan, 1926.

Tillinghast, John. *Mr. John Tillinghasts Eight Last Sermons.* London, 1655.

Tindall, William York. *John Bunyan: Mechanick Preacher.* New York: Columbia Univ. Press, 1934.

A True and Impartial Narrative of Some Illegal and Arbitrary Proceedings . . . in and near the Town of Bedford. N.p., 1670.

Tuve, Rosemund. *Elizabethan and Metaphysical Imagery.* Chicago: Univ. of Chicago Press, 1947.

Tyranipocrit, Discovered with His Wiles, Wherewith He Vanquished. Rotterdam, 1649.

Underwood, T. L., with Roger Sharrock. *John Bunyan: Some Gospel-Truths Opened . . . The Miscellaneous Works of John Bunyan.* Vol. 1. Gen. ed. Roger Sharrock. Oxford: Clarendon, 1980.

Van Dyke, Carolyn. *The Fiction of Truth: Structures of Meaning in Narrative and Dramatic Allegory.* Ithaca: Cornell Univ. Press, 1985.

Walch, Günter. "John Bunyan—Dichter der Plebejischen Fraktion: Revolutionärer Puritanismus und Allegorie." *Zeitschrift für Anglistik und Amerikanistik* 27.3 (1979): 197–207.

Weaver, Richard. *The Ethics of Rhetoric.* Chicago: Henry Regnery, 1953.

Watts, Alan. *Myth and Ritual in Christianity.* Boston: Beacon, 1968.

West, Alick. *Crisis and Criticism and Selected Essays, Foreword by Arnold Kettle, Introduction by Elizabeth West.* London: Lawrence and Wishart, 1975.

White, T. H. *The Sword in the Stone.* New York: Dell, 1963.

Whiting, Bartlett J. "The Nature of the Proverb." *Harvard Studies and Notes in Philology* 14 (1932): 273–307.

Wigfield, W. M. *Recusancy and Nonconformity in Bedfordshire: Illustrated by Select Documents Between 1622 and 1842.* Publications of the Bedfordshire Historical Record Society, vol. 20, 1938.

Willey, Basil. *The Seventeenth Century Background.* 1934. Garden City: Doubleday, 1953.

Wilson, F. P. "English Proverbs and Dictionaries of Proverbs." *The Library,* 4th ser. 26 (1945): 51–71.

————. "Shakespeare and the Diction of Common Life." *Proceedings of the British Academy* 27 (1941): 167–97.

Winstanley, Gerrard. *Works.* Ed. George H. Sabine. 1941. New York: Russell & Russell, 1965.

Wordsworth, William. *The Prelude or Growth of a Poet's Mind.* Ed. Ernest de Selincourt. 2nd ed. rev. Helen Darbishire. Oxford: Clarendon, 1965.

Young, Robert. *Analytical Concordance to the Bible.* 22nd Amer. ed. New York: Funk & Wagnalls, 1955.

Contributors

ROBERT G. COLLMER, Dean of Graduate Studies and Research and Professor of English at Baylor University, has published on Renaissance and seventeenth-century English literature; contributed a study on Bunyan to *Ten Studies in Anglo-Dutch Relations;* and cotranslated and coedited (with A. G. H. Bachrach) *The English Journals of Lodewijck Huygens, 1651–1652.*

JAMES F. FORREST, Professor of English at the University of Alberta, holds the M.Litt. from the University of Glasgow and the Ph.D. from Cornell University; has specialized in Renaissance and seventeenth-century literature; and has published numerous articles in various scholarly journals, critical editions of Bunyan's *The Holy War* and *The Life and Death of Mr. Badman* (Oxford English Texts) in association with Roger Sharrock, and *John Bunyan: A Reference Guide,* with Richard L. Greaves.

RICHARD L. GREAVES, Robert G. Lawton Distinguished Professor of History and Courtesy Professor of Religion at Florida State University, has written or edited nineteen books and some fifty journal articles. His publications include *John Bunyan,* four volumes in the *Miscellaneous Works of John Bunyan,* and (with James F. Forrest) *John Bunyan: A Reference Guide.* His newest book, *Enemies Under His Feet: Radicals and Nonconformists in Britain, 1664–1677,* is forthcoming.

DAYTON HASKIN teaches English at Boston College. His recent articles include studies of the nineteenth-century Donne Revival (forthcoming in *ELH*) and of Milton's portrait of Mary in *Paradise Regained.* Currently he is working on a book about "Milton's Burden of Interpretation," a project that complements an article on *The Pilgrim's Progress* which he contributed to *Studies in Philology.*

DAVID HERRESHOFF, Associate Professor Emeritus of English at Wayne State University, is now residing in the Province of British Columbia, Canada. He has published *American Disciples of Marx* and has contributed chapters to *American Labor in Mid-Passage* and *American Radicals: Some Problems and Personalities.*

BARBARA A. JOHNSON, Assistant Professor of English at Indiana University, holds the Ph.D. from Brown University. She has published articles on Spenser, Shakespeare, and Milton, and has recently completed a book entitled *"Would'st read thy self?": Langland, Bunyan, and the Protestant Reader.*

U. MILO KAUFMANN, Associate Professor of English at the University of Illinois at Urbana-Champaign, holds the Ph.D. from Yale University. He is the author of *The Pilgrim's Progress and Traditions in Puritan Meditation, Paradise in the Age of Milton,* and articles on literary theory and the English Renaissance in a variety of journals.

BRAINERD P. STRANAHAN was Professor of English at Hiram College at his untimely death in March of 1989. His writings on Bunyan included his doctoral dissertation at Harvard University on *The Pilgrim's Progress* and articles in *English Literary Renaissance, Studies in Philology,* and *English Studies.*

GEORGE W. WALTON is Chair and Professor of the Department of English at Abilene Christian University. A member of Phi Beta Kappa, he completed his doctoral dissertation on Bunyan at Texas Tech University.

Index

Hill, Christopher, 4–5, 150, 161, 171–74,
  182, 184, 205, 214, 218
Hill Clear, 110
Hill Difficulty, 28, 193
Histriomastix (Prynne), 96
Hobbes, Thomas, 94, 209
Hold-the-World, Mr., 33, 51, 203
Holmes, Nathaniel, 146
Holy City, The, 15–16, 108, 145–46, 153,
  215

Holy Life, A, 150, 216
Holy War, The, 4, 24, 106, 149–50, 154–55,
  158–60, 166, 210–11, 216; Mansoul, 106,
  149–50, 166
—characters: Atheism, Mr., 150; Conscience, Mr., 150; Diabolus, 149–50,
  158, 160, 166; Emanuel, 106, 150; False
  Peace, Mr., 150; Forget-good, 150;
  Haughty, Mr., 150; Knowledge, Mr.,
  150; Love-flesh, Governor, 150; Love-
  no-light, Governor, 150; Lustings, Lord,
  150; Shaddai, 150, 158; Spite-God, Gov-
  ernor, 150; Understanding, Lord, 149–
  50; Whoring, Mr., 150
Holy Writ, 4. *See also* Bible; Scriptures
Homo Ludens (Huizinga), 96
Hopeful, 29, 32, 44, 50, 53–54, 78, 84, 88,
  109, 124, 179, 204
Horace, 120
House Beautiful, 57, 110
House of the Forest of Lebanon, The, 159, 217
House of the Interpreter, 45, 65, 68, 87–88,
  90, 109
Howell, James, 11
Huizinga, Johan, 96, 105, 210
Humphrys, John, 217
Hussey, Maurice, 8
Hypocrisy, 42, 192

I Will Pray with the Spirit, 143, 215
Ignatius, 79
Ignorance, 16, 35, 52–55
Implacable, Mr., 41, 50–51

Import and Use of Scripture-Metaphors, The,
  134
Inconsiderate, Mrs., 55–56, 204
Interpreter, 27–28, 89
Iron Cage, 87, 110, 209
Isaiah (book of), 47–48, 83, 89, 163
Iser, Wolfgang, 109, 184, 210
Israel's Hope Encouraged, 158, 217

Jack the Giant-killer, 166
Jacob, 74, 86, 203
Jacobeans, 201
James (disciple), 79
James II (king of England), 153, 156–57,
  159, 172
Japhet, 86–87
Jason, 101
Jeremiah (book of), 59, 160
Jessey, Henry, 139, 213
Jesus, 160, 190
Job, 40
Joel (book of), 62, 65, 69, 86
John the Divine, Saint, 84
John, Gospel of, 14, 45–46, 57, 64, 72, 76,
  80, 82–83, 85, 88, 186
John Bunyan Lectures, The (Bedford), 171
John Bunyan: Maker of Myths (Lindsay), 163,
  218
Johnson, Barbara A., 4–5
Jordan (river), 55
Judas, 52, 73

Kairoi, 188
Kaufmann, U. Milo, 2, 5, 19, 115, 206, 211
Keeble, N. H., 62, 72, 207, 209
Keeling, Sir John, 140, 214
Keeper of the Gate, 86–87
Kenyon, Roger, 214
Kettle, Arnold, 167, 170, 174–75, 218
Key of Promise, 108
King James Version (Bible), 36, 39, 41,
  203, 212. *See also* Bible